You Can't Do That on Broadway!

Philip Rose, 1959

You Can't Do That on Broadway!

A RAISIN IN THE SUN AND OTHER THEATRICAL IMPROBABILITIES

A Memoir
by
Philip Rose

Limelight Editions
New York

First Edition March 2001

Manufactured in the United States of America.

Interior design by Mulberry Tree Press, Inc.
(email: Joe@MulberryTreePress.com)

Library of Congress Cataloging-in-Publication Data
available from the publisher upon request.

Acknowledgments

To all the people who for many years asked me to answer the same question about *A Raisin in the Sun,* "How did it happen?" I thank them for asking and apologize for taking so long to respond.

To my wife, Doris Belack, my life's editor who was insistent that the story be told and whose access to me every day was unavoidable. I thank her for her encouragement, her persistent high standards, and her refusal to accept any excuses.

To Courtney Gable, my assistant, and her understudies Jason and Martha, who not only learned to read my handwritten pages but were able to transfer those to a computer and print them so that I could decipher them.

To Mark Grant, the editor who critiqued my first seven chapters and thereby encouraged me to write the following twenty-one.

To Mel Zerman of Limelight Editions, who not only persuaded me to complete the following twenty-one chapters, but agreed to publish them.

To Esther Margolis, for her friendship and many other things too numerous to mention.

To our old friends, Ann and Robert Shanks, who through all my many opening nights of success and failure have been equally supportive of and never embarrassed by either; and for their help in discarding a previous title.

To my old friend Sy Fischer who is not mentioned in this book.

You Can't Do
That
on Broadway!

Prologue

At 8:00 P.M., on the Monday of March 10th, 1959, the curtain rose at the Barrymore Theatre on Broadway. What was about to be presented was the first and only preview in New York of a play called *A Raisin in the Sun*. The play, written by Lorraine Hansberry, an attractive young black woman, twenty-nine years old, had been playing out of town: one weekend in New Haven, two weeks in Philadelphia, and four weeks in Chicago. Now it had arrived in New York to play one preview and to open officially to the critics the following night, March 11th.

The audience at the Barrymore that preview night was largely a theatre party: they were mostly white; knew very little about the play; less about the writer, Miss Hansberry; even less about the director, Lloyd Richards; and nothing about the producer, Philip Rose. Of course, they were familiar with the star, Sidney Poitier, and had heard of Ruby Dee, but not really of anyone else in the acting company. And though the play had received generally good notices out of town, there was little anticipation or excitement about it opening, or even arriving in New York. They also did not know that it had taken years for us to get to this point.

As for Lorraine Hansberry and myself, we were standing in the back of the theatre that March 10th, sharing our fears of this monster, the New York audience: would they eat us up, enjoying every morsel of this *Raisin*, or would they devour us, spitting out what they couldn't swallow?

Now the lights went down slowly and the theatre grew dark. Lorraine and I were holding hands—not just holding, almost breaking each others' fingers. The curtain went up slowly; why was everything happening so slowly? Ruby Dee was slowly coming out of the bedroom, then Sidney Poitier was coming out of the bedroom—slowly. Why was everything taking so long! Why hadn't the director moved them faster? The audience was coughing. Not a word had been spoken and the play was already too long.

But the dialogue began, and we breathed a sigh of relief. The actors had not forgotten their lines; they actually went through the whole first act without missing a single word. Lorraine and I had no idea if the performance was any good. At the end of the first act, there was some applause, not what we were accustomed to out-of-town, but some.

As the audience returned and the second act began, we carefully checked the seats and noticed four empty ones down front. We weren't sure they had been empty at the start, but we didn't panic. Lorraine did remark that maybe New York audiences were different.

The second act, we thought, was playing fairly well, and we were looking forward to the second act curtain, which had always, out of town, brought down the house. When the curtain fell, there was polite applause, and we noticed quite a number of people remaining in their seats during this intermission. Some of them seemed to be crying. Our conclusion was that they were thinking of the price of the tickets. We decided it was safer for us also to stay in our seats rather than mingle with the audience. But the press agent for the show, Jim Proctor, came running down the aisle and grabbed me by the arm, saying to me, "You don't have to watch the third act. We need to talk," as he dragged me out of the theatre and into a bar down the street.

Jim Proctor was a distinguished professional who through the years had worked on some of Broadway's most prestigious shows. He sat me down at the bar, ordered drinks, and proceeded to tell me what options we had other than just getting drunk. "You can open as scheduled tomorrow night, and put up the closing notice immediately. Or, you can postpone the opening for two weeks. I will call Elia Kazan. He knows about the play. You make a deal with him to redirect and do some rewriting. Maybe it can be fixed."

I was stunned. I stared at him, took several more quick sips of my drink, and then said (I thought reasonably) "Jim, even if I had the money to postpone, which I don't, why are you saying this? We've had six weeks out of town, with mostly good reviews and enthusiastic audiences. Why are you telling me this?"

He replied simply, "This is New York. Look at this audience. You think they're enthusiastic?" I got up, finished his drink and mine, and said, "Let me go back and see the end of the play. In any case, I can't accept those options. But I'll think about getting drunk."

At the end of the third act, I thought the applause was certainly decent, but none of us went out to celebrate. Those of us who didn't rush home hung around to pick up a copy of the *New York Times* and other morning papers. That same night, March 10th, as we were previewing, there had been the official opening at the Martin Beck Theatre of Tennessee Williams' *Sweet Bird of Youth*. We read the seven rave reviews and were immediately aware that the critics had used up all of their superlatives for the week, or even for the year. We wondered: even if they liked *A Raisin in the Sun,* what could they have left to say?

The following day, March 11th, Tuesday, our scheduled opening night, Lloyd Richards called a brief rehearsal with the cast. The atmosphere on stage was somber if not quite funereal, filled with stiff upper lips not resulting from makeup. But we all said the usual "Break a Leg" things to each other, with as far as I remember, no new clichés being invented.

Soon it was 6:00 P.M.; flowers and gifts appeared backstage; telegrams were received, some opened, some held for more relaxed reading time. And shortly afterwards, Lorraine and I took fourth row on the aisle seats for the opening night of *A Raisin in the Sun.*

It's hard to nail down what our feelings were, Lorraine's and mine, as the curtain went up. For whatever irrational reason, I was not as nervous as I had been the night before, and I don't think Lorraine was, either. I guess some of it was the realization that we had done everything we possibly could have done, against enormous odds, through years of keeping each other strong and optimistic in our most depressed and hopeless moods. And as we held hands and looked at the audience, they did not seem as terrifying. Then the lights went down, the curtain went up (not so slowly), the actors came on (moving quickly), and the play began.

Everything seemed right onstage that night. The actors were brilliant. But the audience's performance was phenomenal. When the curtain came down at the end of the play, the theatre erupted. As the individual actors took their bows, the applause grew. Mr. Poitier took his call, bowed, and called the company back on stage for the final bow. The curtain closed, but the applause grew. The curtain kept opening and closing; nobody was leaving the seats. The critics, who normally rush out of the theatre, were standing in the rear as the ovation began to verbalize what the audience wanted: they were clamoring and demanding to see the author. "Author!", "Author!" was coming from every seat except Lorraine's. She was resisting getting up. Meanwhile, as the actors were bowing and feeling increasingly helpless, another scene was beginning onstage. Ruby Dee was pounding Sidney's arm and, in a stage whisper, saying to him, "Go get her, you son of a bitch. Go get her." Finally Mr. Poitier jumped off the stage, flew up the aisle as gracefully as only he could, and almost carried Lorraine onto the stage for a bow. The ensuing roar from the audience may well have been heard in every other Broadway theatre that night.

Finally, the audience was satisfied and left the theatre. Through the years, the only regret I've ever had about that opening night was that I was not just a member of that audience coming to see a new play.

Chapter 1

I was born on July 4th, 1921, on the Lower East Side of Manhattan. My family then consisted of my father, mother, two sisters, and a brother. I was soon followed by one more sister. We all lived together for a while in a small three-room walk-up apartment on Columbia Street, a street mostly inhabited by Jewish immigrant parents who proceeded to give birth to first generation American Jews. Meanwhile, in the surrounding neighborhoods, Italian, Irish, and other ethnic groups were going through a similar process. It's interesting that even then, as now, Jews were mostly identified by their religion rather than their original nationality (Polish, Russian, German), while most other groups were referred to by the country of their birth. Each of these groups had their own territory and tended to live within their boundaries or ghettos. Of course, as a child, while I was never aware of any pejorative word like "ghetto," my siblings and I knew—and were told to stay within our borders or be careful when we had to cross them.

The one group that did not much inhabit these areas were black Americans, who were already establishing their hold on other parts of the city. On the rare occasions when black men came to our area, it was for some kind of menial employment. So as a young child, I had no contact with any black Americans.

When I got to be about ten years old, my family began to move around to different apartments, soon leaving Manhattan for Williamsburg across the bridge and finally further into Brooklyn. We were now deep in the Depression of the 1930s and our family moved very often, not because of wanderlust but because it was a way of paying the rent. At that time there was no shortage of apartments, so landlords would offer prospective tenants two or three months rent free, and some of these new tenants would, after living for four or five months, move on to other apartments, going through the same procedure. Our family did that, and there would occasionally be a few black children in the schools I was transferred to; though I might have noticed them, I certainly had no contact with them.

When I was in high school, my brother, the oldest sibling, moved to Washington, D.C. to find work, and did—with the Post Office; my family followed, one at a time; first my father, then my mother, then my sisters. Finally I was left alone in New York to graduate and enter Brooklyn College in 1937, at the age of sixteen. I was living in a single room and after several lonely months, I gave up college and joined my family in Washington, D.C.

Washington, D.C. in the late 1930s was one of the most segregated cities in the United States, comparable to Mississippi, if not as overtly violent in its hostility to black people. Many of the black families lived in Southwest Washington, beginning about three blocks from the Capitol. Their living quarters were mostly shacks with no amenities, some with no streetlights at night, outhouses for toilets, and faulty electricity indoors. This area, in the shadow of the Capitol Dome, included some of the worst slums in the nation. There were also isolated black areas in Northeast Washington and on the fringes of town, as well as a growing black population in Northwest Washington. There stood Howard University and the famous Howard Theatre, Washington's counterpart to New York's Apollo, where white people would occasionally go to see black performers, such as Cab Calloway, Louis Jordan, and Jimmy Lunceford.

Most of Washington's black families had traveled north from southern states, hoping to reach New York City and a better life, and not achieving either goal. They got as far as Washington, where government employment was the major industry but where no black person could be employed by the government or even allowed to take the exams. Outside of government service, the only jobs available were domestic worker for the women at six dollars per week, and custodian for the men at ten dollars per week. Blacks were not allowed into white restaurants, or even at the soda fountains of "People's Drug Stores" (a rather inclusive name for a store that prohibited serving black people), or in the major clothing stores.

As a result of all these restrictions, over several years there began to grow a neighborhood of stores exclusively owned by whites but catering to blacks and poor whites, selling clothing, household needs, appliances, etc. They were known as credit stores, long before the advent of current credit cards, where a black man could buy, for instance, a suit costing about ten to twenty-five dollars, which was more than a poor family could raise at one time. The customer would make a small downpayment and follow it with an agreed-upon one or two dollars per week or bimonthly until the debt was fully paid. Any week that payment was not made, a penalty would be added to the original price. Because there were no government regulations of these stores, the price of a suit or any item originally set at fifteen dollars (and generally worth half that) could balloon up to fifty dollars. The area of 7th Street N.W., extending for several blocks, eventually saw a concentration of these stores, one after another, side by side. It is worth noting that in the upheavals that followed Martin Luther King's assassination in 1968, these were among the major targets of black people seeking revenge. All the credit stores employed several white men as "bill collectors," who would go to the homes or the employment places of their customers to pick up the weekly or bimonthly payments. The largest of them was called Marvin's Credit Department Store.

When I arrived in Washington, my father was still struggling financially, and I had to get a job immediately. My schooling had provided me with no skills that were of any help. I worked as a messenger and did odd jobs for a while. After a couple of years, a friend of one of my sisters who worked at Marvin's told her the store had an opening for a bill collector, which paid a small salary plus a percentage of the money collected each week. Presumably I had all the skills and knowledge required, except for knowing how to drive. I called my brother, who then taught me to drive in one week, with a minimum of patience and a maximum of screaming, while I almost wrecked his car and stripped his gears. One week later I applied for the job, was hired, and bought a used car for $75.00.

At about the same time I found that I had some talent as a singer. I began to study music and was encouraged to work towards becoming an opera singer. Relatively soon I was earning money weekends singing in churches, synagogues, and at weddings and Bar Mitzvahs, and listening to classical music on the radio as I drove around the city.

Meanwhile, at my new job, I saw that Marvin's had numerous bill collectors on the payroll but that few of them lasted very long. Furthermore, they were generally over six feet tall, formidable looking, and very often carried some kind of weapon on their rounds. At five feet, five inches tall, even on my good days I didn't look like that. I also learned quickly that any white person entering these black neighborhoods regularly was soon recognized as a bill collector. At the end of a day or evening, after I finished my collection calls, I would naturally be carrying a fair amount of cash. My fellow workers were happy to inform me how often they had had to protect themselves in the incidence of robbery or worse.

Was I scared as I started to come into these neighborhoods where I had never been before? Unequivocally yes, particularly at night, as I would have to see some clients after their working hours, when the streets were dark. Did I know what to expect? Not from the people and not from myself. I don't think I knew how I would act or feel any more than I knew what would happen to me.

At the beginning, I was certainly not a welcome guest in my clients' homes, arriving by appointment just to collect money. But I was generally not made to feel too uncomfortable when the payment was actually there for me and all I had to do was write a receipt and leave rather quickly. When it was not, I would make another appointment, the late fee being charged to the client by my office. After several missed payments, my employer would either repossess the merchandise and resell it to another customer or garnishee the salary of the husband or wife. In the latter case, I would regularly pick up the payment at the home or office of the clients' employers.

Obviously, all of my visits to clients were quite impersonal, but after a while, my attitude changed. Having experienced no such incidents as I had been warned about, I became much less fearful; indeed, I almost looked forward to making my collecting rounds, because some strange and wonderful things were happening. After a few weeks of visiting the homes of my clients, different relationships slowly began to evolve. I was beginning to know some of these families—the fathers, mothers, children—and specifically to like some better than others. Sometimes, surprisingly, I felt welcome when I arrived. Occasionally, I would even be offered tea or coffee. Often the children were especially friendly, and I even exchanged first names with some of the adults. It took me awhile, however, to persuade the southern black women to eliminate the "Mr." in front of mine.

We began to have real conversations: where they came from, where I came from, that we all came from poor but not similar backgrounds. I was learning things I had never heard of in school, or had heard from a completely different point of view. And then there was the music! In these homes, no matter how poor, there had to be music: not the kind I was now studying, but southern blues singers, early jazz, and gospel, and I would stay on long after I had collected my payment, if I hadn't forgotten it entirely, neglecting my rounds or working later to complete them.

Soon I had formed friendships with some of the young people of my age, late teens or early twenties. That's when I became part of the problem. We could not go to restaurants or movies together except in the specifically black areas. So we would go to the Howard Theatre; we would go to black bars or eating places, where I was a bit of a curiosity; we would go to house parties, being careful, as we drove together in my car, not to appear too social or intimate. The police could easily stop us to inquire why the black man or woman was not sitting in the back. I still remember, vividly, being parked in a dark area of a park with a black woman slightly older than I, and both of us in tears because we were in love and we both knew it would have to end and not because of our age difference. Paralee Morgan—I wonder where she is now. I also had another unforgettable experience, repeated many times, of hearing live gospel music in a black church.

In another part of my life, other things were happening. I was beginning to earn more money as a singer. I now had a job in one of the most affluent Episcopal churches off Connecticut Avenue, as the solo baritone voice and perhaps the token Jew. While I was beginning to wonder in what direction I was going, I knew that at some point soon I would be leaving Washington to pursue my singing career. I began to spend less and less time at my collecting job and more time trying to convince my clients, now friends, not to shop at Marvin's because they were being robbed. I also remember going to the office of a bank president to collect the garnisheed amount from the salary of his "faithful maid." He said to me, "You people at Marvin's store should be put in jail the way you're treating your poor customers." I said to him, "You know, if you gave her a decent wage, she wouldn't have to buy from us." He looked at me as if I'd lost my mind.

Not too long afterwards, when I was almost twenty-one years old, World War II broke out. I was first drafted, then sent home because of my very poor eyesight. This accelerated my decision to return to New York and further my singing career.

In later years, looking back, I realized how profoundly the years and the people I met in Washington changed my life. I have only a vague recollection of what kind of person I was before those years. I suspect I was, in comparison, not really formed, except physically, in any important way. I am sure my parents or family didn't particularly know me. For whatever reason, I had experiences that completely erased the events of my childhood and youth. Why I was so open to becoming this other person, I have no idea. I also don't know why any of those people, given the circumstances under which they met me, cared enough to reach out, to enlighten me, and to point me in a new direction. What I do know is how grateful I am for what was done for me by a group of generous, remarkable people who happened to be black. And while I don't know where or who they now are, I know that for anything important I may have done or will do with my life, I am trying to say "thank you" to them.

Chapter 2

The Broadway production of *A Raisin in the Sun* went into rehearsal on December 10th, 1958. Contracts had actually been signed with our entire cast; Sidney Poitier, Claudia McNeil, Ruby Dee, Diana Sands, Ivan Dixon, Louis Gossett, Glynn Turman, John Fiedler, and Lonnie Elder. We had raised enough money to begin paying rehearsal salaries to these wonderful actors, as well as to the director, Lloyd Richards, set designer, Ralph Alswang, stage manager, Leonard Auerbach, general manager, Wally Fried, and press agent, James Proctor. We were pleased to be rehearsing in the old New Amsterdam roof garden theatre at Times Square where some of Broadway's greatest plays had played but which now served as a rehearsal space because 42nd Street had become a forbidden street.

The first day of rehearsal with a new play is a ritual. In addition to the usual process of getting acquainted, there are generally some remarks from the playwright, the director, and sometimes the producer. On this particular day I was happy to decline and just nod approvingly at anything Lorraine Hansberry and Lloyd had to say. After the remarks, the company gathered around a table to just read the play for the first time. As usual at a first reading, some actors attempt to perform, while most studiously avoid that and just read the words. Occasionally, in spite of any of the actors' predetermined choices, the play takes over and the playwright either begins to get excited about her play or depressed at how the actors are ruining it. On that memorable first day, Lorraine and I may have given the best performances of all as we pretended we never had entertained any doubts this day would come. Of course the actors did their part by being careful not to ask me any questions about what was to happen after the rehearsal period, although it was common knowledge then that I had put the show in rehearsal without having booked a New York theatre.

At the end of the reading, while Lorraine was able to remain outwardly calm, I was walking around with, I was told, the silliest grin on my face. In fact, I was wondering where my third week's company salary would come from.

Technically, the producer was not supposed to spend any of the money raised until the entire budget had been invested. Fortunately, by this point, some of my investor close friends had given me the right to use their funds as "front money," meaning they had faith that the balance would be raised and the show would make it to New York.

During the four-week rehearsal period, Lorraine and I were quite busy. She would be at rehearsal quite often, watching the performers develop; I was there less frequently, as I spent most of my time on the telephone raising money, or having breakfasts, lunches, or dinners with prospective investors, hoping I would not end up even further behind as I picked up the checks. I also had managed to book the out-of-town pre-Broadway engagements for New Haven and Philadelphia.

Meanwhile, after two weeks of rehearsal, problems began to appear, and Lorraine was getting concerned. Ruby Dee, playing Ruth Younger, seemed to be having difficulty creating the character to Lorraine's satisfaction; Diana Sands, playing Beneatha (who, incidentally, is based on Lorraine herself), was finding more humor in her than Lorraine thought she had written. Lorraine was afraid she, Beneatha, would not be taken seriously. Last and most important, Sidney Poitier was beginning to sense that his role, Walter Lee, was as written not a fully developed and realized character.

Lorraine and I had many conversations about all of this. My

feelings were that Ruby Dee was creating a different Ruth than Lorraine had envisioned, and Ruby would be just fine. I also had felt from the beginning that the role of Ruth Younger was the most difficult and thankless part in the play. Lorraine, soon after, began to accept that although Ruby Dee might not turn out to be exactly the Ruth she originally conceived, Ruby was bringing a compelling interpretation to the character. And, indeed, Ruby Dee, playing that most difficult role finally gave an absolutely stunning performance that I don't think anyone else has ever approached. Diana Sands was wonderful, too, and again Lorraine soon agreed with me, although she never was really happy with the degree of humor Diana brought to the role of Beneatha.

With Mr. Poitier, we had a more serious situation. By the time we had finished our last rehearsal in New York and were headed for New Haven, Sidney was more convinced than ever that there was a serious flaw in the writing of his character. Lorraine was trying some rewrites, but as we left for New Haven without any major changes, she was not yet persuaded that the problem was in the script rather than in the direction or acting. She was beginning to be disturbed at Mr. Poitier. She didn't think he was "finding his character," while he was beginning to think it wasn't there to find.

Following is a letter from Lorraine expressing her feelings about the last rehearsal of the play before we left for New Haven. It was the beginning of Lorraine's attempt to cope with her reservations, not just about the performances but the play itself. It also prompted our first discussions about her fears that *Raisin* could be performed or interpreted as though Mama *were* the central character in the play rather than Walter Lee Younger. She wrote more and more about this, as we shall see.

Monday - January 11, 1958

My dears - meaning Lloyd, Phil, Robert (■ in order of possible and probable
tyranny):

It is now the next day since last night you see and as in novels I
have awakened fresh with the dawn and clear headed as a bell about what I
saw and felt last night. (This may be somewhat misleading, ■ insofar as
I did not sleep...)

Any how here are some things for all of you-

OVERALL: I would say that the actors know the pulse and tempo of these
people splendidly. That at this point distortion of intent ■ the written
manuscript is almost impossible - which I consider to be an immense tribute
to Lloyd at this remarkable point in rehearsal. The acting exception remains
Ruby - but I do think that is a problem any longer. Audiences will like her
and care about her to the exclusion of others. She is not Ruth Younger of
the Southside of Chicago - but she is a certain type of American woman that
a hell of a lots of people will identify with - so to that extent it remains an
affirmative distortion and who would complain about that? - ■

sometimes ↑

BENEATHA : ■ Felt nothing in the world for this child last night except
the expectation of laughs. This is wrong and decidely not the margins of Diana's
extraordinary talent. Beneatha must bounce less now, I think. That is to say-
restore, TRUE PASSION AND THOUGHTFUL NESS (as in the God scene forinstance, the
more serious and intellectually appealing she is - the greater the action of
Mama; this has always been the secret of conflict friends. (Everybody involved
try to outdo the other - eh, eh - "like in life"...) (Like Cogan and Rose -_)
Also - Femininity and, if necessary, to achieve the true many sided ness of
■ THIS character - even sweetness? Yes. You see, this has to do with dramatic
truths and with theatricality which are usually wedded I think. That is -
people always laugh with the■ unexpected clown. ■■■■■ She will be splendid.

WALTER: It was just one of those things.

CLAUDIA: Fine.

ABOUT THAT ENDING WHEN BOBB SAYS THE MONEY IS GONE. I should like
to re-state the most serious sense of frustration of the evening which was
involved with this scene: During its happpening it reminded me of nothhng
so much as the fact that I do LIKE chocolate milk - and yet there is nothing
quite so nauseating as ■■■■■■■■■ allowing all ■■ chocolate syrap to
fall in a mere one glass of milk at one time. ALL that chocadate DISTORTS
the whole idea of chocolate MILK. I feel precisely the same about excessive
emotionality in in a deeply emotional play. ■■■■■■■■■■■ I do not feel
these are entirely directorial questions - but having to do with other matters
as well - Anyhow there are too many goddamned people on their knees at the
end of that scene and I do not believe for a moment that it is anything but
an emotional ending of a scene. It has mothing to do with a mirror to life
because Mama would not do that. I never intended to imply that she would.
Now - the high point of that scene in terms of break up is BROTHER. NOT
MAMA but BROTHER. Let us agree on that. In dramatic terms in ■■ view of the
way the play now stands as I have x rewritten it - BROTHER is central and
Mama's actions, speeches and function is pivotal AND expositional.

Therefore - I insist that the climax of the end of that entire scene is
when BROTHER says: that money was made of my father's flesh.   IT IS
WRONG FOR ANYTHING IN TERMS OF DIALOGUE (which does not happen) OR ACTION
TO TOP THAT MOMENT. Mama's lines, ARE, to be sure an impassioned, potent
commentary as written and do close the scene - BUT SHE DOES NOT I enter into
his anguish. NEVER, NEVER NEVER....

When this change is made it will be a superion scene - because when the
audience thinks that the totally understand the nature of Walter"s grief -
-then Mama adds the final cutting dimension in terms of reminding them WITH
IMMENSE EMOTION AND UNBEARABLE RESTRAINT...of the true meaning of that money
in her memory. When she invokes God for strength, she invokes God for strength -
it is not the effor t to give her some dialogue though hysteria. Beneatha
need hardly move at all during this - except if Mama does start to hit him
I like her coming quickly and efficiently and stopping even the first blow-
in fact it might be that which would restraint...

say
If I may so - I consider it a mistake to every put the wail of
TRAGEDY in to a mere drama. I It makes the pot look so very much larger than
the broth that one can loose one's appetite from hunger.

Ivan is so cute.

Cut the stuff in the first scene with Bennie saying Mrs. Murchison
wouldnit like it down to where it would make sense again. And Mrs. Johnson.
Which will inadvertantly loose my only favorite line in the play "I'm old
and corrupted -" well, what you going to do?

Goodbye and thank you for your attention. I am not deeply fond of
this play but I must say that I think it is getting a worthy production.
Love to all of you....

Lorraine

We opened in New Haven in mid-January. It's almost a big blur now: that city, seeing *A Raisin in the Sun* for the first time on the marquee of the theatre, staying up late every night to discuss the play and the performance, and even the opening night. The audience reaction and the reviews were fine. But suddenly Lorraine became even more uncomfortably aware of something. The second act curtain was an opportunity for the audience to explode in approval of Mama, rather than the beginning of the explosion of Walter Lee Younger. Lorraine thought that the scene was directed, and played by Claudia McNeil, overly dramatically; this made it difficult (in Lorraine's view) for the audience to accept Walter Lee as the protagonist; they were instead rooting for Mama. However, what Mr. Poitier had been struggling with was becoming, if not yet obvious to Lorraine, something to discuss with her.

Meanwhile, I had to deal with the uncreative aspects of our production. Though it was true that we had become a reality and were bound for Philadelphia, my manager kept reminding me that two weeks from now we would be in New York with our scenery, lights, and costumes decorating a city street, and with me owing many people lots of money. My publicity agent was avoiding calls from the press, while I was receiving them from investors congratulating me on our New Haven opening but wanting to know where the New York opening night party was to be held.

Things were not dull, and became even less so when I received a call from Martin Baum, Sidney Poitier's agent, saying it was urgent that we meet in Philadelphia the day of our opening, Monday, January 26th. We met backstage in a dressing room and Mr. Baum proceeded to give me all the good news. First, Mr. Poitier had already "in the can" two major films that were about to be released, *The Defiant Ones* and *Porgy and Bess*. As a result, Hollywood was calling to know how soon *Raisin* would be closing and would Sidney be free right after Philadelphia. Also, Mr. Poitier was very unhappy that certain changes had not been made in the play and he would be pleased to leave as soon as possible.

I must point out here that perhaps my two closest friends when I undertook to produce *Raisin* were Sidney Poitier and Lorraine Hansberry. They also knew each other quite well. In addition to the desperate circumstances of the production, I was now right in the middle of a conflict between star and playwright. I could not solve the problem, even though it had become clear to me and to Lorraine that Sidney's instincts had been correct; the audiences were latching on to Mama, and this wonderful, religious, matriarchal authority figure had become the center of the play. For the average audience she could do no wrong. And that was being further underscored by Sidney's realizing that fact but not yet finding the way to cope with it. Meanwhile, after New Haven, Lorraine was still diligently working on rewrites, but quite unsuccessfully.

In the midst of all this potential chaos, while I was still calling all my New York contacts in an attempt to stave off the looming disaster, we opened the show at the Walnut Street Theatre in Philadelphia for our two-week run. The following morning, the reviews were good, and I finally received a return of my many phone calls to John Shubert of the theatre-owner Shuberts. He said he'd heard some interesting things from friends and press contacts in Philadelphia and would like to come down the next day to see a matinee. I said we could find a seat for him.

Sure enough, he showed up at the theatre the next afternoon. He actually saw very little of the play but did watch and listen to the enthusiastic audience going in and out of the theatre at each intermission. At the end of the performance, he turned to me and said, "Well, I guess we'll have to give you a theatre. You can have the Barrymore, but it won't be available for another five weeks. *Look Homeward, Angel* is playing there now and closing then." I said, "That's fine. It's a great theatre, but what do I do with my production for five weeks?" He answered, "Go to Chicago. We have the Blackstone Theatre in Chicago. You can play there for four weeks." I said, "John, if I can get the money together to go to Chicago, we'd have to be there in ten days. There'd be no promotion, we'd open to no advance and be broke in a week." He then said, "Getting there is your problem. We'll provide the theatre and guarantee you against losses for the first two weeks."

After a year and a half of trying to get a theatre, that "negotiation" for two theatres, in Chicago and New York, was completed in about five minutes. I then informed Martin Baum that we were going on with the show and I hoped and expected that Mr. Poitier would stay with us. Almost inevitably, as all the news hit New York, the balance of the budget came in for us and we made plans for Chicago.

Suddenly, from a most unlikely source, I smashed into another barricade. I had called Lorraine to give her all the good news but as soon as I mentioned Chicago, she exploded. "Not Chicago. Not with my play." There was no way she would go there. It was her hometown, where all her family, friends, and enemies lived. But most important, it was the home of Claudia Cassidy, theatre critic for the *Chicago Tribune*, who was the most feared and often most vicious critic in the country. She particularly resisted any new play that came to Chicago after previous tryouts in other places like New Haven and Philadelphia. She enjoyed destroying them. When Claudia Cassidy died in 1999, at the age of 96, her *New York Times* obituary said, "Her scathing denunciation of visiting Broadway productions made her the scourge of New York producers. Some artists left the city vowing never to return."

Nevertheless, I told Lorraine we had no choice, adding "You don't know what she'll write." She said, "Of course I do and I'll show it to you," and hung up the phone. Obviously I had no idea what she meant—until the next day. I then received from Lorraine an advance copy of the Claudia Cassidy review of *A Raisin in the Sun* written, of course, by Lorraine Hansberry, which follows.

Claudia Cassidy review

The Blackstone Theatre has been regrettably dark for a goodly portion of the 1958-59 season, but at no point have the theatre's prospects been murkier than they were last night for the premiere of A RAISIN IN THE SUN.

From the moment Ralph Alswang's gloomy, patch-quilt set is exposed to dim view, and throughout the overdrawn, repetitious mumbo-jumbo that ensues until the salvation of the final curtain, the stage radiates an incredibly detailed experience in tedium. The manufacturers of the play have contrived a sociological treatise of doom and maudlin sentimentality, liberally spiced with an unexpurgated version of Mr. Bones antiquated joke book.

The script by Chicagoan Lorraine Hansberry, successfully encompasses every watery-eyed cliche from the elder Dumas' handbook on Victorian Dramaturgy down to the collectd works of Ma Perkins.

And alas, in this case, the play alone is not the thing. For Lloyd Richards, a newcomer to the directorial chair , has done his best to make us think of him as an old-timer -- about a 150 year old-timer to be precise. He has mounted this play with all the freshness and skill of a palsyed taxidermist (necromancer). His players rant, shriek and suffer with all the guile of a Concord town[redacted] crier done up like Aunt Jemima. And they herald [redacted] dispeptic hysteria signifying nothing. One well may wonder if in [redacted] hands Shakespeare's Ariel could be transformed into that sorely needed star tackle for George Halas' Bears.

Despite its pretense at topical portent, what inhabits the Blackstone is in reality an authentic revival of TEN NIGHTS IN A BARROOM, albeit in blackface. All the elements are there. The villain *Despotic* though his moustachios have been clipped and his black garb replaced by the subtle symbolism of skin pigmentation. Then, too, there is the melodrama of the insurance money; the well-healed, lecherous suitor (son of a landlord, he); a real live genuine imitation prince-charming (in button down armour and singed black hair, if you will). There is the well-meaning, emasculating mamma; her tetched-in-the-head son, a noble swain at heart who's lost in his quest for the golden chalice. In the background there's little boy blue, in this case black, playing sweetly on his stickball club; Little Miss Eva, child in belly, running way from that old devil blues.

And as if history is not sufficiently served by the preceding anachronisms, Ralph Alswang has courageously revived the art of Restoration candle lighting. It would seem that Mr. A. has chosen to gel his lights with pitch. A case of the blind lighting the bland.

If these players can do it there is hope in our lifetimes for a revival of East Lind, starring Jackie Robinson of course.

Whatever their intent, the producers of A RAISIN IN THE SUN have successfully repealed the emancipation proclamation

for this viewer at least. For if the current tenant
of the Blackstone truly represents the negro dream for
America then the KKK cannot be far behind. 'And I for one
say God Bless them for that." ~~The~~ ~~~~

~~~~, ~~~~.

   But lest you get a "shoulda staid in bed" feeling about
this play, I must point out that A RAISIN IN THE SUN stands
a fair chance of revolutionizing the field of Neurology
in ~~our fair city~~ CHICAGO during the next four weeks. I found it to
be a flawless panacea for insomnia.

We left Philadelphia at the end of our two-week engagement, much encouraged by the fact that, barring actual disaster in Chicago, we would get to New York.

There was one last thing to get done and I couldn't do it. It had become clear to Sidney that Lorraine would not be able to solve the problem of audiences embracing Mama rather than Walter Lee Younger as the play's protagonist. The character of Mama was safer for them to accept. Sidney finally concluded that if Lorraine wouldn't or couldn't make the needed changes, *he* would do it with his performance. And that's what he began to do. During previews and with each passing day in Chicago, he became stronger and more commanding of the stage, demanding that the characters in the play accept *his* point of view, that both the audiences and the critics understand and relate to his character, his frustration, his bitterness, and finally his explosion—as in the Langston Hughes poem, and as Lorraine herself had intended.

Having sneaked into Chicago with no advance sale, we did no business at all for the first few days, papering the house, as we say, with Lorraine's family, friends, other well-wishers, and some not-so-well-wishers. Then the Claudia Cassidy review, written this time by Claudia Cassidy, appeared in the *Tribune*, along with good reviews in other papers, and we became an instantaneous smash hit. The real Ms. Cassidy's review follows.

Warm Heart, Backbone, Funnybone
in Blackstone Play and Cast

BY CLAUDIA CASSIDY

A RAISIN IN THE SUN" is a remarkable play, acted to the Blackstone hilt of its warm heart, its proud backbone, and its quicksilver funnybone by a gifted cast headed by Sidney Poitier, Claudia McNeil, and Ruby Dee. It is a new play still in tryout, with time for the cutting and adjusting that can make a powerhouse of its potential strength. More important to Chicago is that it has the fresh impact of something urgently on its way. Lorraine Hansberry can be proud that she wrote it, and her friends, Philip Rose a n d David J. Cogan, that they brought it to the stage.

It was common knowledge in a d v a n c e that the title comes from a poem by Langston Hughes, the one beginning, " What happens to a dream deferred? ", but not all of us knew the poignant irony that gives the final curtain reverberations the second act climax now lacks.

When that second act ends the sobbing son has all but destroyed his mother's dream of a d e c e n t home for the family by losing most of her insurance money to a fast talking fake. It is a scene you expect, you know it will happen, and it happens on schedule. But in theater terms it doesn't come off. You respect it, but you don't feel it so it fails on stage.

But at the end, when the son has reclaimed his manhood, when he has put his dream of quick riches aside for the long haul, and the family has p i c k e d up its

Sidney Poitier

" A RAISIN IN THE SUN "

Play by Lorraine Hansberry's, directed by Lloyd Richards; with setting and lighting by Ralph Alswang, costumes by Virginia Volland. Presented by Philip Rose and David I. Cogan in the Blackstone theater Tuesday evening, Feb. 10, 1959.

THE CAST

Ruth Younger	Ruby Dee
Travis Younger	Glynn Turman
Walter Lee Younger	Sidney Poitier
Beneatha Younger	Diana Sands
Lena Younger	Claudia McNeil
Joseph Asagai	Ivan Dixon
George Murchison	Louis Gossett
Bobo	Lonne Elder III
Karl Lindner	John Fiedler
Moving Men	Douglas Turner, Ed Hall

courage to try its luck in the new home where it isn't wanted, the mother, who has given every cent she has in the world to the new house, is the last to go. And as she stands there you suddenly realize that this ratty apartment, without sun, or a private bathroom, or enough bedrooms, but with cockroaches, is her home. But she leaves it, smiling, taking her puny plant and her far from puny courage, for another stretch in a lifetime haul. This is theater with reverberations, echoes, and a tug at the remembering heart.

As the play ends on that authentic note of nostalgia; it begins with a scene a veteran playwright might envy. In that scrubby apartment a tired woman is trying to get her son off to school, her husband off to work, when neither wants to go. She has inlaws, too. It is a scene of exhaustion, of frustration, of bickering—but also a scene of that quicksilver humor, that sudden shifting into grace, that ability to laugh at itself that makes good company. You care about these people from that first scene, which is half the battle of a play.

As the angry young man who happens to be a Negro, Sidney Poitier strides a wide range from the one who wants something for nothing to the man who will try it the hard way. Claudia McNeil is the matriarch with depth and humor except when the director has her turn coy for her daughter's beau. Ruby Dee is the one most touching, the young wife who almost loses, Diana Sands as the rebellious sister, Glynn Turman as the small boy of the house, Ivan Dixon and Louis Gossett as the callers — all hold their own, tho the two men suffer from scenes that try to stuff too much into the play John Fiedler is the white man who comes from the new house community to pay the Negro family to stay away. The neutral "inoffensiveness" of his casting is as interesting as the scene in which Poitier tells him the payoff is rejected, and why.

In general, Lloyd Richards' direction is so right that the false spots are probably on their way out this morning.

Chapter 3

In late 1943, when I left Washington and returned to New York, I moved into a six-room apartment on Hudson Street in Greenwich Village. I shared this space with three other occupants at a total rent of $32.00 per month. This came to eight dollars for each of us, which was actually more than we could afford. However, when necessary, if one person couldn't come up with his share, the others would pool their resources and bail him out.

I continued to take singing lessons, paying for this with jobs in choirs of synagogues and churches around the city and by performing at weddings and funerals. I was also lucky enough to sing in choirs that accompanied artists like Richard Tucker, still a cantor then at Brooklyn's Eastern Parkway Jewish Center; Jan Peerce, at a synagogue on Rivington Street in Manhattan; and, for a brief period, on radio's Bell Telephone Hour with singers like the great Jussi Bjoerling, among others. Meanwhile, I would spend some evenings in Harlem listening to talent at the Baby Grand on 125th Street or, naturally, the Apollo Theatre. At the Baby Grand I became friendly with their perennial emcee, Nipsey Russell, and I was introduced to many of the young artists, both amateur and professional, who would appear there. I remember being surprised and impressed with how many young black people would, instead of singing, recite either their own poetry or that of better known black poets in this noisy nightclub. Occasionally the stage musicians—sometimes just the rhythm section—would improvise music behind the poetry. It's obvious to me now, in retrospect, that I was hearing the beginning of "rap music." It was also the beginning of my acquaintance with well-known (but to me then unknown) black poets.

During this period I auditioned for a Gilbert and Sullivan company at the Provincetown Playhouse in Greenwich Village, and I became briefly a member of that company which included a very talented, very, very young actress named Doris Belack. We double-dated occasionally, she going out with the leading tenor while I escorted a soprano. Some weeks later, when I auditioned and received an offer to go on tour with an opera company, I had already been with Gilbert and Sullivan long enough for Miss Belack to realize that she had much more in common, intellectually, with a baritone than with a tenor (since, as I pointed out to her, it was well known that singing all those high tenor notes often addled a tenor's brain). In any case, we had come to know each other well enough to continue a somewhat intimate correspondence while I was on tour. Those letters will not be published here.

I left New York for the opera company tour in March of 1945, singing in the chorus. This was my first experience travelling all around the country on one-nighters, visiting cities I had never been to. I was looking forward to new experiences and new acquaintances. I thought that since I would be seeing the country and its people during a world war, there would be many things to talk about with perhaps new friends. I soon discovered that almost without exception the company members had no interest in any minor current events such as World War II or the race relations in the cities we were visiting in 1945. With no black performers in our opera company and certainly no shared relationship to the war, there was little of that nature to discuss. The conversation backstage in the dressing rooms or on the bus was generally about which tenors in the company could hit the high C, or which basses could sing the low F. I was getting a little concerned about spending my next thirty years in such company when a shattering event took place on April 12th, 1945.

Our group had arrived in Memphis early that morning. I had the afternoon free and went to a film matinee. When I left the movie house I became aware that people walking the streets looked peculiar, carrying handkerchiefs over their eyes, some even obviously crying. After a short walk I stopped a woman, asked her a question, and the answer was, "The President is dead."

That evening, I expected and needed to talk about Franklin Delano Roosevelt, the only president I had ever really been aware of. And sure enough, when I got to the theatre, the conversation *had* altered somewhat. Now they were talking about the sopranos. I managed to get through the performance and then called my family and discussed the day's events.

The following night we were not scheduled to perform and I had no desire to spend the evening with my fellow artists. I had been on the phone most of the day talking to friends and listening to the radio, trying to absorb the impact of the president's death and Harry Truman's accession, but as evening came and I lay in bed I couldn't get over my loneliness and depression, so I went out and walked to a taxi stand, got in a cab, and asked the driver where I could go to hear some music, preferably jazz. After a bit of conversation, he said there was no place in the heart of Memphis, but he could take me to a remote area called Forest Park, which had a nightclub. We then went on a long drive to the now very dark outskirts of the city, and there he dropped me.

I stood in front of a very impressive building surrounded by deep forest and hesitated briefly before being assured by a black doorman that I would have no problem calling a cab when I wanted to leave. I then entered a very large, ornately decorated restaurant with lots of tables and a dance floor jammed with people, who were all white. On a music stand, playing for the dancers and diners were four black musicians, on piano, drums, saxophone, and trumpet.

I was shown to a small table near the bandstand, at my request, and soon began to enjoy wonderful music by this terrific group playing all the well-known pop standards, with no music being read and with great jazz improvisations. I was having a great time listening while I had a drink, ate a sandwich, and had another drink. There was no vocalist with the band, so after still another drink I approached the pianist, obviously the bandleader, and asked if I could sing a number. After a brief hesitation he said yes. I stepped up and following a brief consultation, sang a song.

I received a surprised but pleasant reception from the musicians and the audience. The bandleader then offered me a chair to sit among them. I happily agreed and as he seated me he asked, "You're from New York, right?" I said yes and he said that's where the band hoped to be one day. As I sat and sang and drank occasionally, I began to dream about never going back to the opera company but staying in Memphis—and in the middle of my fantasy, the bandleader asked me if I would like to join them after closing time, 2:00 A.M., in somebody's home for a jam session. I excitedly agreed, wondering if I was being offered a contract.

A few minutes later I began to notice a slight change in the atmosphere in the audience. And at one point a gentleman who was obviously part of the nightclub staff came up and whispered something to the pianist. At the next break the leader approached me and quietly said he thought it might not be such a good idea if we left together, maybe not too safe for the band or for me. I realized then I'd been having such a good time that I had been unaware that some of the guests might have been less than enthusiastic about my singing or my presence on the bandstand being social with these four black men. I expressed my regrets and real disappointment to the musicians at not being able to continue the night into the morning, begging off with the excuse that I had a rough day ahead, which we all understood was not the reason for my leaving. I finished my drink, was escorted to the front door by the staff member waiting nearby, put in a cab which the management had already called for, and dropped off at my hotel. Along the way I realized that I had neither paid the check nor been offered one, but I decided not to return to protest this.

After that first and last experience as a band vocalist, I finished the opera tour, and immediately landed an engagement with the St. Louis Municipal Opera Company which was scheduled to last through the summer. But after about only the third week of my contract, I received a phone call from Boston from a former New York neighbor of my family. This gentleman, now running a burlesque house in Boston, knew of my singing ability, having heard me sing around the apartment across from his own. My mother had kept him informed about my career, and the fact that (in her eyes) I was becoming a star. He had called to ask if I would be interested in joining his burlesque company, with a nice lucrative contract and perhaps some incidental perks. That I had no particular experience as a stripper or even as a dancer would be apparent to the casual observer even to this day. However, he hastened to assure me that my job would simply be to stand on stage right with a microphone in soft light, fully clothed, to sing such songs as "A Pretty Girl Is Like a Melody" while the pretty ladies did what they were presumably better suited, or unsuited, for.

I immediately ran to our Muni Opera conductor, Edwin McArthur, an incredible musician who had hired me for my previous opera tour and then brought me to St. Louis, and told him of the offer. His response was immediate and unequivocal: "Philip, you've got an important career ahead of you as an opera singer. Don't throw it away." Mr. McArthur had been the accompanist and conductor for the great Kirsten Flagstad, and his reply was enough for me to easily turn down the offer of burlesque singer/ emcee. I was very young at the time and I've often wondered and fantasized about how much influence I might have had in perhaps integrating an all-white burlesque tradition with some black dancers. Perhaps fantasized is the operative word. In any case, I completed my St. Louis contract and returned to New York. It was during that summer (and briefly noted by the company) that the atomic bomb was dropped on Hiroshima and the war ended.

During the next few years, while still singing, I began to supplement my income by working in the music and record industry, at first as a salesman for a record distributor who represented small independents specializing in what was then called "race records"—that is, recordings by black artists sold exclusively in black communities around the country. These recordings of the late 40s were played only on small radio stations that catered to a black audience. They were actually called and listed in the trade papers as "race records" until, under pressure from organizations like the NAACP and similar groups, the industry came up with the phrase "rhythm and blues." That identification still exists, along with country music, rock, rap, classical, etc.

Working for a record distributor was now bringing me to Harlem not only evenings for recreation, but during the day, as I made the rounds of the record stores on 125th Street and elsewhere, selling "Rhythm and blues." I became particularly friendly with Bobby of Bobby's Records on 125th Street, one of the few stores in Harlem owned and run by a black man. I also met Willie Bryant, a black disc jockey who hosted the major night radio show devoted exclusively to rhythm and blues. I appeared on his show to discuss how impossible it was to get recordings of black artists played by the white disc jockeys on major station programs like WNEW's *Make Believe Ballroom*.

Meanwhile, in the late 40s, I had become actively involved with many civil rights groups. As a result, I became aware in a much more political sense of the ongoing struggle for freedom for black Americans and also of the many extraordinary people involved in that struggle. As has happened to me so many times in my life, I was fortunate enough over the next few years to meet and shake hands with two contemporary giants in the battle for civil rights, Paul Robeson and W.E.B. Du Bois. And I also met two artists who through their writing and acting not only altered the country's vision but also dramatically changed, once again, the course of my life. They were Lorraine Hansberry and Sidney Poitier.

Chapter 4

During the spring of 1949, I auditioned for a job at a summer camp in Wingdale, New York. Camp Unity, about one hundred miles from New York City, was very much the sort of family resort which typified that general area. What distinguished this camp from the others was that black families were as welcome as whites, making it almost unique among the famous Catskill resorts, as well as less expensive. Its openness carried over into the camp's personnel, including the waiters and waitresses, the cleanup crews, the entertainment staff, and just generally the faces to be seen around the grounds. I auditioned in the spring and was asked to be the featured male singer throughout that summer.

That season's cultural director was Herschel Bernardi, then a struggling actor, who years later went on to star in television and theatre, including Broadway, where he became the longest running Tevye in *Fiddler on the Roof.* Bernardi's camp job required him to create at least one hour of after-dinner entertainment for the guests five nights a week. I performed regularly with a partner, a lovely black soprano, Geraldine Overstreet, doing folk songs, theatre songs, opera duets, and, when required, some acting. We also put on classic one-act plays as well as contemporary pieces.

Some of those pieces were by an aspiring young writer at the camp named Lonnie Elder, Jr., whom Bernardi would also call on to act on stage. Lonnie and I started out as card-playing buddies, sometimes recklessly losing as much as two or three dollars at a single two-hour session. Our friendship continued all the way through 1958, when he was cast as Bobo in the original production of *A Raisin in the Sun*. Lonnie also went on to success as a writer, particularly with a play called *Ceremonies in Dark Old Men*, which is still performed today.

Among the guests was a black man named Bumpy Johnson, who was quite famous or notorious, depending on your point of view. He was known as (and admitted to being) the man who defeated Dutch Schultz for control of the numbers racket in Harlem. That much-publicized battle was not conducted through peaceful negotiations, as the authorities were well aware. But during that summer, while constantly under surveillance, Bumpy was still a free man. Though he could have well afforded to frequent the most expensive resorts (assuming they would have had him), he chose Camp Unity for two basic reasons: it was close to New York City and, more importantly, he liked to be surrounded by both black and white families. He loved playing chess and would sit on a porch challenging anyone who walked by to a game. From his pitchers of vodka and orange juice, continually refilled, he would pour freely and offer a drink to anyone who was thirsty. He would start and entertain political discussions with any man or woman who was interested. But he had one basic rule if the conversation became heated: when there was a woman present or within earshot, no strong or obscene language could be uttered or even suggested. It was a rule you ignored at your peril. This remarkable man, raised on the streets, had become known as the toughest and most dangerous man in Harlem—and yet he had the manners of an old world gentleman. He supported and contributed generously to many civil rights organizations and often entertained for such causes at his Harlem apartment. A fascinating man, full of contradictions, he died years later in prison, having been convicted on a drug charge, which he always insisted, and I believed, was a frame-up.

There was another unusual person at the camp that summer. I may not have noticed her immediately. I believe we first met in the dining room, when I was having dinner soon after arriving at the camp; she was a waitress at the table. I don't remember whether it was during the first course or dessert but, as I seem to recall, my first impression was that rather attractive as she was, she was not a very competent waitress. And she certainly didn't seem to be enjoying her work. But, in fact, I didn't pay her too much attention then, being more concerned about my own job and getting acquainted with the people on the cultural staff.

On Sunday afternoons, all the guests were invited to gather together on a large lawn where anyone so inclined could entertain or start a discussion about current events, which quite often dealt with the race situation in the United States. Employees were encouraged to take part in the discussions, and at one of them the not very good waitress surprised everyone not only by joining in but by electrifying the audience, including me, with her intellectual facility, her poise, and her intense emotional fervor. Afterwards, as I quite deliberately introduced myself to her, I was aware that while she accepted my enthusiastic compliments gracefully, she was obviously amused by my surprise that such an attractive, young (19), black "girl" waitress could speak so eloquently. But, in addition to her smile, she gave me her name, Lorraine Hansberry, and informed me that she might also be involving herself with the culture staff in her free time. She also assured me that waitressing was not to be a large part of her future. Two days later we met at the ping-pong table, and when she bragged about her game and confided that she enjoyed ping-pong much more than waitressing, I was quick to advise, after beating her, that ping-pong should also not be considered as a career.

During that summer the entertainment staff worked very hard and Lorraine would often critique our presentations. I began to see that while she could be very constructive, she could also be very dismissive of another point of view. She was brilliant, perceptive, incredibly articulate, well informed in the literature of theatre, and certainly freely expressive of her very strong opinions. Along with this almost overwhelming package came an ability to laugh at herself and to see humor in her most serious points of view. She was unflinchingly passionate about where this country was delinquent on civil rights and delightfully hysterical when beaten at ping-pong.

As our friendship deepened, we began to discuss how we personally felt about civil rights and what might be our individual roles in that struggle and about what we planned or hoped to do with our careers. I was sure then that I would be a famous singer, and Lorraine knew she would be a writer but was less certain of achieving success.

Lorraine had come to New York from Chicago a short time before, and had been working part-time as a waitress in a Greenwich Village restaurant close to her small apartment. At one point during the summer she said if we stayed in touch she might show me some of her writing after we were back in New York. Indeed, when the summer was over I had become, and was to remain friends not only with Lorraine but also with Lonnie Elder, Herschel Bernardi, and several of the guests at the camp. All of us returned home vowing to stay in touch and, surprisingly, we all did. Of course neither Lorraine nor I realized how important our commitment was destined to be.

Chapter 5

Upon returning to New York at the end of that summer, I was forced to realize that while I loved singing, I didn't wish to starve, and that would require some additional income. So while I continued doing various gigs in and around the city, I searched for other employment. I knew, however, that for my peace of mind, my day job would have to be in the entertainment or music area. A friend in Harlem who owned a record shop advised me about a new record distributor who handled small independent recording companies with mostly black artists. I set up an appointment with Jerry Blaine, the owner of Cosnat Distributing Company, located on 10th Avenue at 52nd Street, and was immediately hired as a salesman to cover the Manhattan area record stores, uptown and downtown, and a short time later I was promoted to sales manager of this small but fast-growing company. Soon after my promotion Mr. Blaine and I were chosen to be the New York distributor for a new label, Atlantic Records. This company was soon to become the leading label recording black artists. Owned by Jerry Wechsler and Ahmet Ertegun and under their guidance and genius, Atlantic Records discovered artists like Aretha Franklin, Ruth Brown, Dinah Washington, and many, many others. As a result, I found myself increasingly associated with black music and artists, appreciating and learning more each day.

Some time later Larry Newton, who owned Derby Records, offered me the job of chief record producer, in charge of artists and repertoire. Since Derby was being distributed by Jerry Blaine's "Cosnat," I would be in familiar hands. I accepted and stayed with Derby until 1954, when I left to start a label of my own called "Glory Records," with which I had some success over the next few years.

Meanwhile, since the summer of 1949 and all through the years that followed, Lorraine Hansberry and I would see each other quite often. She took great pleasure in my new and presumably permanent career. When we went to the theatre we would agree or disagree vehemently about the plays we had seen. Although I enjoyed the arguments, they sometimes left me feeling somewhat insecure. I, who had never seen a Broadway play until I was in my twenties, was talking to a young woman who could recite and critique Shakespeare, Chekhov, O'Casey, Tennessee Williams, Arthur Miller, and many other classic and contemporary poets and playwrights. On many occasions while I was getting an education from her, I did a great deal of vamping, but we would generally end up laughing at and with each other.

Lorraine had begun to show me samples of her writing, at the same time observing how dismal the prospects were for a beginning serious writer, particularly a playwright. A couple of her articles were printed in a little newspaper called *Freedom*, published by Paul Robeson, and her writings and speeches on civil rights were certainly impressive. One day she asked me to read her play about three girls living in the Village, and while I thought it had some decent writing, it was not passionate. Lorraine knew it too, but seemed not to know in what direction to go with her writing in order to have anyone pay attention.

By 1949, I had gotten to know several of the struggling young black actors for whom there was very little work in the commercial theatre and almost none in film or television. Many of them worked with a group in Harlem called the American Negro Theatre, founded by Frederick O'Neal, who in later years was to become very well known as an actor and an official at Actors' Equity. I also met an actor named William Marshall who was achieving some prominence. A handsome, very tall black man with a booming voice, who at one point had played "De Lawd" on Broadway in a revival of Marc Connelly's *The Green Pastures*, Marshall had also co-starred with Dale Robertson in a film called *Lydia Bailey* with Marshall playing the part of King Dick in a film about Haiti. I was invited to the opening of the film at Radio City Music Hall, where in the audience was Paul Robeson, one of my then-and-now idols. At the end of the screening, Bill Marshall asked if I could drive him and a friend up to Harlem. Three other people had come to the screening with me, so I said I wouldn't mind but it would be a tight fit in the car. Leaving the parking lot with my three friends in the back seat, I drove to the front of Radio City. There, Marshall was signing autographs, and waved to me indicating that he would get away as soon as he could. I then noticed that a few yards beyond, Paul Robeson was also signing autographs, for many more people than Marshall.

Soon Marshall, having finished with his signings, walked over to Mr. Robeson, took his arm, cleared a path for him, and they both walked over to my waiting car. Mr. Robeson got in first, sitting next to me, and Marshall followed. These two men, both six feet four were now squeezed with me into the front seat of my car. Moving the front seat as far back as possible to make room for their legs, I could barely reach the gas pedal or brake, which served as an excuse to drive very slowly. As we pulled away, after shaking my hand, Mr. Robeson leaned towards me (not a very long move) and stage whispered in that incredible voice, "I know you've got a big star in your car, this Bill Marshall, so you've got to drive carefully. But, by the way, did you notice who the crowd was going to for autographs?" So I not only had the ordinarily very serious Mr. Robeson in my car but I was also privileged to enjoy his sense of humor. And hearing that voice, Mr. Robeson's, from no more than inches away, on that trip to Harlem, is something I have never forgotten.

Bill Marshall did something else for me. I was having some people over to my apartment one Sunday afternoon, and when Marshall arrived he was once again with a friend. He and this very tall young man walked in, both having to stoop to get under the very low doorway, and I was then introduced to Sidney Poitier. The year was 1949. Mr. Poitier had just returned to New York after a three year off-and-on tour of *Anna Lucasta*, and as with all young black actors of that time, he was struggling to build a career.

I would like to boast that upon first meeting Mr. Poitier I knew immediately that I was in the presence of a man who would one day be Hollywood's number one box-office attraction. But actually I remember thinking, as we discussed the particular civil rights issues of the day, that he was a rather tall, good-looking young man destined for nothing but frustration and defeat in seeking an acting career. I did, however, feel it was gracious of Bill Marshall to encourage his competition, since it hardly seemed likely there would ever be room for two black leading actors in American theatre or film.

Over the next few years, however, Sidney began to achieve some success in film, while he and I also moved from bachelor to marriage status. So in addition to our increasing activity in the civil rights movement, we became a social foursome that included his wife, Juanita, and my wife, the actress Doris Belack. Through the decades our friendship has lasted and deepened. We joined the Poitiers in celebrations of the growth of their family with four beautiful daughters. In later years Doris and I would meet and come to adore Sidney's second wife, Joanna, and to share the joy in the birth of their two lovely, talented daughters, Anika and Sydney. During all of this, Doris and I had been so busy admiring and enjoying the growth of Sidney's families that we never got around to starting our own.

As Sidney and I became busier through the early 1950s, we also developed mutual friendships with quite a number of people. Among them was a writer-actor named Julian Mayfield, whom we met separately, but we each learned to know and love him. Julian was a good-looking, talented young black man in his twenties. He was a leading man on Broadway in *Lost in the Stars* and wrote several books, but finally, frustrated by conditions here, he left this country to live in Ghana for a while. There he became a government head of cultural affairs, and then returned to the United States to become a professor of literature at Howard University. Two incidents during my long friendship with Julian are particularly vivid memories.

The first occurred in New York on a Friday evening when Julian had been visiting some friends in Greenwich Village. He left their apartment at about 11 P.M., walking up to 14th Street to catch a subway going uptown. As he approached the station stairway he noticed a policeman at the top of the stairway who seemed to stare at him, or so he imagined. But as he reached the bottom, another policeman, waiting with his hand on his holster, ordered Julian back up the stairs. The two then escorted him, not too politely, to a squad car, and ordered him inside, all this while even less politely refusing to answer any of his questions. They drove a few short blocks to a movie house on Greenwich Avenue and brought him into the lobby and then to the manager's office, where a very disturbed white man was seated. With Julian held between them, the police asked this man, "Is this the guy?" The man stood up, stared at Julian for a moment, and answered, "No, he was much older, nothin' like him." The cops looked at each other, then said to Julian, "OK, you can go." When Julian demanded again to know why he had been brought there, the disturbed man, not the police, apologized, adding that he had had his wallet stolen in the theatre by a black man. The cops, now anxious to get rid of Julian, just ordered him to leave.

As Julian walked back to the subway, his anger was heightened by the realization that if upon his earlier arrival there, he had heard the rumble of a subway train and decided to run down the stairs to catch it, there's no telling what either of those cops might have done. Julian wrote the headline that he was sure would have appeared in the morning paper, "Thief shot while trying to escape by subway. Two cops lauded for their great detective work and bravery."

Another incident that I shared with Julian, took place on the night Sugar Ray Robinson fought for the sixth time the great white boxer Jake LaMotta. Julian was at my apartment on West 68th Street and we decided to watch the fight on television. Since at that time I didn't own a television set, we went to a local bar on Broadway to see it. We walked into the bar, ordered our beers, and may or may not have noticed that Julian was the only black man in the crowded room. That was not unusual in the early 1950s at Broadway and 68th Street. As the fight progressed through the early rounds, it was clear that unexpectedly, Sugar Ray was being beaten, and rather badly. It was nevertheless an exciting fight and everyone in the bar was having a good time. At about the eighth round Julian and I ordered two more beers and even had a bit of friendly conversation with the bartender and two patrons about the great fight we were seeing.

Around the tenth round, somehow the fight began to go the other way. Sugar Ray was now not only outboxing LaMotta, but by the eleventh round was beating him unmercifully. Suddenly the atmosphere in the bar changed. First it turned softer, then ominously quiet, except for stage-whispered remarks like "Kill the nigger," aimed presumably at Sugar Ray but growing deliberately loud enough for Julian and me to hear. We both continued to drink our beers and stare at the television screen, making sure our eyes did not meet those of any of the other patrons. All the while we were both communicating with glances: "Should we try to get out now or do we dare wait till it's over?" And if Sugar Ray were actually to win, would their celebration be over our dead bodies?

After two more bloody rounds LaMotta was helpless, the fight was stopped, and Sugar Ray won it on a technical knockout. All eyes turned toward us. We had both been absolutely silent during the last three rounds. We knew this was no time for us to celebrate a victory. We just quietly put our beers down on the bar, walked slowly to the doorway, crossed the threshold, and raced back to my apartment, where we collapsed.

As we laughed our way through the rest of the evening, I admitted having considered at one point edging my way to the "white" section of the bar and pretending Julian and I had just met. He said he was thinking at that same time about going to the men's room and escaping out a window, but he was afraid the men's room might have a sign saying "For Whites Only" and he wouldn't be able to get in.

Julian died many years later while still a professor at Howard University, and I still miss him.

During the early 1950s, Sidney met Lorraine Hansberry and we spent some evenings together. One night Lorraine asked Sidney for advice and encouragement about how to sell television scripts. Sidney corroborated how difficult it was to sell anything to television about black characters or families. But it was equally hard for black writers to ignore or resist such subjects. For instance, Sidney said, "Once when I wasn't getting work as an actor I decided to write a television play just for the money. And I finished a play in which there was nothing about race or black people. As I started to reread what I had written, in one scene I have these two guys having a conversation and I see this one white boy saying to another white boy, 'Joe, how come these white folks treat us so badly?' So you see, it's hard to get away from the subject."

At the same time, I came to know the work of many black poets and met and spent time with Langston Hughes. Also, with my own recording company set up, I thought it might be a good idea to do an album of poetry by black poets. Of course, that was the time of the LP, long before the days of tapes or CDs. I asked Sidney if he would be interested in recording some poetry and he agreed. For the content and the liner notes I asked Lorraine to help me choose the selections and write the cover copy. I added an actress, my wife Doris Belack, and we proceeded to record.

While the recording received some good press, it obviously did not appeal to a mass market and so enjoyed only limited sales. But in Lorraine's liner notes she revealed her writing talent so dramatically that it may have implanted in my mind the possibility that one day this woman might really write a play someone would produce. In any case, here is a copy of the cover of *The Poetry of the Negro* and the notes written by Lorraine Hansberry in 1955.

POETRY OF THE NEGRO

PAUL LAURENCE DUNBAR
At Candle Lightin' Time
When Malindy Sings
An Ante-Bellum Sermon
The Debt
Ere Sleep Comes Down to Soothe the
  Weary Eyes
We Wear the Mask

JAMES WELDON JOHNSON
The Creation
Lift Every Voice

COUNTEE CULLEN
To John Keats
Yet Do I Marvel

LANGSTON HUGHES
I, Too
Blues at Dawn
Mother to Son

GWENDOLYN BROOKS
When You Have Forgotten Sunday

M. CARL HOLMAN
Debate of the Dark Brothers

ARMAND LANUSSE
Epigram

> *Green trees a-bending*
> *Poor sinner stands a-trembling*
> *The trumpet sounds within-a my soul*

SOME NEGRO SLAVE once lifted his voice and sang those lines for the first time. Somewhere else, miles away or perhaps on the very next plantation, another dark brother in chains parted his lips and challenged the heavens with:

> *King Jesus rides a milk white horse*
> *And no man works like him!*

In such moments was born the "POETRY OF THE NEGRO"

Unquestionably the earliest expression of the Negro as poet in the United States lies embedded in the depths of the great and beloved music of the spirituals. The "black and unknown bards" created patterns of imagery and structural tradition in the "sorrow songs" which have been directly and indirectly an artistic foundation for the development of Negro poetry.

Having inherited this tradition, two great poets of the Negro people, PAUL LAURENCE DUNBAR and JAMES WELDON JOHNSON, wrestled mightily with the problem of the utilization of the folk idiom in their poems.

Dunbar, the Ohio born son of former slaves, first wrote simple "straight" English verses. He was later captivated by the living color in the speech of his people and consciously incorporated it into his famous humor poems and mood-monologues.

His mastery of "dialect" verse gave him a ready entry to the white literary publications of the time. The same editors, however, were not inclined to publish the poet's haunting lyrics about love or loneliness written in the classical traditions, though many of Dunbar's lyric poems take their place easily among America's finest.

Dunbar was obliged to spend much of his creative talent writing innocuous short stories which, for the most part, merely sustained the notion of the Negro as buffoon. The restrictions forced on him by publishers and a lifetime of poor health combined to make a tragic figure of the man who was probably America's greatest humor poet.

American Negroes remember Paul Laurence Dunbar largely for poems and monologues such as: LIZA; THE PARTY; and the three dialect poems included in the album. They have long been favorite repertory items of the "dramatic-reader" at church socials and teas.

Still, it was this same poet who sang so sadly and chanted out the beauty of ERE SLEEP COMES DOWN TO SOOTHE THE WEARY EYES. And before he died, at 34, he had already shared with his people, a thought charged with bitterness: WE WEAR THE MASK.

JAMES WELDON JOHNSON, who was throughout his life deeply involved in the political life of his people, evolved a more sophisticated approach to the problems of folk material. Like Dunbar, he felt that in it lay the source of great poetry. He respected the efforts of Dunbar toward what he called "mechanically" trying to achieve "Negro sound". But he repudiated the mere "mutilation" of English for the achievement of the folk spirit in composed work.

He wrote: "What the colored poet in the U. S. needs to do is something like Synge did for the Irish; he needs to find a form that will express the racial spirit by symbols from within rather than by symbols from without . . ."

He sought an artistic fulfillment of a marvelous beginning: "I felt that this primitive stuff could be used in a way similar to that in which a composer makes use of a folk theme in writing a major composition."

A finer tribute to his theories cannot be found than that presented by THE CREATION, originally published in GOD'S TROMBONES.

It is virtually impossible to separate the artistic strivings of and experiments of the Negro poets from the social experiences of their people at corresponding periods. For three centuries racists had hurled slander and insult at Negro speech and insisted that its unique nature was the product of tongues which were incapable of mastering a European language. Thus, "dialect" became a despised stigma to millions of Negroes. Negro intellectuals rejected even the charm of Dunbar because he employed "slavery-talk"; and James Weldon Johnson, sensing the richness of the material, sought to find a new but faithful way to present it.

Today we can see both poets sought truth, and that their classical, folk and "transformed-folk" poems are by and large the products of agitated genius.

Of the World War I Negro migrations from the South, the distinguished Negro critic, the late Dr. Alain Locke, wrote that the movement involved: "A new vision of social and economic freedom. A deliberate flight not only from countryside to city—but from medieval to modern."

James Weldon Johnson, for many years General Secretary of the National Association for the Advancement of Colored People, wrote a poem full of "hope and faith" which was set to music and promptly swept through Negro communities North and South until it was finally designated by the NAACP as the "national hymn" of the Negro people. This, of course, was LIFT EVERY VOICE which concludes the album. It is presented by the artists in the final stanza with a stirring martial intonation which is an accurate reflection of the time and spirit of its creation.

THIS TOO, was the period of the "New Negro Renaissance" in New York. A group of poets emerged with fresh talents and fresh ideas. For them the New Negro had to have a New Song to sing.

Sometimes, the song was sheer bitterness.

Sometimes it was militant and angry, even violent.

Yet again, it was but artistic anguish, put down in language the world would find difficult to forget:

> Yet do I marvel at this curious thing,
> To make a poet black—and bid
>   him sing!

But while the black poets marvelled, they did continue to sing. A supreme talent appeared in the author of the last lines. The young Countee Cullen, who offered his first volume of poetry at 22, is considered by some critics as perhaps the finest of the poets to come out of the period. Two representative Cullen works are presented in the album: YET DO I MARVEL and TO JOHN KEATS, POET AT SPRINGTIME. Of the latter, listeners will doubtless share the collectors' opinion that neither Keats nor spring have been saluted more nobly.

By the 'Thirties several currents had run through the moods of intellectual black America. Africa was unearthed and celebrated in politics and verse. A former unknown, unloved and unsung "homeland" became the dream. Black beauty, black thought and black culture underwent a poetic re-examination and gained exaltation. Inadvertently the Negro poet had a new consciousness and identity.

It was from this period that a young Missouri-born poet came into full glory singing songs to black washerwomen and putting the meter of the blues into poetry. In his work was a culmination of many attitudes in the historical development of Negro poetry. Whatever remained of self-consciousness; of apology; of back-handed defense of Negro speech—melted away under the pen of Langston Hughes.

Hughes wrote as his people spoke and the color that Dunbar, so loved leaped to life again. He wrote as the people thought, and the "symbols from within" which Johnson promoted sang from his verses. Few could doubt when he wrote on behalf of his 15,000,000—

> Someday . . .
> You'll see how beautiful I am

Hughes is probably one of the country's most popular poets today with an immense audience, Negro and white. His poetry has kept pace with the times, trying out new rhythms in verse as promptly as they emerge in Negro life from blues to bop. His facility for the street-corner or laundry-room phrase is sometimes deceptive. Behind the simplicity of statement:

If I thought thoughts in bed, them
thoughts would bust my head
So I don't dare start thinking in
the morning.

—lies a profound sensitivity to ordinary despair and the occasional beauty of everyday.

THE THREE LAST POETS included in the album testify to some of the earliest and the most recent developments in the poetry of the Negro.

EPIGRAM, is the work of ARMAND LANUSSE, a free Negro of 19th century New Orleans who taught school, participated in the literary pastimes of his group, and wrote his little known and apparently whimsical verses in French. (Translated here by Langston Hughes).

WHEN YOU HAVE FORGOTTEN SUNDAY is by the leading Negro woman poet, GWENDOLYN BROOKS. In this representative poem she gives us a statement of remembered love which, through her spectacular gift for the unembellished, is strangely familiar and sentiently personal.

DEBATE OF THE DARK BROTHERS by M. CARL HOLMAN offers a rather muted and dual judgment on the nature of reality.

To be sure, this set of 16 poems by 7 representative American poets will be, for the uninitiated, a splendidly entertaining introduction to an immense body of work which represents some of America's finest poetry. For those who already know and love Negro verse, it will be an experience of heightened and lasting satisfaction.

LORRAINE HANSBERRY

SIDNEY POITIER—The slim young star of "BLACKBOARD JUNGLE" and "CRY THE BELOVED COUNTRY" is presented here in his first recording. It was felt that Mr. Poitier's remarkable, controlled registry of the spoken word and his robust and proper sensitivity for the "tenderest of folk statements" made him a natural for this album.

Mr. Poitier, winner of the Sylvania television award for best actor of the year, 1955, is soon to be seen again by motion picture audiences in the forthcoming "A MAN IS TEN FEET TALL".

DORIS BELACK — Miss Belack, a talented young New York actress, has been gaining increasing attention for her work in T.V. and Theatre productions. On hearing her splendid performance at early test auditions, Mr. Poitier felt that Miss Belack's interpretation of the material was precisely what was wanted and she was accordingly his personal choice for assisting artist.

Chapter 6

With Lorraine's continuing theatre interest and my increased, if somewhat vicarious, involvement through my growing circle of actor friends, Lorraine and I would see more and more off-off-Broadway plays together. In that period of the mid-50s, we could afford to go as often as we liked since ticket prices for the plays were generally no more than voluntary contributions. As she continued to show to me, as a friend, some of her writing, I was aware of her deepening frustration at not having anything produced in spite of her efforts to write "commercially."

On one occasion, we attended a performance at a church in Greenwich Village of a new play written by a black writer. It was about a black family and was getting positive word-of-mouth and some press attention. Afterwards, Lorraine, while pleased to see a play by a black writer, was not particularly impressed, and she remarked off-handedly, "Well, if I were going to write about a black family, I could do better than that." My response—just as casual—was, "So, why don't you try it?" We had no further conversation on the subject until one Saturday evening, months later, when Lorraine invited me to her apartment for dinner and to hear her read several scenes from a play she was working on, temporarily entitled *A Raisin in the Sun*. At that reading were also a mutual friend, Burt D'Lugoff, and Lorraine's husband, Robert Nemiroff.

The play, even though not completed, had an enormous effect on me, and we talked about it far into the night. When I finally left her apartment to return home, presumably to sleep, I found that sleep was impossible. I kept hearing Lorraine's characters and feeling the emotions the play had aroused in me. I began to realize that I had to meet this family again. I had to get to know them better, and to know what was going to happen to them. At about 6:30 Sunday morning, I gave up trying to sleep and called Lorraine.

My first words to her were, "Lorraine, I think I want to produce your play." Her first words to me were, "Are you nuts? It's the middle of the night!" My incoherent response was, "No, that's another play. I mean your play, *A Raisin in the Sun*. I really want to produce it—and I can't sleep." She said, "I'm sorry you can't sleep. It's probably my cooking. Call me when it's daylight, or when you feel better, whichever is later. And take a Tums." When I called her back, she finally accepted that I hadn't gone mad, and said I was welcome to become her producer.

But how, when or where does one learn how to produce a play? I made the very shrewd guess that in order to produce a play I would have to acquire some kind of ownership in it. The word "option" occurred to me as something I had heard but didn't fully understand. I briefly had assumed when Lorraine, that Sunday morning after my sleepless night, had said, "OK, go ahead, produce it," I was ready to put out a shingle saying, "Philip Rose, Producer," and to respond to the many calls which would undoubtedly come in from eager investors, actors, directors, theatre owners, etc. I did realize it might take me a few weeks to accomplish all this, but I was prepared to work hard.

But then I thought I'd better telephone my friend Sidney Poitier for help. When I told him, with no specifics, about my plans to option a play, he didn't laugh out loud but he did suggest I see an attorney. He recommended his own, Harold Stern, who, it turned out, was quite prominent in the theatre as well as the film industry. I called Harold the next day and, knowing that I was a friend of Sidney's, he set up an appointment for me almost immediately. I then informed Lorraine of this and we arranged to meet at Mr. Stern's office.

There, without waiting, we were ushered into Mr. Stern's private office and I introduced Lorraine and myself. I could see that while he was very gracious, he was nevertheless surprised to meet such a very attractive, very young black woman who had written a play presumably good enough to open on Broadway. He was equally gracious in not emphasizing his opinion of the very slight possibility that such an event might ever take place with me as the producer.

After chatting amiably for a few minutes, with Lorraine probably the least nervous, we got to the purpose of our visit. I explained that since Lorraine and I had decided I was to produce her play, it seemed we should have a written agreement. He thought that was a wise first step, and asked Lorraine who would be representing her. Lorraine responded that we thought he could represent both of us. Mr. Stern pointed out that Lorraine and I, at some point during the production might develop an adversarial relationship. When Lorraine and I both denied that possibility, he asked us to think the matter over for a few days, and then if we were still comfortable with joint representation he would draw up a simple option agreement.

After we left Mr. Stern's office, Lorraine over coffee expressed her amusement at Mr. Stern's reaction to her and the very idea of my producing a play on Broadway. She did say, however, that as an efficient and well-informed theatre attorney, he was probably right, and I might have to lower my aspirations a little. She then said, "It doesn't matter. I'm writing this play in the hope that it might be performed, maybe in some little theatre or even a black church somewhere." She did admit, however, to her excitement that we were taking this first step and to how much work she still had to do on the play itself. Just before we left the coffee shop, standing at the table and still laughing at Harold Stern's reaction to the two of us, I remarked, "Wait 'til he hears that I'm going to get Poitier to play the lead and he'll have to represent another adversary." Lorraine fell right back down in her chair saying, "You're kidding; are you really going to ask Sidney?" I answered, "You'd better go home and finish the play." She jumped up, calling over her shoulder as she ran, "Call Harold Stern back right now."

I waited a few days before calling Harold as I began acquiring all the information I could from friends and acquaintances about theatre producing in order to be a little more knowledgeable at our next meeting. I read some books, switched my subscription from *Billboard* and *Cash Box* to *Variety*. I discovered lists were available of investors in all the Broadway shows, including addresses; as well as lists of directors, set designers, actors, and, of course, other producers.

Armed with all of this incredible knowledge, I went to my second meeting with Harold Stern. He was fully prepared with an agreement for Lorraine and me to sign, but he also informed me of some of the obstacles I would be facing, namely, the odds against even an experienced producer ever getting a play to Broadway, much less having a success. He gave me a complete lesson in the legal and practical aspects of raising money, the papers to be filed before I could even approach people, the bonds for the unions, and the money required for the fees of a press agent, a company manager, and himself. He kept me for as long as I could bear it. He was very generous, I thought, with his time, but he assured me as I left that I would receive a bill for all the hours we'd spent together. I recall now that, years later, when Harold Stern was negotiating with Columbia Pictures for the sale of the rights to *A Raisin in the Sun* and represented David Susskind and myself, who were to co-produce the film, someone from the studio said, "Philip Rose doesn't know a damn thing about producing a movie," and Stern was able to brag honestly, "When I met him, he knew even less about producing a play."

Everything that Harold Stern revealed and indeed taught me would of course turn out to be true and applicable to *any* play being produced. What he was not discussing (or perhaps was deliberately avoiding) were the difficult circumstances peculiar to this play.

Lorraine started writing it in 1955. Those were the pre-civil rights days, when segregation and worse were firmly entrenched in the South and existed a bit more politely in the North. In the theatre community, while many people did not overtly share these prejudices, a Broadway play was (and is) after all a business, with its success or failure determined by its profit or loss. In that context, the *presumed* obstacles this play faced would soon become obvious. Some of them were:

1. It would be difficult to find a group of experienced black actors, much less a black star, to appear in it.
2. No one was likely to invest in it.
3. Who would go to see it? Black people didn't go to Broadway plays and whites weren't likely to come to this one, unless Lorraine added the singing and dancing usually associated with black shows.
4. If the play did manage to attract black audiences, wouldn't that scare away the white audience whose attendance was essential for the play's success?
5. Since all the above comprised a generally accepted point of view who would rent us a theatre?

Absurd as they may seem today, these and many other similar attitudes were not regarded as unreasonable at that time. Moreover, the play could easily be dismissed or ignored in view of the following additional irrefutable facts: This was a new play, a serious play, not a comedy, about a black family, written not by a man, but by a woman, a young black woman with no apparent writing credits. And who supposedly was going to produce the play? A young white man, a struggling singer who had absolutely no producing credentials, apparent or otherwise: "Forget the names Lorraine Hansberry or Philip Rose. You'll never hear them again."

Fortunately, since I had neither knowledge nor the experience to acquaint me with all these presumptions and precautions, I could only proceed, with the advantages of naiveté and ignorance.

Chapter 7

Lorraine and I signed our initial option agreement on December 3rd, 1957. Harold Stern cautioned me that before I could begin to raise money, I needed to complete an offering circular, legally prepared and registered with the appropriate government agencies. Meanwhile, I began to talk to friends about the play. Several of my closer friends just naturally assumed, since the playwright was a black woman, that I intended to produce it as a political statement about the civil rights struggle, and they were prepared to make a contribution to that effort. When I explained that I saw it as a potential profit-making production, many of them withdrew their offers, since as a business investment it seemed to them to make no sense.

Mr. Stern also informed me that in order to prepare an offering circular, I would need a budget for the production, and that would require my hiring a general manager to estimate the show's production and operating expenses. He also thought it would be a good idea to acquire a press agent to announce the existence of the play in the *New York Times* theatre column. However, given an unfinished play by a new writer with an unknown producer, and, most crucially, no star, my calls to theatre professionals went unanswered. I then realized that even though Lorraine was still working on the play and had yet to produce a third act, I would have to test my offhand remark to her that I was going to try to get Sidney Poitier to star in it. I called Sidney to ask if he would come to my apartment for a social evening and to listen to a reading of the play. He seemed surprised to hear that the play still existed, as I had not mentioned it since the phone call some weeks before, when he had recommended Harold Stern to me. I did not tell him the author was anybody he knew, saying only that Lorraine Hansberry was going to read all the parts as a favor to me because the playwright was not available. I was devious only because I thought it essential that Sidney feel free to express openly his feelings about the project, whether positive or negative, and without embarrassment. He agreed to come to my apartment and we set a date for late December.

I arranged a very private reading in my living room and I tried to create a relaxed social atmosphere with drinks all around before we began. Lorraine made some veiled remarks about some of the problems in the play that she thought the playwright had not solved, and she joked about her attempt to try to play all the different characters. She then began to read, and after a few pages, her hesitancy at trying to act all the roles began to disappear. Her familiarity with and passion for all these characters took over, and so did the play. By the second act we seemed to forget that Lorraine was reading, and we were removed from Central Park West to a small apartment in Chicago.

Lorraine went right through the first two acts without a break. At the very emotional ending of act 2, I suggested, and Sidney seemed to want, an intermission. Watching his visual and sometimes audible responses during the reading, I felt he had been both affected and entertained. He confirmed this by asking immediately where I had found the play and who the writer was. I hoped that we could postpone the rest of the reading, knowing as I did that Lorraine was unprepared to present a third act and would have had to improvise it. In any case, Sidney was obviously excited and insisted that we identify the playwright, and when we hesitated, he tried to guess. He began by naming the many black writers we mutually knew, starting with Alice Childress, going on to John Killems, followed by Langston Hughes. And as Lorraine and I progressed from shaking our heads, to broadening our smiles, to laughing loudly, he shouted with us, simultaneously and incredulously, "Lorraine Hansberry?!"

Sidney was stunned, embarrassed, and excited, apologizing for not being aware of the brilliance of Lorraine's talent. Of course there was no way he could have been, but that did not dilute his surprise. With all the time he spent congratulating her, Sidney had to rush off to another appointment. So fortunately we had to postpone reading the nonexistent third act. But Sidney was eloquent in his praise of Lorraine's writing and her intelligent reading, and he left with words to me, at the door, to call him the next day.

After he was gone, Lorraine, well aware of how charming and kind Sidney could be and would have been even if he had hated the play, was calmly of two minds about his reaction. Her opinions were, first, he may have thought she was the greatest new playwright of the century, and second, he would never speak to me again for embarrassing him so profoundly by making him come to this reading. I said I thought the truth might lie somewhere in between, and after a few drinks we ended the evening feeling generally up and somewhat hopeful.

Of course I spoke to Sidney the next day, just before he was to return to Los Angeles. The conversation was mostly positive, to the degree that he said he would like to see the completed play. I promised to arrange this as quickly as possible. He also mentioned in passing how busy his schedule would be for the next few months: he would soon be involved in the filming of *The Defiant Ones* and *Porgy and Bess*. While Sidney's attitude was encouraging, it in no way invited my association of his name with the play publicly. I informed Lorraine that we needed an acceptable completed script for me to pursue him further. The trouble was that she was struggling with the third act and had been for some time.

When Lorraine had first begun to write about the Youngers, she called upon her life experiences in Chicago, where her own family was being vilified for using their real estate interests to fight to open white neighborhoods to black families who could afford them. Drawing upon these experiences, she had planned to have the last half of the play take place in the new house to which the Younger family would already have moved. This would inevitably lead to racial incidents created by their new neighbors. But racial incidents were not what Lorraine wanted to write about. What she had written and created so eloquently in the first half of the play was a black family whose every member had individual hopes, dreams, and frustrations; and whose center, her protagonist, Walter Lee Younger—a son, husband and father—worked as a chauffeur but had ambitions to provide a better life for himself, his son, his wife, and his mother. His frustrations, his (in our society) dangerous dreams, and finally his explosion had to be the core as well as the story of the play.

One day Lorraine expressed her dissatisfaction with her story line and the way the racial events in the new neighborhood were interfering with the development of her characters. I casually asked, "What if they never had moved to the new neighborhood? What would have happened to them?" Lorraine jumped out of her seat, and later, by the time we had the reading for Sidney, she had already recast the main story line. It would not deal with the Youngers in the new neighborhood, but with whether, as a result of an ill-conceived action by Walter Lee, the family might be destroyed and never move out of their sordid surroundings or realize any of their dreams. The final scene, the most difficult for Lorraine to solve, was how to have Walter Lee effectively control the resolution of the play.

When, after my conversation with Sidney, I told Lorraine we had to have a completed script as soon as possible not only to show to him, but for potential investors, I was pleased to hear that she was already rushing through the third act and hoped to have it in a few days.

In a short period of time Lorraine did indeed deliver the third act to me, and while we were not satisfied with the very last scene, she felt it was good enough to show to Sidney. Since he was then unavailable, I decided instead to hold another reading at my apartment, this time with a cast of actors. I would invite friends, some potential investors, and, also, on the recommendation of Harold Stern, a prominent general manager and a press representative. I also invited Sidney Poitier's agent, Martin Baum. Mr. Baum had been a very powerful friend, supporter, and promoter of Sidney's career from its beginnings and, incidentally, continues to be to this day. I hoped that somewhere along the way I would negotiate with him and have him as an ally.

On April 23rd, 1958, I finally received from Harold Stern a completed offering circular for *A Raisin in the Sun*, which meant I could now legally begin to raise money for the show. Until then raising money had not been an issue because my attempts to do so were so ineffectual I couldn't even get people to call me back to turn me down. Now, at last, we were legal and I set the date for the reading for April 27th, 1958.

On a lovely Sunday afternoon we had about sixty people sitting on chairs, stools, couches, and the floor of our living room at 50 Central Park West, while a group of actors were gathered around our dining room table to read the play. The guests included friends and strangers. Among the actors reading were Ruby Dee and Ivan Dixon, both of them destined to be in the play on Broadway. Lorraine was reading the role of Mama, a role we would later have some difficulty casting.

Although I was generally nervous about all the reactions and I was beginning to sense what producers go through on opening nights, I was most anxious about the reactions of Sidney's agent, Martin Baum, and particularly the esteemed general manager and press agent I was hoping to hire after the reading. At the end of the first act my anxiety was reduced, or heightened, as both of these esteemed professionals suddenly and simultaneously discovered they had other engagements and had to leave.

These gentlemen shall remain nameless, not because I don't know their names, but because they are still involved in theatre and I would not want to embarrass them further.

That aside, the audience at the reading seemed enthusiastic and emotional, with wet handkerchiefs waving like flags around the room. Furthermore, the response was clearly all-inclusive— covering equally male and female, young and old, and black and white members of the group. While Lorraine still sat among the actors, slowly recovering from being "Mama" rather than the playwright, and before she left her chair to receive congratulations and embraces, she stared at me, her eyes communicating what I was feeling: "My God, we may really have something here." I did not choose that moment to point out that the only people to leave after the first act were the two "professionals" whom I had been prepared to offer rather than ask for money. To anyone who might ask me who these men were, I was prepared to reply that they were both surgeons who had to rush off to perform emergency operations. Overall, the afternoon was unquestionably very encouraging, and a few people requested copies of the offering circular.

Of course, Sidney had not yet agreed to do the play, though there were rumors floating around about him, particularly among the actors at the reading. But I did make our intentions known to Marty Baum, who promised to discuss the role with him.

A few days later Mr. Baum volunteered that while there could be many schedule conflicts preventing a commitment, Sidney certainly was intrigued by the character and the play. "But," Marty said, "you know and he knows that you have no third act ending." I told him that Lorraine was actually rewriting the last scene at the moment, and he suggested I get it to him quickly.

Well, Lorraine and I both knew that until a short time ago we'd had no third act at all, much less an ending. In the script at the reading, Walter Lee resolved all of his and his family's problems by finding religion at the play's conclusion. This was a holdover from a previous third act and was certainly not going to be retained. When I told Lorraine we really would have a chance of getting Sidney if we hurried, she informed me that she had already solved the problem and I would have the new and completed script within days. Also, over the last few days Lorraine had received a letter from Langston Hughes giving her the right to use *A Raisin in the Sun*, a line from his poem "Dream Deferred," as the title of her play. (Until then we had been using it without official authorization from the poet.) A very few days later, as promised, I received the newly finished script, with a truly shattering last scene. We now had a complete play with an official title, and I sent it out to Sidney immediately.

In early May I suddenly became ill with what my doctor diagnosed as a severe and contagious case of flu with a danger of progressing to pneumonia. Obviously everything that I had been doing to raise money came to a perceptible slowdown. One day, as my fever went up and my spirits went down, my wife informed me that I had a visitor, and into my bedroom walked Sidney Poitier. He was in town, heard I was ill and decided to come over. He said he would have come sooner but he was delayed, searching for a protective mask to wear. Since he didn't find one I suggested we forgo any embrace unless we had an overwhelming reason for one. He looked at me as if he were trying to judge how serious my illness was and said, "I've read your play. How sick are you?" "Sick enough," I said, "that it won't matter what you think, so take your best shot." "Well," he said, speaking very slowly, "I have to tell you that I've decided, regretfully—to play the part." It took a brief moment for me to absorb what I had heard. I then tried to execute a jump from the bed into his lap but I barely made it to the floor. Sidney was already racing down the hallway, yelling at me over his shoulder, "Talk to my agent."

I didn't bother to get up but crawled to the nearest phone and put in a call to Marty Baum to begin negotiations. I was pleased to hear Marty say it was the new last scene that made the difference. We agreed to discuss all the contractual items when I was feeling stronger and able to defend myself. Many times in later years I have accused Sidney of agreeing to do the play that day because he thought I was too sick to recover and it wouldn't ever get produced. He has never quite denied this.

Chapter 8

It did not take long to complete negotiations with Marty Baum for Sidney's written commitment to star in the play. Marty did caution me that I had better move rapidly, since Sidney was getting offers to star in more major films after completing *The Defiant Ones* and *Porgy and Bess*. So now, blessed with the very positive element of having a star, I was feeling increasing pressure to collect all the other elements of a production: director, cast, set, lighting, costume designers, stage manager, general manager, press agent, and a place to house the play—preferably in a theatre. Just to begin hiring all these people would require signing contracts, paying some advance fees, putting up bonds with unions—and therefore having to accelerate the money raising.

By signing Poitier I was able to obtain the services of two prominent theatre professionals: a general manager, Walter Fried, and a press agent, James Proctor. As general manager, Wally would be responsible for negotiating, with my approval, the terms of all future contracts, while Jimmy as press agent would now handle the promotion of the show in conjunction with a theatrical advertising agency. As mentioned earlier, both of these men had been involved with such successful producers and plays as Kermit Bloomgarden's original production of *Death of a Salesman*. They agreed that *Raisin* contained excellent writing as well as timely social content. They were also intrigued by the combination of a play written by an unknown young black woman and the first Broadway effort of an unknown young producer. Both Proctor and Fried agreed to start with no more than a handshake deal.

As Proctor sent out press releases announcing the play with Sidney Poitier as the star, Fried began putting together a list of Broadway theatres that I hoped would be offering us a home. Meanwhile, I began to move on to the other elements of the production. I knew many of the black actors who were part of the New York theatre scene, and indeed some of them had participated in the reading at my apartment, but I knew it was now urgent that I at least interview some directors. Once again I turned to Sidney. He suggested I see and consider Lloyd Richards, a young man with whom he had studied at the Paul Mann Actors Workshop. I knew Richards only as an actor whom I had seen and admired in a Broadway play called *The Egghead*. He and I had a brief meeting in my office, and I didn't hesitate to make an immediate decision, offering him the job as director. I would like to say it was an easy choice because I was so prescient that I knew Lloyd would turn out to be, through the years that followed, one of our most important theatre directors and teachers. But the fact is the reason I had no trouble deciding was simply that I knew Richards would make Sidney comfortable. Much later, many well-established directors were still questioning their agents as to why they had never had a shot at or been interviewed for the play. Meanwhile, as general manager Wally Fried began negotiating with Lloyd Richards's agent, he reported to me that while he was not making much progress in nailing down a theatre in New York, there were out-of-town possibilities as soon as we were ready for production.

After the *New York Times* announced Sidney Poitier's involvement in the play, it was a bit easier to contact seasoned theatre investors, and I began to send out scripts to sophisticated and affluent individuals whose names I secured through various sources. While I was having some success with friends who believed everything they read in the *Times*, I was making very little progress with the well-known angels. Fortunately, around that time I was earning income from my music publishing and recording company and thus was able to advance the front money we were beginning to expend. My wife and I were getting a bit concerned about this, but I expected that as word got around, I would begin to get more responses. Then, suddenly, I received some return calls, from David Susskind and Roger Stevens among others.

David Susskind at the time was a prominent television producer who had presented many of the best original dramas written by the medium's most accomplished writers. One of these plays was *A Man Is Ten Feet Tall,* by Robert Alan Aurthur, which starred Sidney Poitier and won awards for both the play and Sidney's performance. I knew that Mr. Susskind, who also hosted *Open End,* one of television's first serious talk shows (unfortunately, called by some *David Susskind's Open End*), was interested in expanding into theatre and film production. When I received a message to come to his office, I was sure I'd found a co-producer who would solve all my problems. Since we were both friends of Sidney's, it seemed as if it would be an ideal relationship.

Before we met at David's office, I had told Lorraine things were looking up, and she, knowing well who David was, shared my optimism. Susskind was very friendly, introducing me to his chief assistants before he escorted me into his inner sanctum. He then proceeded to tell me how much he admired my courage in trying to do this play, but that he could not be involved because it was not "commercial." To participate in a Broadway production, he would have to be sure it would be a hit. He could not stake his reputation on such an extremely risky venture. I said, "But David, you've promoted your television reputation on just such risk-taking and you've achieved and received much success and admiration just for that." He responded, "Yes, but in television you do it and if it doesn't work you've already got your next one on. When I get involved in theatre I'll know I've got a commercial hit that runs for a long time—and you don't have that."

I left his office a bit stunned, but I had to rush back to my own office to return a call from Roger Stevens. Mr. Stevens was one of Broadway's most successful producers and was later to become head of the Kennedy Center theatre operation, financing and co-producing original plays both on Broadway and at the Kennedy Center. I was pleased to have him take my call immediately and to hear him echo David Susskind's admiration for my courage in trying to produce *Raisin*. But then he went on: "I can't get involved in this one. You see, Walter Lee Younger, your hero, is not an admirable character. He does a terrible thing to his family, and I can't approve of that." "But," I said (fighting a lost cause), "he is forced into doing that out of desperation and even if what he's done is not admirable, many figures in very successful plays do things we don't approve of, as in *Death of a Salesman*, or *Hamlet*, or . . . ." He interrupted me with, "But this is a poor black family and he shouldn't have done that to them." I hung up the phone as graciously as possible, but was increasingly resentful of all the admiration I was getting and ready to exchange it for some money, even if it were accompanied by contempt for my naiveté or stupidity.

I called Lorraine and she was able to make both of us laugh at my restrained reaction to the comments about the play. Meanwhile, I said, I would soon be organizing casting sessions for the three of us (Lloyd, Lorraine, and myself). I had already hired a stage manager, Lenny Auerbach, who had been recommended by an old friend, Morty Halpern, one of the most sought-after stage managers back then and until his recent retirement. He helped and taught me a great deal. Lenny turned out to be a wonderful choice, and before too long also a very good friend. It was Lenny who set up the procedure for the casting sessions.

At about that time I received a phone call from David Cogan, to whom I had sent the play. His name had appeared on one of those many lists of Broadway financial supporters. He had been a major investor in the recent, very successful *Two for the Seesaw*, the play written by William Gibson that starred Henry Fonda and made a star of Anne Bancroft. David invited me to visit him at the Empire State Building, headquarters of his very prestigious accounting and money management firm. His first words as I accepted his invitation to disappear into a very large, too comfortable chair, were how much he admired me, which was enough for me to try to extricate myself from the chair and head for the door. But then he said, coming toward me and extending his hand, "I like the play very much and I think it should be produced. I would like very much to be a part of it." I now lapsed back to be comfortably ensconced in my chair, estimating in my mind what percentage of the needed one hundred thousand dollars he would commit. But as I reached up for his handshake, he returned to his desk and continued. "So I'm prepared to give you immediately a check for five hundred dollars with just one provision: that you do the play off-Broadway. It will never work otherwise." I left his office politely mumbling something about considering his very valuable advice, but articulating something much more clearly after getting out the door.

Chapter 9

We had now sent out lists of the character breakdowns to Actors' Equity and to all the agents for casting suggestions. At that time, the summer of 1958, the role of the independent casting agent had not yet reached its current prominence, and audition appointments were generally set up directly between the actor's agent and the producer's office. Actors who had not yet acquired agency representation would make the rounds of all the producers' offices hoping at least to be seen, if not read, for a part. That practice by struggling actors of "making the rounds" has largely been eliminated as producers and directors generally only see actors who have first been screened and selected by an independent casting agency. This has substantially reduced the time spent on seeing too many actors, and has made it easier for directors and producers. I'm not sure it has made it easier, though, for young, old, unknown, and sometimes talented actors to begin their careers.

In any case, the actors we saw for a role in *Raisin* either were submitted to me by their agents, recommended by Lloyd Richards or Lorraine Hansberry, or had come on their own to the very accessible and now official office of the *Raisin* production company at 157 West 57th Street. This was the location of my "rhythm and blues" recording company, which was already receiving a steady stream of young aspiring black performers, mostly singers, who would audition for me with my office piano. I might also occasionally use that piano to rehearse an operatic aria and to further offend my neighbors.

My office for *Raisin,* as well as for future productions, soon enjoyed a reputation for being open to any actor to visit, with or without an appointment. That would seem to welcome chaos, but a young woman, Lynda Watson, just out of high school, who came to work for me at the time of the *Raisin* production, became my assistant for more years than she might want known. Linda soon learned to welcome visitors when I was available in my office, knowing that I would be able to cope with any actor, attitude, and behavior short of violence. She stayed with me for over thirty years, a figure she admits to, though sometimes underestimates.

Through the many years after *A Raisin in the Sun,* as I began directing as well as producing, my accessibility to young talent has been important to me both professionally and personally. Once again, the opportunities I may have offered to some have rewarded me with joyful dividends many times over, and much more profoundly, particularly in the area known as non-traditional casting. I'll have more to say about that later.

Obviously, the casting search began with the comforting knowledge that we already had filled perfectly our starring role, with Sidney Poitier. So what very often becomes a major problem in many potential Broadway productions was already solved, and the rest of the cast, we assumed, would fall into place fairly easily. We began, then, with the role of Ruth Younger, Sidney's wife in the play. Ruby Dee, an extraordinary young actress, had already appeared in many films with Sidney, playing both his sister and his wife. She had also, at my apartment, done the original reading of the play before we had a commitment from Sidney or a director. Lloyd, Lorraine, and I were in unanimous agreement about Ruby, and I don't recall that we even read anyone else for the part. The one person we had to convince was Ruby Dee, who freely admitted to no confidence that *A Raisin in the Sun* would ever get to Broadway, with all the obvious obstacles, including the producer, her good friend Philip Rose. Since that time I've enjoyed having

Ruby star in two more of my Broadway plays, including *Purlie Victorious*, written by Ossie Davis, a friend of mine and a husband of hers, not in order of importance. Later on, when Sidney had to leave the cast to do a film, Ossie replaced him, thereby playing Ruby's husband onstage as well as off. He seemed to get along very well in both roles.

Lou Gossett was a very talented young actor who had appeared on Broadway in a play called *Take a Giant Step,* and after hearing him read as George—the upper-class college boy somewhat contemptuous of the Younger family, particularly of Sidney's character—we all agreed he could take the giant step with us.

Casting Asagai, the young man from Africa who falls in love with Beneatha and teaches her and the audience many things, was also relatively effortless. Ivan Dixon had been in a film with Sidney and had become a friend of his. Ivan, who read for us beautifully, was an easy choice. Of course, the fact that he studied acting with Lloyd Richards didn't hurt his chances.

Lorraine and I knew Lonnie Elder from our days at Camp Unity and he seemed to us to have the personality of someone likely to encounter disaster of one kind or another. He seemed just right to play Bobo, Sidney's crony in their ill-fated scheme to become millionaires. And after having him read, Lloyd fully agreed.

We were quickly able to cast the small roles of two moving men with Ed Hall and Doug Turner. Mr. Turner also became understudy to Sidney Poitier, and while to the best of my recollection Mr. Poitier never missed a performance, Doug Turner went on to do the lead in our first road company, and later to create the Negro Ensemble Company, which lasted for years.

Finding Beneatha, Sidney's very contemporary and intellectual younger sister, was to emerge as the first serious casting problem, particularly for me and, later, for Lorraine. Diana Sands was a skillful young actress who had appeared in a very successful off-Broadway production of *The World of Sholom Aleichem*, in which she had replaced Ruby Dee, who was moving on to other projects. Another actress in that play, Doris Belack, had recently become my wife. (Doris, while appearing regularly on stage, screen, and television, has also chosen to perform offstage all these years in the role of my wife. She may have had the wrong agent.) In any case, Doris and Diana Sands became very close friends during the run of the *Sholom Aleichem* play, and Doris would often console her when Howard Da Silva, the director, would discourage and disparage her for not immediately reaching the level of Ruby Dee's performance. I, on the other hand, who was often at the theatre to see Doris, was very impressed with Diana.

After the production of *Raisin* and the casting of Sidney Poitier had been announced, Doris and I went to Brooklyn to see Diana Sands in a way-off-Broadway play. While we were backstage, and Doris was talking to Diana, Diana saw me in conversation with several of the other actors in the company. In her funny, flippant, loud, voice she asked Doris, "What's everybody talking to Phil for?" Doris replied, "They're talking to him about *A Raisin in the Sun*, obviously." Diana demanded, "What's he got to do with it?" Doris: "He's producing it." Diana, who knew me only as Doris's husband and some kind of music person, said, "He's *that* Philip Rose? I want to be seen for that, but how do I get to read for it?" Doris said, "Just be nice to me. Why do you think we're here?"

So when we got to seeing people for the role of Beneatha, I arranged an audition for Diana Sands immediately. I knew, of course, that Beneatha, while a fictional creation of Lorraine's, was also the most autobiographical character in the play. She had some of Lorraine's humor but, most crucially, Lorraine's seriousness and intensity. Lorraine liked Diana but I knew she had reservations, particularly a concern that Beneatha might emerge as primarily a comic character. I believed that Lloyd

Richards would be able to work with Diana to eliminate those reservations, but, in fact, I wasn't sure how strongly positive his opinion of Diana was. Diana's last reading for us was on a Friday. When I left to go to a money-raising meeting, I let it be known that of all the actors we had auditioned, Diana was absolutely my first choice. Lorraine and Lloyd said they would discuss it further between themselves and would call me at home that evening.

All through my meeting, as I tried to keep my mind on the money, I was wondering what my position would be if Lorraine and Lloyd were to say no, they wanted another actress. To this day I don't know if I was prepared to have my first serious casting argument with both of them. But the phone rang at my home at six and my stage manager informed me that they had decided to go with Diana. At two minutes after six I called Diana, and her scream of delight must have frightened her entire neighborhood.

For many days we saw actors for the role of Lindner, the only white character in the play, a man selected by the white community to persuade the Younger family, by whatever means necessary, to stay out of their neighborhood. We had been auditioning actors very large in stature, and potentially threatening in personality, and were not very enthusiastic about any of the possible choices. One day Charlie Dubin, an old friend and a prominent television director, called to ask if I would see an actor named John Fiedler, who had heard about the role of Lindner. I agreed to have Mr. Fiedler come to my office to pick up a script and arrange a reading time.

When Johnny walked in I saw a person who seemed an exact incarnation of the proverbial Caspar Milquetoast, a little cherub of a man with a high, squeaky, but pleasant voice, who it seemed wouldn't frighten a baby, much less an entire black family. He was, however, charming and immediately likeable, and we set a date for his audition.

When Fiedler first walked onstage, the initial reaction, like mine, was that this was nothing like Lorraine's image of Lindner. But as he began to read and then follow some direction from Lloyd, Lorraine and I looked at each other and knew that there was more dimension, and perhaps less of a stereotype, to this character than Lorraine had imagined. This may also have been my first move, if a very short step, toward atypical and perhaps even nontraditional casting. Johnny was wonderful in the part and in many other stage and film roles afterwards.

Having cast the only white actor, we then moved on to the role of Travis, the ten-year-old son of Sidney Poitier in the play. We began by seeing the usual submissions of "professional" young boys, some with longer résumés than the adults. Of the boys we auditioned, many had talent but in some cases the mothers seemed more interested in being in the theatre than their sons were. Lorraine was particularly dissatisfied with the candidates and even suggested that we start seeing some undersized adults. One day she called to tell me that in her neighborhood deli she had run into an acquaintance who had heard and congratulated her about the play. When Lorraine told her of our problem casting the young boy, Mrs. Turman volunteered that she had a son of that age. "So," Lorraine said, "what could I do? She's a neighbor. I told her we'd be happy to see him." Glynn Turman walked onto our audition stage and I'd say after about one minute Travis was born and grew to be ten years old. Our only fear was how to keep him from growing if the play was a hit. Glynn did grow to be a very fine mature actor, on stage, television, and film.

Throughout the period spent in casting all these other characters, we were, of course, reading actresses for the role of Mama, the antagonist to Sidney's protagonist, her son Walter Lee Younger. Mama is a woman in her late fifties or early sixties. Her husband died some years before and she raised her son and daughter to be decent adults with religious backgrounds. She had done so against all odds without making any serious errors, and she still rules her family, now including her daughter-in-law and grandson. In other words, she is this wonderful, nonthreatening cliché that any audience, white or black, can respond to. She can do no wrong. But in the course of the play she can and does.

We needed an actress in the appropriate age range and with the look and the power to play against Sidney Poitier. The obvious choice then was the star Ethel Waters. She was very much considered in our discussions, but Lorraine and I felt strongly that we would be adding another easy choice for the audience to love and thereby do a disservice to the play.

But time was running out and we needed a "Mama." We had seen many actresses before Claudia McNeil's name was submitted to us by her agent. Her reputation was mostly as a singer, but she had played a small dramatic role in *The Crucible*, the Arthur Miller play produced by Kermit Bloomgarden. When she came in to read for us, everything about her, from her voice to her physical stature and movement, said, "This is Mama." If any of us had reservations at that moment they were not expressed. We were sure we had the "Mama" for the Younger family and for our audience.

*Diana Sands
and Louis Gossett*

*Diana Sands,
Claudia McNeil,
and Ivan Dixon*

*Diana Sands
and Sidney Poitier*

Ruby Dee,
Claudia McNeil,
Glynn Turman,
Sidney Poitier,
and John Fiedler

Ruby Dee,
Sidney Poitier,
and Lonnie Elder

Diana Sands,
Ruby Dee,
and Sidney Poitier

Glynn Turman and Sidney Poitier

Ruby Dee, Louis Gossett, and Sidney Poitier

From left: David Cogan, Lorraine Hansberry, Lloyd Richards, Philip Rose, and Sidney Poitier

Chapter 10

We now had put together what we were convinced was a brilliant cast headed by an extraordinary star, Sidney Poitier. We were ready to sign each of the actors to Equity contracts, which would preclude their accepting other employment from the first day of rehearsals through the out-of-town openings and would extend their obligation to the run of the play in the New York theatre. Beyond putting up bonds at Actors' Equity to guarantee everybody at least two weeks' employment, some problems remained: we had not set a date for the start of rehearsals for our out-of-town opening, and certainly not for a New York opening. I therefore informed my general manager to proceed immediately to book the required theatres; we would then time our first rehearsal to conform to the availability of a Broadway house. After the press announced our completed cast, I assumed that booking the theatre and finding the additional capital to eliminate our budget deficit would fall into place, as was apparently happening for many other plays scheduled for the 1958–1959 season.

I had to concentrate first on raising more money. Among potential investors, I still found some degree of disbelief in my assurances that our play was definitely coming to Broadway. After all, we had not announced a Broadway opening, just a cast. But at last I received some good news from my general manager, Wally Fried: we were penciled in for opening in New Haven and Philadelphia with firm dates in January and February, and we could open in New York in March. Of course, I would have to put up financial guarantees for the theatres to confirm those dates. This fit in perfectly with my commitments to the actors and indeed to Lorraine to have the play in rehearsal by December of 1958.

While I struggled to control my excitement and to concentrate on expressing approval for what he had accomplished, I asked Wally the name of the New York theatre. Wally then said, "Well, that's the problem. We don't have one. And the Shuberts do not see anything available in the foreseeable future. So there's no point to booking the out-of-town theatres. We'll just have to postpone rehearsals." The pitch of my excitement descended a bit as I asked, "How long do they mean by the foreseeable future?" He answered, "My guess is somewhere just short of never." He continued, "You know there are no secrets in this business. Everybody knows you haven't raised the money and John Shubert is not about to hold a theatre for you even if he wanted your show, which is a whole other story." With very little excitement left I inquired, "So what do you suggest I do?" "Give it up, kid" he said, "postpone it; maybe ten, twenty years from now it might work."

As I hung up the phone I tried realistically to assess my situation. I seemed to have several problems. First, after eighteen months—from early 1957 to the fall of 1958—I had raised only $20,000 of a needed $100,000. At that rate I could easily have the required $100,000 by the year 1964, by which time all the actors currently cast in the show, with the possible exception of Claudia McNeil, would be too old for their parts. But we could then recast and, assuming the racial climate in the country would have improved sufficiently, some theatre owner might be persuaded that the walls of his theatre would not come crumbling down if it housed this play. Also, instead of a young black Lorraine Hansberry, we would have an older, safer black woman playwright, with an older, gray-haired Philip Rose as her producer, who might one day even buy a theatre in which to produce a play. So things might not then be as black (a pun in-

tended?) as they seemed now. After arriving at this realistic assessment, I decided to continue my fund-raising efforts for as
long as I could hold on to my cast and my sanity.

A very few days later, my press agent, Jim Proctor, who had
become much enamored of our play, called me after hearing
from Walter Fried about our current dismal situation. He
asked me for permission to show the script of *A Raisin in the
Sun* to Kermit Bloomgarden, then the most prestigious producer on Broadway, with successes that included the original
productions of *Death of a Salesman*, *The Crucible*, *The Diary
of Anne Frank*, and the currently-running *The Music Man*. I
gave my consent willingly, if not hopefully, and went on with
my own efforts. About a week later Mr. Bloomgarden's assistant called requesting that I meet with Mr. Bloomgarden in his
office the following Wednesday.

Of course, as soon as I hung up the phone, I called Lorraine.
"What do you think he wants?" she asked. I said, "I haven't got
a clue. Maybe he's looking for an intern for his office and thinks
I can type." She said, "I'll recommend you. If you're seeing him
next Wednesday I presume I'll hear from you a week or two after
that." "Very possibly even sooner," I said, and then we both
laughed uncontrollably.

During the days waiting for Wednesday to arrive, a week that
for some reason was a month long, I received a return phone call
from William Gibson, who wrote the big hit, *Two for the Seesaw*,
then running on Broadway with Anne Bancroft and Henry
Fonda. I had called to ask if he would take the time to read
Raisin. In truth, I wasn't sure of how he could be of help, but
I was reaching out wherever I could. After a very pleasant conversation, he agreed to read it and I sent it off to him. Meanwhile, the following Wednesday finally dawned and I went off to
the office of Kermit Bloomgarden.

I entered an office whose walls were decorated with posters
of some of the most impressive theatre events of the past sev-

eral years, plays that had also succeeded financially. I shook hands with Mr. Bloomgarden, who after introducing himself wasted no time on small talk. As I sat down in the offered chair, he said, "You've found a very interesting play. I'd like to co-produce it with you. Tell me something about yourself and Lorraine Hansberry." I felt a little like the salesman in Arthur Miller's play fearing that I'd already made the biggest sale of my life and anything further I'd say or do would kill the deal. But I overcame that to relax sufficiently to tell him how and where Lorraine and I had met, which seemed to intrigue him. I wondered for one brief moment whether I should ask him to tell me something about himself, but didn't feel quite secure enough to test his sense of humor. We talked for a short while longer, after which he somewhat abruptly said, "Come back to my office next Wednesday and I'll have a contract for you. Everything between us will be evenly split and the billing will be Kermit Bloomgarden and Philip Rose present, my name first." He then stood up, extending his hand. For a second I was almost tempted to kiss it rather than shake it, but decided, wisely I think, to deliver a very strong handshake and leave. I ran to the nearest functioning street telephone and called Lorraine. We both agreed to postpone our celebration until after the following Wednesday, when we could enjoy our drinks knowing our contracts with Mr. Bloomgarden had been signed.

I returned to my office to find a message to call William Gibson, which I did immediately. I was then stunned to hear him say, "This is a wonderful play by an extraordinary writer. It *must* be seen *on* Broadway. If there's anything I can do to help, call me. In the meantime you'll be receiving a check from my business manager for an investment in the play."

With all this occurring within a one-week period, I continued my money-raising attempts with much more confidence and encountered a slight rise in the degree of interest, particularly when I inadvertently dropped the names of Bloomgarden and

Gibson into the conversation. One evening during the course of that week, Doris, Lorraine, and I spent a social evening at Sidney Poitier's home, at that time in Mount Vernon, New York. Among the guests was Archie Moore, the light heavyweight boxing champion of the world and also at that time Sidney's brother-in-law. I don't recall (or choose not to remember) who suggested that as part of the evening's entertainment we read through *Raisin* in celebration of Sidney's forthcoming starring appearance on Broadway. We gathered in a very warm den, and Mr. Moore sought out and seated himself in the most comfortable chair, looking very formidable even as he sank into it. Of course Lorraine was to do the reading, which went very well for the first ten or fifteen minutes.

It was then that a sound came from the general area of Archie Moore's chair. As we all turned that way, it had become obvious that Mr. Moore was fast asleep and snoring from time to time. Lorraine paused and looked at me; Sidney also looked at me, smiling broadly to keep from laughing out loud, and then raised his arms sort of helplessly; I turned to Lorraine with the same gesture, but indicated she should just continue reading. For the next hour or so Lorraine did that but had to stop whenever there was a sudden surge of sound from the chair. Mr. Moore joined us again for about the last half-hour and at the end seemed quite enthusiastic about the entire evening.

There were two things I learned from that evening and noted for future reference. First, one never disturbs a heavyweight champion who happens to be napping in your home; and second, we probably should not plan to recruit much of our audience from the boxing community.

Chapter 11

The following Wednesday I proceeded to Mr. Bloomgarden's office at twelve noon to pick up our co-production contract. During the previous week I told Wally Fried of my meeting with Kermit Bloomgarden, and he had congratulated me and confirmed that now not only would my money problems vanish, but that Mr. Bloomgarden's name as co-producer would get us a New York theatre immediately. However, Wally expressed surprise at Mr. Bloomgarden's generous offer to share everything with me equally. As it happened, Wally had been half of a similar co-producing agreement with Bloomgarden years before on *Death of a Salesman*, and things had not quite turned out as anticipated. He cautioned me to be aware that Mr. Bloomgarden was a very tough negotiator and a sometimes difficult partner. I told Wally that anything else that I owned outside the play that Kermit might want to acquire, with the possible exception of my wife, would, in my current situation, be negotiable.

I arrived promptly for my 12:00 appointment, and was kept waiting for about fifteen minutes. The receptionist was very friendly, and kept assuring me that Mr. Bloomgarden would be off his very important phone call shortly. I was then ushered into his office, greeted warmly, and offered any kind of drink, which I politely declined. As I sat down, I glanced at the many papers on his desk, trying to guess which of them was the contract I would be taking home with me. Mr. Bloomgarden walked slowly to his desk chair, seated himself, fumbled with several papers as he apologized for keeping me waiting, and then pushed the papers aside and said, "Phil, shall I call you Phil or do you prefer Philip?" I responded immediately, "Everything's negotiable, but whichever you prefer." He then continued, "Phil, I don't have any paper ready yet for you to sign because there are some things we didn't get to talk about in our first meeting which we need to discuss before we can go forward." He paused and continued. "There are two artistic agreements that you have already concluded that I have problems with, and we have to agree on them before we can go any further. The first one is the role of Mama, for which you've chosen Claudia McNeil. Claudia McNeil did a small part in my production of *The Crucible*. She is competent, but that's all. The role of Mama requires a star, and we need someone to co-star with Mr. Poitier, who is not yet a star stage attraction. I have investigated, and know that I can get Ethel Waters to play that role and we'd be guaranteed a hit show." While I was taken aback by his vehemence, I was nevertheless prepared and willing to discuss Ethel Waters. But before I could, he asked me to let him go on to the next problem, which he immediately proceeded to do.

"The other major problem is the director. You've hired a gentleman named Lloyd Richards who I understand is a good actor. But his background as a director is limited to some work in Detroit and his additional credit as an acting teacher. Therefore, what I would have to add to our agreement is my right unilaterally to dismiss him either before rehearsals or anytime before we open in New York. These two elements we would have to agree on before I could move forward with you. Now tell me what you think."

Ethel Waters was a fine actress and a great star, and an obvious choice for Mama. As I've mentioned, Lorraine and I had considered her in many of our conversations. But since the beginning, *Raisin*, particularly from Lorraine's point of view, needed protection from becoming a play about Mama rather than her son, Walter Lee. Casting Ethel Waters in the role would have compounded the problem, which was, to be sure, never entirely eliminated from the play. Thankfully, we had, in Sidney Poitier, not only a star but an actor with every element—the strength, the talent, and the charisma—to retain control of the play and bring it as close as possible to what Lorraine had intended to write. I tried as well as I could to get all this across to Mr. Bloomgarden but was not sure I had succeeded as I moved on to discussing Lloyd Richards.

I told him that Lorraine and I had spent enough time with Mr. Richards to feel absolutely certain he was the ideal choice for director. I pointed out, too, that he was the suggestion of Mr. Poitier, a fact, I thought, certainly worthy of consideration. I then mentioned that, at any time during rehearsals, or even while out-of-town, if it was evident that Mr. Richards was not doing a good job, both Lorraine and I would surely agree with Mr. Bloomgarden and indeed be anxious to replace him. Why should we now assume the worst, or that this would even be a problem? Kermit listened attentively, interrupting very briefly at times, and then said we both should think it over and meet again on Friday. He also asked me to bring Lorraine along, since he had not yet met her and was looking forward to that.

I left his office somewhat confused, and certainly disappointed. Before calling Lorraine, I called my manager, Mr. Fried, and my press agent, Mr. Proctor, and briefly filled them in on the meeting. They both congratulated me on my success, and seemed shocked that I was at all disappointed rather than jumping for joy. Their response, then, was one of amazement that I seemed to be on the verge of closing a deal, with very minor concessions, and could now move forward with the play. After all, Mr. Bloomgarden was not asking for a larger financial share but just for some artistic changes that in their view would actually help the play.

When I spoke to Lorraine, I tried to make it clear that we were in a negotiation and that I hoped with our mutual points of view, Lorraine's and mine, I had made some impact on Mr.

Bloomgarden with respect to Ethel Waters and Lloyd Richards. In any case, we agreed we could go to the Friday meeting, and I hoped that Lorraine might be able to convince Mr. Bloomgarden where I might have failed.

When we arrived at his office on Friday, again at twelve noon, I was pleasantly surprised to be greeted by a most charming, almost courtly Kermit Bloomgarden, who couldn't wait to shake Lorraine's hand and tell her how honored he was to meet her. I attributed this almost new personality, and his holding her hand perhaps longer than necessary, to the fact that she was obviously younger and much prettier than I, which he might not have anticipated. He finally let go and guided her to a chair at one side of and quite close to his desk, and he motioned me to a chair on the other side. He began by congratulating Lorraine, but she interrupted to express her admiration for his contribution to theatre, particularly *Death of a Salesman*, which was, in her view, one of the great American plays. They discussed this briefly, after which Mr. Bloomgarden volunteered his pleasant surprise that the writer of *A Raisin in the Sun* should turn out to be so young and so attractive. I sat quietly throughout all this, wondering if this was the usual beginning of a negotiation, and assuming that, if so, it was going very well. Then there was suddenly a pause in the outpouring of mutual admiration. Mr. Bloomgarden turned briefly and looked at me, then swung back to Lorraine, leaned closer to her, and in a very quiet, serious tone said, "Miss Hansberry, you have written a wonderful serious play. I want to wish you the greatest success with it. I would have liked to be associated with you. Unfortunately, Mr. Rose and I don't see things eye to eye, so I will not be able to work with him. But I do want to wish you the best of luck, and if I can be of any help, please feel free to call me." As he rose from his chair, signifying the end of the meeting, he nodded to me. "And you too, Phil, call me any time."

Lorraine and I entered an elevator filled with people whom

we had no desire to bring into our conversation. Therefore we were quiet until we reached the nearest coffee shop. As we sat down and ordered our coffee, we were still too stunned, I think, to begin talking. Finally she said, "OK, you first." I said, "Let me get out of the way quickly how shocked I am at how he chose to do this. Obviously he could have phoned me and said, 'Look, these are my terms, take it or leave it. If you'll accept my position, bring Lorraine in and we'll have a deal; otherwise, cancel the meeting.' That would have been brusque, but straightforward. What he opted to do was appeal to you directly. He is exactly what I was warned he would be: a very tough and even devious negotiator. But," I added, "that doesn't make him a bad producer. He wants your play, but on his terms, and he'll do whatever it takes to get it."

I paused, waiting for some response from Lorraine, and was rewarded with a silent look which, on her face, could sometimes be more formidable than anything she might say. So I went on:

"Lorraine, here are the facts of where we are. We are about two months away from our rehearsal date. I have raised approximately $20,000 of a required $100,000 budget. I have, as far as I can see, very little chance of raising the additional money. Mr. Bloomgarden wants the play. He will produce it if we agree to his demands. I'm sure I would end up with nothing to say artistically. But I'm sure he won't deny me my share of any financial success, and my name would be up there alongside his. We would have Ethel Waters, and probably lose Lloyd Richards. I'm not sure what Sidney's reaction would be to these possible changes. But I would be out of the woods financially, and you would probably have a big hit. After working together on *Raisin* for three years I would guess that in another three years I might recover from the emotional pain and disappointment. But I think I must call Mr. Bloomgarden back and say, 'OK, Kermit, you've got a deal. It's your play.' And now will you please stop looking at me that way and say something."

She rose from her chair, said, "I'll call you later," and left the coffee shop. I knew she was going to rush back to her flat on Bleecker Street to talk to her husband, Robert Nemiroff. He was currently an employee of mine in my publishing and recording company. I knew him well, and there was very little question in my mind that he would be advising Lorraine to call Bloomgarden and agree to anything he asked for.

As it happened, later that afternoon my wife and I had a date with Ellis Baker, an old friend who was also my accountant. We were meeting at the bar at the old Astor Hotel to celebrate our anticipated deal with Kermit Bloomgarden. Already a supporter and investor in the play, Ellis was overjoyed at the news, but he sensed we had some reservations as he said, "At least you'll be off the hook financially." We cut short the "celebration" and I rushed home to wait for a call from Lorraine, which finally came at 7:00 P.M. that evening. She said quite succinctly, "You know, Phil, when you first woke me up that early Sunday morning to tell me you wanted to produce the play, I assumed we'd be doing it in some little church somewhere. So let's do it in some little church somewhere." When I hung up the phone, I was amazed at my own positive sense of relief, followed by an almost hysterical determination that I would raise the balance of the money needed without Mr. Bloomgarden's help.

Chapter 12

Monday morning came along in its usual time, though it seemed to take much longer to arrive than normal. I couldn't wait to get on the phone, because I was now determined to harass people into investing in *Raisin* by any means necessary: threats to their person or standing outside their homes with a cup and a gospel choir. But as I made my first more rational telephone approaches, I heard, surprisingly, much more responsive answers to my pleas.

In numbers, the theatre business is a very small community and holds very few well-kept secrets. Well, it seemed that during the three weeks after I first learned of Mr. Bloomgarden's interest in our play, many other people had heard the same news from various sources. Certainly my press agent and manager had let it slip into their conversation as often as possible when talking to their respective colleagues; after all, press agents are not paid to keep their mouths shut. I also suspect that Mr. Bloomgarden was not shy about letting it be known he was about to produce next season's "wonderful serious play," acquired from a writer who happened to be a beautiful young black woman. In any case, whatever scenario may have been responsible, I was getting some believable promises of checks in the mail from possible investors.

I received a call from a Mr. Kenneth Schwartz, who ran a theatre in Detroit at which Lloyd Richards had directed several plays. He promised to raise $10,000.00. He indeed did, and received associate producer billing along with his financial interest in the play.

I called the playwright William Gibson, whose previously promised check had not yet arrived. He seemed quite surprised that I hadn't received it and said he would call his accountant immediately to make sure it was sent. "Incidentally," he volunteered, "if you don't get the check in the next few days please call my accountant. His name is David Cogan and here's his number." I did not mention to him my meeting with Mr. Cogan some weeks before, but I did call Cogan three days later.

He apologized for the delay, telling me how busy he had been, and suggested I come by his office and pick up Mr. Gibson's check at my earliest convenience. I informed him that I, too, was so busy that my earliest convenience would be within the next half hour. We agreed on meeting that afternoon, and off I then went to his office presumably to pick up the check.

When I arrived I was welcomed very enthusiastically. David emphatically reminded me how much he had liked the play and how he had offered me some money to take it off-Broadway. "But now," he went on, "since you've got Sidney Poitier and some people in the industry are talking about it, I'd like to be involved. I can raise money for you from my clients; several of them have already made money in *Two for the Seesaw* and they'll come along if Bill Gibson and I do." After just a few minutes David and I shook hands on a deal in principle, and we left it to our attorneys to draw up the papers. Then, within weeks, David brought in several investors for a total of about $30,000. In return, he received a pro rata financial interest in the show and co-producer billing. He was not, however, a party to artistic decisions, which remained exclusively with me and Lorraine. (Sometime later David, who was deeply involved in several nontheatrical business enterprises, offered me the opportunity to join him in some Manhattan real estate investments. Though he sent me relevant material, I turned him down. David has at times reminded me how he could have taken me out of show business and made me rich. I guess I should have read *his* script more carefully.)

Shortly after what turned out to be my final meeting with Mr. Bloomgarden, checks began to come in, and while we were still waiting for investments even after opening in Philadelphia, the fund-raising pressure was greatly alleviated and I was better able to concentrate on other, more welcome tasks. Incidentally, I never called or heard from Mr. Bloomgarden again until I ran into him in Chicago, where *Raisin* opened before coming to New York. He was there for his own Chicago opening of a touring company of *The Music Man.* We met at a restaurant hangout for theatre people. He approached me, held out his hand, and said, "Congratulations. I think I made a mistake." I shook his hand, thanked him effusively for all he had done for me, and walked away leaving him looking confused and unenlightened.

Soon I began to actually enjoy my meetings with my manager and my press agent: now I could tell them to stop worrying about money, to go ahead and pay the outstanding bills for costumes, scenery, advertising, etc., and to concentrate on our openings in New Haven and Philadelphia and, of course, New York. They were very pleasantly surprised to know their weekly paychecks would be forthcoming and they could proceed to assure everyone that the budget for *A Raisin in the Sun* was now guaranteed. However, they also jointly pointed out, "We still can't go into rehearsal until we've been offered a New York theatre." "And when might that be?" I asked. When they responded, "We have no idea," I said, "We're going into rehearsal December 10th. Please let that be made public and emphasized. The actors' bonds are being put up and I would like to announce the New York opening date, but for now, please make certain that everything is set for New Haven and Philadelphia, including as much publicity as we can get." "But what will we do if we close in Philadelphia and don't have any place to put the show?" I was asked. "That's easy," I said. "We'll have a joint suicide pact and I'll cover all the expenses."

Of course, I kept Lorraine completely informed of all the encouraging events over some celebratory drinks. We both expressed relief, amid some incredulity, that it finally was all going to happen—we were going into rehearsal. The only new guarantee she demanded was to be included in the suicide pact.

So we moved forward. All the actors were bonded. Scenery and costumes were being designed, and, while the checks weren't pouring in, they were certainly "in the mail." Suddenly people who were investing or involved in other ways began raising questions about the title of the play. What did it mean? Where did it come from? How would people remember it? All of which inevitably led to suggestions of other titles. Soon even Lorraine and I, feeling uneasy about this, started throwing titles at each other. After waiting anxiously for approval from Langston Hughes to use *Raisin in the Sun*, which came, as mentioned, in his cordial letter in April, now we were questioning our decision. In our spare time we would present ideas to one another, but as we spoke them we recognized and dismissed them as ridiculous.

One night, lying in bed, I suddenly thought I heard an unusual noise and running steps outside our window. I jumped up and yelled, "flight has a sound." My wife awoke and as I tried to explain my outburst she looked at me strangely, then graciously accepted my apology and went back to sleep. I rushed into another room, closed the door, and called Lorraine, who was not yet asleep. I paused after our mutual hellos and then intoned, *Flight Has a Sound*. There was a moment's silence and then she said, "Say it again." *Flight Has a Sound*, I said again, giving it a somewhat different reading. Then she began to repeat it slowly with various approaches—happy, sad, questioning. Finally Lorraine said, "That's it! Can we get it changed right away and notify the press?" "Of course," I said, "first thing tomorrow I'll call Jim Proctor to make the announcement." We went to bed at about 11:30, congratulating each other for having solved our title problem.

The following morning, as Doris and I sat down to have our coffee she asked me, "What was that all about last night?" I told her that we had been looking for a new title and I had been inspired to come up with *Flight Has a Sound*. She looked at me and asked, "So when does the inspiration come?" and went back to her coffee. After breakfast and more coffee I printed the title in different styles, so as to visualize the newspaper ads. I also read it aloud several times, and suddenly I was a bit uneasy. I called Lorraine. As she said hello I could tell something was wrong. We both hesitated, discussing how we each had slept, until finally Lorraine said, "Phil, what are we doing?" I said, "I don't know. I think we've both lost our minds." Then, over rather mindless laughter, she asked, "Flight has a sound?" and I answered, "Yes! flight has a sound!" We gave it several more readings before deciding that our mutual acceptance of this title had been prompted by a need to release the tension of the past months, triggered by the good news of the last few days. That morning, we made a pact: if anybody ever again suggested changing our title or proposed any other nonsensical idea about the play, we would only stare at them and say very seriously, "Flight has a sound," and walk away. This served us very well over the months that followed.

LANGSTON HUGHES
20 EAST 127TH STREET
NEW YORK 35, N. Y.

April 5, 1958

Dear Mrs. Nemiroff:

I can't recall whether I answered your
letter of February 8th requesting permission to use the line: "a raisin in
the sun", as a title for your three-act
play. ✕

I am happy to give my permission for its
use and send you all my good wishes for
its success.

Sincerely yours,

Langston Hughes

Langston Hughes

Mrs. Lorraine Nemiroff
337 Bleecker Street
New York City 14

✕ *I was in the hospital
when your note
arrived — and then
everything got
piled up.*

Chapter 13

We did go into rehearsal December 10th with a fair portion of the budget in the bank and much of the balance believably promised. During the rehearsal period we had the usual problems that any new play encounters, some not so usual, and many that I've already discussed, including Lorraine's reactions and her writings about them. As we neared the end of our rehearsal period and the tensions and excitement heightened, we decided to invite an audience to the play's last run-through before leaving town. This procedure, quite common in those days before shows left for out-of-town tryouts (if a show was a musical it was called a "gypsy run-through") was an opportunity to give the actors and staff some idea of what to expect from an audience. Since that audience generally consisted of friends of the actors and investors in the show, reactions might well range from extra enthusiasm from the friends to excessive nervousness from the investors. But while most of these reactions could safely be ignored, others might be worthy of consideration. The response at our final run-though was much as we expected, and we were quite pleased. The small audience was generous with both their laughter and their increasing use of tissues, particularly as the play came to an end.

There was a moment which I would say startled us all equally. It happened just before the curtain was about to fall on act two and the audience has cried and applauded the Youngers' decision to move. As the family is preparing to leave the old apartment, Mama rushes to get her little window plant which, we have been told, has been dying for years. When Beneatha ridicules her for wanting to take "that raggedy old plant to the new apartment," Mama says simply, "It expresses me." This line is a playback of something Beneatha said when Mama ridiculed her guitar playing hours before, during the first few minutes of the play. Mama's repetition of that line with reference to herself displayed a surprisingly sophisticated understanding of her own character, and was greeted with laughter and scattered applause. We were all pleased that the audience obviously had remembered the earlier scene and that it resonated so well for them. But Lorraine was a little concerned about their reaction, and having already been a bit perturbed by laughs that Diana Sands was getting, she wondered aloud whether Claudia was doing something irrelevant just to get a laugh.

We moved to New Haven in mid-January to open on Wednesday the 21st and continued through the Saturday night performance on the 24th. I can only describe my memory of that very brief engagement as a vivid blur. As we arrived in town, of course the first notable image we saw from a distance was the marquee of the Shubert Theatre with the words *A Raisin in the Sun* large enough to be seen, I thought, in Philadelphia, the site of our next engagement. We were booked into the old Taft Hotel, a "landmark" building unfeelingly torn down years later, along with some of our memories. Also long gone is the restaurant across the street, whose name I can't remember, though we spent our nights meeting there after each performance until closing time, when we would move to one of our suites to continue talking until we retired to our individual quarters. The word "retired" is used loosely since we generally got to our suites just in time for a bath and breakfast.

The opening night performance in New Haven I can describe as perhaps the most intense three hours of my life. Never having had the experience of asking a thousand strangers to approve what I had spent or wasted three years of my life doing, I remember being actually frightened by what they might do if they disapproved. I wasn't aware of any safety precautions my manager had taken to get Lorraine and me out of town in a hurry. I believe I spent the last half hour before curtain time getting increasingly well acquainted with the men's restroom. Finally, with all those people sitting there, I was left with no choice but to tell the stage manager to raise the curtain as I ran back to my seat.

It didn't take long for me to realize that my fears were unfounded. The audience was obviously having a good time, enjoying the humor at the start of the play and getting involved with the characters and in the story. The first-act intermission buzz was encouraging and the second act went far beyond what we had expected or even hoped for. Mama's line "It expresses me" got the biggest laugh of the evening, the audience response indicating Lorraine just hadn't realized that, while a very serious writer, she could also be funny. At the final curtain there was an ovation, and we were sure we had a show that could capture audiences in New York if we could get to them.

Then began the out-of-town ritual to which I was to become accustomed through the years. Loosely speaking, I could describe it as, "If it ain't broke, fix it anyway." I don't mean to imply that Lorraine and Lloyd and I thought that everything was perfect and there was nothing to be done, but I did find that people from all quarters—professionals, civilians, investors, our general manager, press agent, a few ushers (all prefacing their remarks with their enthusiasm for the play)—were now prepared to tell me, Lorraine, and Lloyd how to "fix it." What was amazing to me, and has remained so, is how many people, including theatre professionals, when seeing a new play either out-of-town or in previews, feel free to make unsolicited suggestions to a director or producer or even the playwright. Inherent in these suggestions was the suggester's tacit assumption that they would never have occurred to the writer in the entire five years she had spent writing the play. Furthermore, along with the remark that "of course this is only one person's opinion, and you all must know what you're doing," came the warning that, "if you don't make these changes, well—you'll be facing disaster."

What we did learn from the run in New Haven was that one scene between Walter Lee and his son hurt the flow of the play, and we all agreed to excise it. One other scene, which included a neighbor, had already been cut during rehearsals, eliminating that character, and that proved to have been an excellent decision. The two cuts were made with the unanimous agreement of Lorraine, Lloyd, and myself, solely for the artistic improvement of the play. I mention this because after Lorraine's death, her husband, the late Robert Nemiroff, chose to rewrite and republish her play with the two scenes reinstated. (Mr. Nemiroff's name will come up again in this memoir.)

Though the reviews we received in New Haven were very encouraging and the audience response unquestionably positive, the fact remained that we had no New York theatre and no further response from the Shuberts. So we moved on to Philadelphia with great hopes and greater fears. Fortunately, our fears were somewhat lessened after we opened in Philadelphia to very enthusiastic reviews, and John Shubert arrived for the Wednesday matinee. He offered us a New York theatre with a not-so-perfect solution to our problem: after Philadelphia, we would have to go to Chicago. While this certainly came as relief from the immediate pressure of finding the final home for our production, allowing us to plan for our New York opening, it also meant we had to work feverishly to alert Chicago about our unexpected and imminent visit.

Meanwhile, it was a source of personal distress to me that Sidney Poitier, while still committed to opening the play in New York, was not happy. Also, Lorraine continued to struggle with the problem posed by much of the audience and some critics in their acceptance of Mama as the presumed—though certainly not the intended—protagonist of the play. Although she kept trying to change that, from time to time submitting new pages to me and Lloyd, nothing she wrote was satisfactory, let alone worth showing to Sidney. On one occasion she forced us to read a scene written by her husband—which did serve to relieve some tension by reducing us to laughter.

We left Philadelphia and opened in Chicago with Sidney feeling that we were either ignoring him and his justifiable reservations about the play by attributing them to a "star turn," or were simply unwilling to make changes because of a belief that we had achieved perfection. The one thing Lorraine and I failed to understand at the time was why Sidney did not throw aside his discontent and, by his onstage performance, deliberately take the play away from Mama. Lorraine and I both knew that he had the talent and power to do that; all he needed was the determination, and the direction.

When we opened in Chicago, not only had I been unable to ameliorate the situation, I felt a growing sadness that something negative had come between me and Sidney, something that could extend far beyond *A Raisin in the Sun*. Looking back from today's vantage point, I regret that I did not have the experience or confidence to go to Lloyd Richards directly and raise the question with him about Lorraine's feelings and mine. I just assumed that Sidney was resisting the director. This assumption came as a result of Lorraine's reporting of a conversation with Lloyd, who indicated as much to her. In any case, I thought it was not the producer's right to interfere. I have had several occasions to learn and to act differently since.

We opened in Chicago with no advance sales but to largely enthusiastic reviews, and after a nervous few days we were selling out. Each morning at breakfast my manager, press agent, and I discussed plans for the New York opening. We made the decision to open the show in New York after only one preview because we knew we would have a very small advance, and it was the critics who would determine whether our show lived or died. Lorraine, obviously interested in our decisions, would usually join us for breakfast, but one morning, a very few days after our opening, she did not appear, and I had to explain that she had gone to New York. Wally Fried assumed she had a crisis of some kind and asked when she'd be returning. I answered that she might be coming back for the closing and that I would also be returning to New York the following day. Wally asked, " Is she ill?" "No, she just wanted to go home," I said. Wally and Jim Proctor stared at me and then at each other. Then Wally asked, "Who's going to do the rewrites?" "What rewrites?" I asked. Wally said, "We've got three more weeks here in Chicago. You've got to do rewrites." I responded, I thought reasonably, "The reason we're in Chicago is because we couldn't get a theatre in New York. Not because of rewrites. Now if you tell me what you think she should be rewriting, we'll discuss it, and if I agree I'll talk to Lorraine and if she agrees she'll try it and if necessary I'll bring her back. But can I have some coffee first?"

The play was by then, to use the theatre vernacular, "frozen," with no more writing changes made. But something else did change during the run. And here I will be relating a conversation I was not a party to and only learned about years later from Sidney Poitier's wonderful autobiography *This Life*. Sidney wrote in his book that Lloyd and Lorraine and I were happy with the play as it was being performed and with having the focus on Claudia McNeil as Mama. Well, I cannot speak for Lloyd because as mentioned earlier, I did not have much direct contact with him. But, as I also mentioned, while Lorraine was trying vainly to help build Sidney's character with her unsuccessful and unusable rewrites, both Lorraine and I wished fervently that Sidney would take the play over and away from Mama, which we were convinced he could do. Moreover, to the very end of the play's run, and indeed to the end of her life, Lorraine hated the staging of the second act curtain because she thought it corrupted the essence of what she was saying by having the scene emphasize Mama's grief rather than Walter Lee's anger and frustration.

To continue Sidney's storytelling: one day in Chicago, after Lorraine had returned to New York, he and Ruby Dee were discussing the play and the question of whether Walter Lee is a weak or a strong man and how the audiences were seeing him. As a result of that conversation, Sidney goes on, he made the decision to play him as a man fighting for his life against "the racism of his environment"—and with no help from Mama. In other words, he started to do exactly what Lorraine and I had been hoping he would do. And on opening night in New York he was magnificent. Nobody who has played this role since has come close to him. But if Denzel Washington would like to try, I'd be happy to produce it with Sidney Poitier directing.

Chapter 14

As the Prologue recounts, our opening night in New York, on March 11th, 1959, seemed to be a triumph from the standpoint of audience reaction. After the curtain came down, we began what was then an obligatory ritual observed at every important Broadway premiere. It would begin with the arrival at Sardi's restaurant of the usual first-nighters, followed by the show's management and creative team and its acting company, with the stars almost invariably the last to appear; they were greeted by their friends and relatives, the show's investors, a flock of celebrities, and other VIPs who managed to get a table reservation from Vincent Sardi. What followed was a party that continued until close to midnight, at least for those who waited for the morning papers—specifically, the *New York Times* and *New York Herald Tribune,* which carried the reviews of Brooks Atkinson and Walter Kerr, respectively. Depending on the opinions of those two critics, the mood of the crowd would then either rise to a new height of celebration or fall to a hush, with a subdued procession exiting the restaurant.

Lorraine and I did not arrive at Sardi's immediately. We were delayed at the theatre by congratulatory greetings from friends and investors; and, of course, we went backstage to thank everybody in the company for an extraordinary performance. We then got into a limousine and traveled from the Barrymore Theatre on 47th Street to Sardi's on 44th. During the three-block ride, we contemplated all the possible scenarios that could happen within the next few hours. Lorraine thought she had been through enough for one evening, and even talked of transferring to a cab and going home to throw the covers over her head, to be awakened in the morning from this three-year-old beautiful dream or horrible nightmare. But in fact we made it to 44th Street together, stepped out of the limousine, and paused at Sardi's entrance, where we lingered briefly.

During my previous three years of getting somewhat involved in the theatre community, I had attended several Broadway openings and come to Sardi's afterwards. So I had some idea, in kind if not degree, of what to expect on our entrance. I assumed that some people might recognize Lorraine but, after all, she was not a starring actor, just a writer. At the door, Lorraine looked at me with the unspoken question: "Do we really have to go through this?" But with the doorman opening the door for the third time, and with my arm firmly around Lorraine's waist, we crossed the threshold, at which point I removed my arm and gently nudged her forward.

What happened then, just like an hour earlier at the theatre, was quite different from any ovation I had ever heard. It was not just that every person in the restaurant exploded into applause, waiters and busboys included (while Lorraine turned around to see what great star might be behind her), but that they were responding to a breathtaking image. Here was this very young, very beautiful black woman standing alone in the doorway who suddenly looked ten feet tall. And for the first time it entered my mind that this event I was so deeply a part of was much more than what would perhaps be a successful play. Those people in the restaurant that night, looking at Lorraine in the doorway, recognized that they were also looking at the face of change, a face of strength and dignity that was truly black and beautiful, and that some things and some feelings might never be the same. I finally stepped over to Lorraine and, arm in arm, we proceeded to our table. It was only after Lorraine sat down that everyone else did.

While Lorraine and I were at Sardi's, our official opening

night party for several hundred invited guests was beginning at the Plaza Hotel. We had first planned this party when we received our good reviews in Chicago, and our many investors expected it. Even general manager Wally Fried felt we owed them that. Though of course there was no guarantee the Chicago reviews would be matched or even approximated in New York, we just couldn't disappoint the many who had invested, in some cases, their hard-earned money. So we stayed at Sardi's long enough for Lorraine to accept the personal congratulations of the many who came to our table and to sign the proffered *Playbills* or Sardi's menus as souvenirs, which she did very graciously. Finally, our waiter brought the check, which I signed (not quite as graciously), and we left for the Plaza.

By the time we reached the Plaza ballroom, partying was well underway, with many of the celebrants way past their first drinks. All the same, Lorraine's entrance received the now-expected standing ovation from those who were still standing. Again, many guests (mostly investors and their families) were anxious to get Lorraine's autograph. As they crowded around Lorraine, our press agent arrived to inform me that while he hadn't yet seen the actual reviews, he knew that the major newspapers were all positive, at which point I loudly called for "Quiet" and announced the news to the crowd. After a roar of approval, many of them rushed toward me, now demanding my autograph. I soon realized that they wanted it not for posterity but to visualize it as a signature on the checks they were certain they would start receiving from me the next morning. Well, those investors who stayed late enough to pick up the morning papers on their way home were able to top off their celebration with a good night's sleep and a dream—not only of a return on their money but possibly even a profit. And that, indeed was to prove a dream come true.

The following morning, we began the work of promoting the show by choosing the appropriate quotes for the advertisements.

Fortunately, we had many good choices. We also got reports from the Barrymore box office that phones were ringing and lines were forming for tickets. In spite of our small advance sale, we would begin to sell out within two weeks.

We also had one more party to throw. Because of the large number of investors, our actors were almost lost in the crowd at the large Plaza ballroom, and we planned another party for them the following Saturday night. We decided to have a more intimate celebration in an upstairs room at Sardi's just for the company, the staff, and a few close friends. This turned out to be a wonderful, relaxed evening, with the actors aware they now were in a Broadway hit (a first for nearly all of them), had no need to worry about a job for awhile, and, on top of that, were in a show they could all be proud of.

The evening was memorable in many ways, but two events remain particularly vivid. As noted, the part of Sidney Poitier's ten-year-old son was played by Glynn Turman. During the evening's festivities, which included singing around the piano by the likes of Claudia McNeil, Harry Belafonte, and others, our stage manager announced that Glynn Turman and his understudy would like to play a scene for us that would require absolute quiet and complete attention. As soon as we met those requirements, the two boys took center stage and proceeded to perform the second-act curtain of our play, with Glynn playing Sidney Poitier as Walter, and his understudy portraying Claudia McNeil as Mama. Their heightened emoting approached perfection. Perhaps perfection is not the word; since they had obviously decided between them that Claudia as Mama sometimes tended to overact a bit, they wanted to make sure we all got the point. It was a riotously funny scene, played as freely as only two talented children could have done, and it was greeted with enthusiastic applause by everyone, with the possible exception of Claudia.

My other favorite part of the evening was the entrance of Miss

Lena Horne. I had met her briefly at the theatre on opening night, when she had expressed her enthusiasm about the play and given me a phone number where she could be reached. I had then called to invite her to the cast party, and she agreed to come in spite of a previous engagement, saying she would not be able to stay too long. Well, she arrived and for a moment stood at the door of our party room. I remember that she wore a clinging gold lamé dress, but I won't attempt to describe how she looked, trusting the reader's imagination to do justice to that vision. She stayed to be introduced and to talk to everybody in the company, saying how proud and excited she had been by Lorraine's writing and the performances of all the actors, and how important she felt the play was. Later, when she was preparing to leave, I was standing next to Sidney and she came over for the second time to congratulate us and say goodnight. She shook my hand and then, standing close to Sidney, who held her hand in his, she once again apologized for leaving early. Thereupon I watched Sidney turn on his more-than-considerable charm and, his eyes staring intently into hers, he said, "I'm so sorry to see you go. But you'll still be with us in spirit." And Miss Lena, staring just as intently at him, paused and said, "You mean in body, don't you, baby." She had to remind him then that in order for her to leave he would have to release her hand. I had never before seen Sidney outcharmed by a woman.

For many years after that, I always invited Lena Horne to my opening nights, and she came whenever she was available. One of my personal disappointments occurred when, long after *Raisin*, I wanted to make a musical out of the film *Marriage Italian Style*, and I thought the only person who could play the Sophia Loren role would be Lena Horne. When I called her to discuss the possibility, she invited me to her apartment where we talked and she expressed a great deal of interest. Unfortunately, though I spent months trying, I was unable to obtain the rights, which were tangled up in ways too numerous to mention.

On the morning of March 12th, 1959, seven very positive reviews appeared in the major New York newspapers, each in its own way glowing. On Broadway they were referred to as "money reviews," which meant that we had a hit. I am reproducing here reviews from the *New York Times* and *Herald Tribune*, because without strong reviews in those two, any serious play, and certainly *A Raisin in the Sun*, would have had a hard time finding an audience. I have also reprinted an article by Kenneth Tynan, the British critic then writing for *The New Yorker* who was to many the most respected theatre commentator of that era, as well as a sermon preached in a Chicago synagogue that prompted the response from Lorraine also printed here. The choices I've made here relate to or have bearing on many events to be considered later in this book.

The Theatre: 'A Raisin in the Sun'

Negro Drama Given at Ethel Barrymore

By BROOKS ATKINSON

IN "A Raisin in the Sun," which opened at the Ethel Barrymore last evening, Lorraine Hansberry touches on some serious problems. No doubt, her feelings about them are as strong as any one's.

But she has not tipped her play to prove one thing or another. The play is honest. She has told the inner as well as the outer truth about a Negro family in the southside of Chicago at the present time. Since the performance is also honest and since Sidney Poitier is a candid actor. "A Raisin in the Sun" has vigor as well as veracity and is likely to destroy the complacency of any one who sees it.

•

The family consists of a firm-minded widow, her daughter, her restless son and his wife and son. The mother has brought up her family in a tenement that is small, battered but personable. All the mother wants is that her children adhere to the code of honor and self-respect that she inherited from her parents.

The son is dreaming of success in a business deal. And the daughter, who is race-conscious, wants to become a physician and heal the wounds of her people. After a long delay the widow receives

The Cast

A RAISIN IN THE SUN, a drama by Lorraine Hansberry. Staged by Lloyd Richards; presented by Philip Rose and David J. Cogan; scenery and lighting by Ralph Alswang; costumes by Virginia Volland; production stage manager, Leonard Auerbach. At the Ethel Barrymore Theatre.
Ruth Younger..................Ruby Dee
Travis Younger..........Glynn Turman
Walter Lee Younger......Sidney Poitier
Beneatha Younger..........Diana Sands
Lena Younger..........Claudia McNeil
Joseph Asagai..............Ivan Dixon
George Murchison.......Louis Gossett
Bobo.....................Lonne Elder 3d
Karl Lindner ....John Fiedler
Moving Men....Ed Hall, Douglas Turner

$10,000 as the premium on her husband's life insurance. The money projects the family into a series of situations that test their individual characters.

•

What the situations are does not matter at the moment. For "A Raisin in the Sun" is a play about human beings who want, on the one hand, to preserve their family pride and, on the other hand, to break out of the poverty that seems to be their fate. Not having any axe to grind, Miss Hansberry has a wide range of topics to write about —some of them hilarious, some of them painful in the extreme.

You might, in fact, regard "A Raisin in the Sun" as a Negro "The Cherry Orchard." Although the social scale of the characters is different, the knowledge of how character is controlled by environment is much the same, and the alternation of humor and pathos is similar.

If there are occasional crudities in the craftsmanship, they are redeemed by the honesty

Sidney Poitier and Claudia McNeil as they appear in play by Lorraine Hansberry, "A Raisin in the Sun."

of the writing. And also by the rousing honesty of the stage work. For Lloyd Richards has selected an admirable cast and directed a bold and stirring performance.

●

Mr. Poitier is a remarkable actor with enormous power that is always under control. Cast as the restless son, he vividly communicates the tumult of a highstrung young man. He is as eloquent when he has nothing to say as when he has a pungent line to speak. He can convey devious processes of thought as graphically as he can clown and dance.

As the matriarch, Claudia McNeil gives a heroic performance. Although the character is simple, Miss McNeil gives it nobility of spirit. Diana Sands' amusing por-

trait of the overintellectualized daughter; Ivan Dixon's quiet, sagacious student from Nigeria; Ruby Dee's young wife burdened with problems; Louis Gossett's supercilious suitor; John Fiedler's timid white man, who speaks sanctimonious platitudes—bring variety and excitement to a first-rate performance.

●

All the crises and comic sequences take place inside Ralph Alswang's set, which depicts both the poverty and the taste of the family. Like the play, it is honest. That is Miss Hansberry's personal contribution to an explosive situation in which simple honesty is the most difficult thing in the world. And also the most illuminating.

═FIRST NIGHT REPORT═
WALTER KERR
'A Raisin in the Sun'

ETHEL BARRYMORE THEATER

A new play in three acts and six scenes by Lorraine Hansberry, staged by Lloyd Richards, settings and lighting by Ralph Alswang, costumes by Virginia Volland, presented by Philip Rose and David J. Cogan with the following cast:

Ruth Younger .... Ruby Dee
Travis Younger .... Glynn Turman
Walter Lee Younger (Brother)
　　　　　　　　　　　Sidney Poitier
Beneatha Younger ....Diana Sands
Lean Younger (Mother) .... Claudia McNeil
Joseph Asagai .... Ivan Dixon
George Murchison .... Louis Gossett
Bobo .... Lonne Elder III
Karl Lindner .... John Fiedler
Moving Men ..... Ed Hall, Douglas Turner

THERE is nothing more moving in "A Raisin in the Sun" than the spectacle of Sidney Poitier biting his lip, clutching the back of a chair, and turning himself into a man —and we'll come to that in a moment. What is really astonishing, along the way, is how completely touching a trivial, almost shrugged-off, implication can be.

* * *

Claudia McNeil does it fairly early in the evening at the Barrymore. As the solid rock on which a Chicago Negro family is founded, Miss McNeil holds in her hand the one thing that will give all of them a tardy toehold on their dreams. Her dead husband, who spent most of his life coming home from work to stare in desperation at the eternally fading carpet, has left behind him an insurance legacy of $10,000.

The house is alive, and edgy, with anticipation. The check comes. With no one on the premises daring to breathe, the youngest child is asked to count the zeros—to make sure there has been no mistake. As relief and a promise of glory fill the air, Miss McNeil suddenly—and simply—fail to share it. Without speaking, and merely staring at the check, she tells us—unforgettably— that the check isn't a promise; it is her husbands. As she moves away, a lifetime turns over—and so does something or other in your throat.

Ruby Dee is, in a very quiet way, doing it all the time. Miss Dee is the pregnant wife who must act as peacemaker between generations: a generation that has been willing to settle for a very modest survival and a generation that looks at smokestacks and looks at farms and demands the right to own a share of them.

Wan, winsome, holding back the tartness that is always ready at the edge of her tongue, this wraithlike figure slowly comes into focus as the bond between embattled souls who cannot help betraying one another. With a light shift of her voice, she commands a rebellious child to kiss her goodbye; with an unobtrusive gesture, she flicks an ironing-board from a sofa so that a lounging and slightly fatuous college boy can relax in a tenement. Miss Dee is lovely to watch, if you can catch her rustling from mood to mood as the bitterness around her grows.

* * *

Mr. Poitier, too, can bring instant illumination to the most fleeting of transitions. A time comes when the money that means freedom for everyone seems, without warning, to vanish into thin air. The incident is really over, doom has sounded with an unmistakable blast, the scoundrel who has absconded

Claudia McNeil and Sidney Poitier in "A Raisin in the Sun."

with every last cent is irretrievably gone.

But time stands still for a moment in Mr. Poitier's glazed eyes, his arms rise in a limp and helpless arc until they seem to embrace a whole defeated race, and a sound that is only a meaningless echo comes out of him ("Don't-do-it-Willie!") with a fervent intensity and an impossible longing that are shattering.

* * *

Lloyd Richards has directed Lorraine Hansberry's first play for the theater with a fluid, elusive, quick - tempered grace that permits no moment—and no shade of desperation—to pass unexamined. Miss Hansberry has, it is true, driven her desperation to too unrelenting a pitch somewhere in the second act. Blow follows blow, snarl follows snarl, and we are

threatened with a monotone of defeat; the relieving and wonderfully caustic comedy that his enlivened the earlier stages ("he doesn't care how houses look— he's an intellectual") is mysteriously missing.

* * *

But the threads are caught up again in a savage final scene that finds Mr. Poitier taut and trembling in a limbo between violent surrender to a hostile world and a shaken reassertion of a "pinch of dignity." In the summation, Mr. Poitier is superb—and a cumulative swell of emotion reaches back over the evening to surround, and bind up, an honest, intelligible, and moving experience.

"A Raisin in the Sun" is an impressive first play, beautifully acted.

KENNETH TYNAN

Pundit, producer, and panjandrum of England's National Theatre, Kenneth Tynan was The New Yorker's man on the aisle from 1958 to 1960.

———

THE supreme virtue of "A Raisin in the Sun," Lorraine Hansberry's new play at the Ethel Barrymore, is its proud, joyous proximity to its source, which is life as the dramatist has lived it. I will not pretend to be impervious to the facts; this is the first Broadway production of a work by a colored authoress, and it is also the first Broadway production to have been staged by a colored director. (His name is Lloyd Richards, and he has done a sensible, sensitive, and impeccable job.) I do not see why these facts should be ignored, for a play is not an entity in itself, it is a part of history, and I have no doubt that my knowledge of the historical context predisposed me to like "A Raisin in the Sun" long before the house lights dimmed. Within ten minutes, however, liking had matured into absorption. The relaxed, freewheeling interplay of a magnificent team of Negro actors drew me unresisting into a world of their making, their suffering, their thinking, and their rejoicing. Walter Lee Younger's family lives in a roach-ridden Chicago tenement. The father, at thirty-five, is still a chauffeur, deluded by dreams of financial success that nag at the nerves and tighten the lips of his anxious wife, who ekes out their income by working in white kitchens. If she wants a day off, her mother-in-law advises her to plead flu, because it's respectable. ("Otherwise they'll think

you've been cut up or something.") Five people—the others being Walter Lee's progressive young sister, and his only child, an amiable small boy—share three rooms. They want to escape, and their chance comes when Walter Lee's mother receives the insurance money to which her recent widowhood has entitled her. She rejects her son's plan, which is to invest the cash in a liquor store; instead, she buys a house for the family in a district where no Negro has ever lived. Almost at once, white opinion asserts itself, in the shape of a deferential little man from the local Improvement Association, who puts the segregationist case so gently that it almost sounds like a plea for modified togetherness. At the end of a beautifully written scene, he offers to buy back the house, in order-as he explains-to spare the Youngers any possible embarrassment. His proposal is turned down. But before long Walter Lee has lost what remains of the money to a deceitful chum. He announces forthwith that he will go down on his knees to any white man who will buy the house for more than its face value. From this degradation he is finally saved; shame brings him to his feet. The Youngers, move out, and move on; a rung has been scaled, a point has been made, a step into the future has been soberly taken.

Miss Hansberry's piece is not without sentimentality, particularly in its reverent treatment of Walter Lee's

Claudia McNeil, Ruby Dee, and Sidney Poitier in "A Raisin in the Sun."

mother, brilliantly though Claudia Mc-Neil plays the part, monumentally trudging, upbraiding, disapproving, and consoling, I wish the dramatist had refrained from idealizing such a stolid old conservative. (She forces her daughter, an agnostic, to repeat after her, "In my mother's house there is still God.") But elsewhere I have no quibbles. Sidney Poitier blends skittishness, apathy, and riotous despair into his portrait of the mercurial Walter Lee, and Ruby Dee, his wife, is not afraid to let friction and frankness get the better of conventional affection. Diana Sands is a buoyantly assured kid sister, and Ivan Dixon is a Nigerian intellectual who replies, when she asks him whether Negroes in power would not be just as vicious and corrupt as whites, "I *live* the answer." The cast is flawless, and the teamwork on the first night was as effortless and exuberant as if the play had been running for a hundred performances. I was not present at the opening, twenty-four years ago, of Mr. Odets' "Awake and Sing!," but it must have been a similar occasion, generating the same kind of sympathy and communicating the same kind of warmth. After several curtain calls, the audience began to shout for the author, whereupon Mr. Poitier leaped down into the auditorium and dragged Miss Hansberry onto the stage. It was a glorious gesture, but it did no more than the play had already done for all of us. In spirit, we were up there ahead of her.

Author Salutes Reviewer

By LORRAINE HANSBERRY and RABBI JACOB J. WEINSTEIN

Sabbath Service, March 13, 1959

By Rabbi Jacob J. Weinstein

It says in *Proverbs* 13:12 "Hope deferred maketh the heart sick. But desire fulfilled is a tree of life."
And in the poem which prefaces the script of *A Raisin in the Sun*, the same truth is expressed:
"What happens to a dream deferred —
Does it dry up
Like a raisin in the sun?
Or fester like a sore
And then run?
Does it stink like rotten meat
Or crust and sugar over
Like a syrupy sweet?
Maybe it just sags
Like a heavy load
Or does it explode?"

This poem by Langston Hughes provided the title for the play which had such a remarkable three-week run in Chicago. Not since Carl Sandburg, Theodore Dreiser, Edgar Lee Masters and — yes, and Harriet Monroe, set the literary style for America have we Chicagoans been privileged to send better theatre to New York than New York has sent to us for some time now.

But Lorraine Hansberry Nemiroff has borrowed more than the title from Langston Hughes. She has manifested something of his spirit, too; for Langston Hughes has been interpreting the ways of black folk to white folk for 30 years. And while at times his bitterness and fear show through, he rarely forgets that he is talking about human beings lost in the human situation — each one of us a mixture of good and evil, the difference being only that some of us have the happy illusion that we are masters of our fate and some the dour certainty that we are not. Reading this play and reading Langston Hughes, one is impressed with how much more one can say about the most sensitive problems of our lives, if only one remembers to smile, or laugh, or drop the subtlest insinuation that the prophet of righteousness isn't above stealing a glance at a well-turned ankle.

Yes, this play, the first to be produced by Lorraine Hansberry, deals primarily with the dreams of a Negro family residing in a rather typical kitchenette apartment on the crowded South Side of Chicago. The family hailed from the deep South and before that, who knows? The Negro community does not have *landsmanschaften* in the manner of the Jews. They are not too anxious to remember the *Yikhus* (ancestry) of the family in Vicksburg or Yahoo and they simply don't know what part of the Old World they came from. If they did, we might find that some could claim a common descent from the Ethiopian princesses that came to Solomon's most accommodating bed.

The father of the Younger family has died after a life of constant labor, so that his son and daughter might have some of the opportunities he did not have. The widow Lena remains and she is the dominant character of the play. She dominates it so completely that even the Academy Award nominee, Sidney Poitier, is eclipsed by her massive strength. Not since Ma Joad in *The Grapes of Wrath* gave an incredible security to her Oakie brood has the mother strength so completely pervaded an entire family and so heroically shored up that family from the engulfing floods as does Lena Younger in this play.

I rummaged among my notes on *The Grapes of Wrath* to find these lines, the relevance of which will be apparent in a little while:

"Her full face was not soft; it was controlled, kindly. Her hazel eyes seemed to have experienced all possible tragedy and to have mounted pain and suffering like steps into a high calm and a superhuman understanding. She seemed to know, to accept, to welcome her position, the citadel of the family, the strong place that could not be taken. And since old Tom and the children could not know hurt or fear unless *she* acknowledged hurt and fear, she had practiced denying them in herself... Imperturbability could be depended upon. And from her great and humble position as healer, her hands had grown sure and cool and quiet... She seemed to know that if she swayed the family shook, and if she ever deeply wavered or despaired the family would fall, the family will to function would be gone."

Listen now to the author's (Hansberry's) script note on Mother Younger:

"She is a woman in her late 60's, full bodied and strong... Her dark brown face is surrounded by the total whiteness of her hair and, being a woman who has adjusted to many things in life and overcome many more, her face is full of strength. She has, we can see, wit and faith of a kind that keep her eyes lit and full of interest and expectancy...

"Her bearing is perhaps most like that of the Herero women... rather as if she imagines that as she walks she still bears a basket or a vessel upon her head...."

Let me make clear what the crucial action of the play is. Lena has been left an insurance policy of $10,000. Walter Lee, her son, who is married to Ruth and has a 10 year old son and another child on the way, and who lives in this small apartment with his mother and his 20-year old sister Beneatha, a college girl with the ambition to become a doctor, knows that this check is due... He dreams of going into business for himself, a liquor store, with two partners, Willie and Bobo.

Walter Lee finds his job as a chauffeur stifling and he buttresses his own discontent with feelings of anguish for his wife's need to work in white folk's kitchens and the certainty that his own son will not rise above the poverty of the Negro ghetto... His mother and wife, however, have their own dreams of a two story house in some sunlit suburb.

Beneatha, who is intent on becoming a doctor also thinks her brother's plan is completely crazy and refuses to help him....

Lena does put a down payment of $3,500 on a house in... a suburb up to now all white. The remaining $6,500 she entrusts to Walter (for himself and for his sister's education, after she realizes he is at the point of exploding or drying up within and needs the assurance that he is the man of the house). Walter immediately delivers the whole $6,500 to Willy to do his politicking in Springfield. He is so sure that he has taken the first step toward affluence that he becomes a changed being, smiling and confident, present-buying and even loving. Give a man a check book, as Sholom Aleichem would say, and he becomes Rothschild's uncle.

Then the blow falls. Willy skips with the money. The scene where Bobo reveals this awful truth to Walter Lee has all the power of a Greek tragedy. Not since the denouement in Sholom Asch's *God of Vengeance,* when the father discovers that his own daughter has become a prostitute, even though he has installed a Torah in his own home, have I felt the impact of doom descend upon a whole family, as it did here when this news lights a devastating fire under the dreams of (every one of them).

This dismal sub-climax underlies the social realism of the play and serves as a solid foundation which grandly sustains the depth psychology, the folk lore and the symbolism. It also helps to make the play universal, since everyone of every color can feel the cold terror of poverty. It is a rare thing indeed to find a play these days which puts in proper balance the inner-directed motives of men and the outer forces which play and press upon them. Either we get subtle delvings into a psyche that reacts in a vacuum or the breakdown of an organization man — a mere extension of our mechanical gadgetry. Lorraine Hansberry has adroitly balanced the economic deterministic forces and the conscious and subconscious psychological ones.

Still this catastrophe does not destroy the family. They do not walk into doom as they would in a Greek tragedy or in a Chekhov or an Ibsen play. There is still that $3,500 down payment on the house. And Mama

Lena, when she has recovered from the shock of her son's foolishness, begins to make plans to use that money to refurbish and decorate the old apartment where she came as a bride with big Walter. They might even win it from the rats and cockroaches and make it attractive. But this plan is changed when a representative of the Clybourne Home Owners Association comes to offer Lena a bribe if she will take her money back and not intrude on a white man's neighborhood.

I imagine this scene will make a lot of people uncomfortable; but if a play is to be a real catharsis, it must build up some tension and some guilt. I don't think people in lily-white neighborhoods will like this scene. And yet it answers the segregationists in the best and most effective manner. In this scene, Lorraine Hansberry shows her honesty, her compassion, her maturity. She could have had the white man, the only white character in the play, a bit of a cracker, with all the vulgar prejudices of the bigot. She chose rather to represent him as a kindly person who hates violence and who represents modest people like himself, who have put everything into their homes and want to preserve their investment and their way of life. Deeper fears and deeper differences are revealed only in side remarks; as when Ruth asks, "Are the white people afraid that we are going to eat them?" and Beneatha's answer, "No, they are afraid we are going to marry them."

Well, after a very subtle kind of roll call, the family decides unanimously to move into that two-story at 406 Clybourne Street. They move from the rat-infested kitchenette, where they have known so much of anguish and so much of terror, into the sunlit, all-white neighborhood. The curtain comes down on Ma Lena Younger taking the little scrawny plant which she has nurtured in the narrow slant of sun coming through the one stingy window of her apartment; and everyone in that audience catches the meaning of that symbol.

And each and every member of that audience knows that the plant is the hardy perennial we call brotherhood and whether it lives or dies at 406 Clybourne is going to depend not only on the loving care of the Youngers, but on the attitude of their neighbors. If the people in 404 and 408, and the people across the street in 407 and 409 open their hearts and treat the Youngers as fellow human beings, that plant will grow and become a great tree and give us all of its fruit and its shade. But if they receive them with bricks and stink bombs, the gall and bitterness which the white neighbors will engender in the black soul will spill over and the plant will wither, shrivel up and die, "like a raisin in the sun."

The movers who take the Younger family from their South Side rat-hole to their new suburban home are the vanguard of an exodus as significant as the one we celebrate in scripture and song tonight. The children of slaves are moving from a station in their journey from the land of Pharaoh. Under the great Lincoln, they lost their chains and came to the Cis-Jordan, where they could see the promised land but not enter it.

It will be recorded that it was often more bitter to have had the name of free men without the substance, than to have had neither the name nor the substance. It will also be recorded that the fetters — the invisible, inchoate fetters — of unspoken prejudices, of social conventions, of property covenants, were much more corrosive in the flesh than the visible chains of tyranny. It will also be recorded that in being despoiled, they often turned about and despoiled their neighbors, so that the viciousness of a white con man reaped an act of violence or brigandage against an innocent white man; but God's justice is often hard cutting and inexorable. As both Amos and Lincoln have reminded us, in a world where God is One amd indivisible, where each man is involved in mankind, Justice is a pooled justice and retribution spreads to the innocent, even as the pain of man-made wrong descends upon the undeserving.

But the moral, good friends, is this: that all men are God's children and when God wants his children free, no one is going to stop them. "God's love was not all on Israel spent," Paul Laurence Dunbar reminds us; and "He will send some Moses to set his children free." It is the glory of such talents as that of Lorraine Hansberry Nemiroff that they can make so many Toms, Dicks, Harrys and Jakes feel that they, too, can be a Moses and make a way in the neon wilderness to that long-promised land. ∎

Mrs. LORRAINE NEMIROFF   337 Bleecker Street, New York 14, N.Y.
                                                              May 5, 1959
Dear Rabbi Weinstein:
    This is the first opportunity I have had to send you some expression of the appreciation I felt when a copy of your March 13th Sabbath Service reached my hands. I read it through once and was astonished at what a relatively few pages had apparently encompassed. I was, in fact, so impressed that I read it aloud to my husband that evening and, later, to our producer, Mr. Philip Rose. They concurred with me that it is undoubtedly the most significantly perceptive discussion of *Raisin* that any of us have read or heard of anywhere. This is particularly true because your commentary transcended the play and drew upon the most pertinent aspects of American society and literature as a frame of reference. I was particularly moved by your gift for uniting dramatic analysis with clear and necessary human objectives.
    I was considering requesting your permission to use parts of it as either an appendice (sic) or preface in the published version (Random House), which will appear nationally by early summer. I have since been advised by the publishers that this is contrary to contemporary play publishing — whatever that means.
    In any case, all of us connected with the production are inspired by your interpretation and brilliant use of our effort. Please accept my very best wishes, I am
                                                              Sincerely yours,
                                            Lorraine Hansberry

On the morning after the opening, I attended a meeting at the Blaine Thompson advertising agency, then the largest and almost the only agency specializing in theatre advertising. Joining me in attendance were the entire staff of the agency, plus my press agent and general manager. We were all there to discuss our advertising campaign with regard to style and budget, while the immediate task was to design a *Raisin* logo and choose the review quotes for the first newspaper ads to run since our opening. Back in 1959, nobody gave much thought to radio or television as media for theatre ads.

When I arrived at the meeting, everyone was in an expansive mood. The art department had already come up with several ideas for the logo, and the writing team was having a hard time deciding what to omit from any of the reviews, since they were all so enthusiastic. With some of my later productions I would find these morning-after meetings to be mostly about extracting phrases or a word or two that would hide or even contradict the reviewer's original intent. But on *Raisin* we had no such problems. Indeed, the artwork for the logo already existed in a graphic I had chosen many weeks before: a drawing of Sidney Poitier's head in a burst of sunlight. And with our quotes it was great fun choosing the best among the best. The only question I raised, which Lorraine and I had already discussed, was why Mr. Atkinson chose to use the word "honesty" or some variation of it six times in the course of his review. Possibly, in writing against a deadline, he might not have noticed it, but then why didn't his editor point it out? These are the phrases: "The play is honest," "the performance is also honest," "the honesty of the writing," "the rousing honesty of the stage work," "[Ralph Alswang's set] . . . . Like the play, it is honest," and last, "Miss Hansberry's . . . simple honesty is the most difficult thing in the world." At the time, I thought perhaps there might have been validity to the first three or four mentions, but when I got to the Ralph Alswang set—not that I thought Ralph Alswang was anything less than reputable—my reaction was that had I thought too much about his set's possible dishonesty I might not have used it. The last and most disturbing reference was to Lorraine's "simple honesty." While I may have considered Lorraine as honest as the next person (whoever that person was), in no case, whether she was being painfully honest or brazenly lying, would she ever be simple. Lorraine and I wondered about this for some weeks, until a succession of events that ended in a meeting between Lorraine and Mr. Atkinson, but more about that later.

Following is a replica of the ad approved at the advertising meeting which appeared immediately after our opening, and was repeated when *A Raisin in the Sun* won the New York Drama Critics award for Best Play of the Year.

"BEST PLAY OF THE YEAR"

NEW YORK DRAMA CRITICS AWARD

UNANIMOUSLY ACCLAIMED!

"AN IMPRESSIVE PLAY, BEAUTIFULLY ACTED"

"A cumulative swell of emotion reaches back over the evening to surround, and bind up, an honest, intelligible and moving experience. An impressive play, beautifully acted. Mr. Poitier is superb."
—Kerr, Herald Tribune

"BOLD AND STIRRING"

"Miss Hansberry has a wide range of topics to write about—some of them hilarious, some of them painful in the extreme. Lloyd Richards has directed a bold and stirring performance. Likely to destroy the complacency of anyone who sees it. Mr. Poitier is a remarkable actor with enormous power. Claudia McNeil gives a heroic performance."
—Atkinson, Times

SIDNEY POITIER

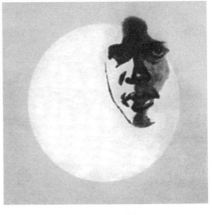

a raisin in the sun

SIDNEY POITIER

a raisin in the sun

"A WORK OF THEATRICAL MAGIC"

"A beautiful, lovable play. It is affectionately human, funny and touching. Shows us what the theatre should be at its best. The acting company, under the direction of Lloyd Richards, is flawless. A work of theatrical magic."
—Chapman, News

"ANOTHER SMASH HIT"

"A moving play wonderfully acted. Miss Hansberry is the most gifted dramatist to reach the Rialto in several semesters. Miss McNeil can make you roar with laughter one moment and reach for your handkerchief the next. Not only good fun but gripping theatre as well. Another smash hit."
—Coleman, Mirror

"IT WILL MAKE YOU PROUD OF HUMAN BEINGS"

"The number of tears shed by presumably wordly first nighters must have set a new record at the Ethel Barrymore last evening. They dropped in tribute to Lorraine Hansberry's 'A Raisin in the Sun'. It may rip you to shreds. It will make you proud of human beings."

—Aston, World Telegram & Sun

"A STUPENDOUS HIT"

"A small hunk of history was made at the Ethel Barrymore Theatre last night. Written with humor, pathos and good sound dramatic insight. 'A Raisin in the Sun' is a wonderful emotional evening."

—McClain, Journal-American

SIDNEY POITIER

a raisin in the sun

SIDNEY POITIER

a raisin in the sun

"MOVING AND IMPRESSIVE DRAMA"

"Miss Hansberry brings to her work a fine sense of character, a gift for wry humor, the ability to give a scene emotional impact. Miss McNeil and Mr. Poitier have the dominating roles and play them splendidly. Excellent acting, a moving and impressive drama."

—Watts, Post

a raisin in the sun

A new play by LORRAINE HANSBERRY

with

CLAUDIA McNEIL   RUBY DEE
LOUIS GOSSETT   DIANA SANDS
JOHN FIEDLER   IVAN DIXON

Directed by LLOYD RICHARDS
Designed and Lighted by RALPH ALSWANG
Costumes by VIRGINIA VOLLAND

Chapter 15

By the end of March we were a smash hit. We were receiving many requests for interviews with Lorraine, Sidney, and other cast members. All kinds of stories were being written about the Broadway miracle, and the largely white audiences who might have stayed away were paying ticket brokers high prices for their choice seats. But it took a while for us to attract large numbers of black theatregoers for several reasons. Among them were the cost of tickets; a lack of interest in the usual Broadway product; and a historic failure on the part of Broadway's establishment to even attempt to reach potential black patrons. It took me some time to deal with this, and not until 1961, when I produced *Purlie Victorious,* was I able, with the help of Ossie Davis, to create a special mechanism to bring black groups to the theatre through their various organizations, especially their community churches. Today this is standard procedure for any Broadway show which wants to expand its audience.

I enjoyed going to the Barrymore Theatre quite often to watch the *Raisin* performances and occasionally to hang out in the lobby. I was fascinated to eavesdrop on the audience during each of the two intermissions and at the end of the show. They seemed to be experiencing something quite unlike what they had anticipated. As the play proceeded, they were anxious to talk about it to their companions or even to strangers like myself. It was amazing to me how rarely I would hear conversations in the lobby about anything but the play. But one day at the first act intermission, a white gentleman, quite nicely dressed, approached the box office window and I heard him ask in a well-educated, perhaps slightly southern accent if he could change his seat. The box office person asked if the seat was broken or there was some other problem. The man said no, he would just like to change his seat. The box office attendant looked at his ticket stub and saw that it was for a fourth-row center seat, an ideal location, and probably purchased at some expense from a ticket broker. He returned the stub and informed the gentleman that the house was completely sold out and nothing could be done. The gentleman then asked if he could stand in the back and, after consultation with the house manager, was told he could for the last two acts.

Just before the house lights dimmed for Act II, I walked down the aisle to check the now empty seat. On either side of it was a well-dressed black couple. I decided to sit in that seat for the last two acts and even engaged in some slight conversation with them each time the lights went up. I gathered they'd had no contact of any kind with the previous occupant or taken any particular notice of him. As the lights went up at the end of the performance, I looked back and saw that the gentleman— who in 1959 obviously had been uncomfortable sitting in a seat sandwiched between two black couples, but had been much too interested to leave—was now applauding enthusiastically from his place at the back of the theatre. (Perhaps he had concluded that when attending a "black play" all the white people should be kept at the back of the house.) In any case, I tried to rush up the aisle to talk to him, but by the time I got through the crowd, he was gone. I wondered later if he might one day return with a companion to see the entire play from a seat. Maybe he would even bring along a black friend.

Jumping forward now briefly to 1963, after the New York production closed, we put together a road company of *A Raisin in the Sun* that traveled the country encountering all the usual "inconveniences" a black touring company had to deal with at that time. We were booked into the National Theatre in Washington, D.C. While they were no longer legally segregated, theatres in Washington were not considered particularly welcoming to black audiences. We were touring without Sidney Poitier, who had long since left the New York production and whose part on the road was being played by Doug Turner, a fine but relatively unknown actor. The opening night audience was primarily white, well-dressed, and no doubt upper-class.

Washington at that time was becoming aware of an emerging black middle class, the result of federal government jobs that became available in the wartime 1940s. The many black families now striving to live in nicer homes were slowly, in the parlance of the time, "invading" white neighborhoods. Consequently white families were selling their homes as soon as there was even a rumor in their neighborhoods that a black family might be moving in. This, as in many other cities, was the beginning of "white flight": white families deserting the cities for the suburbs. Perhaps worse than those who left were those who stayed on and threatened the first black family who even dared to try to buy.

At the Washington premiere, when Walter Lee Younger made his compelling speech about how he and his family were going to move into a white neighborhood because it was "our right to do it and we have earned that right," the entire audience seemed to applaud in acclaim. The next day a local newspaper, in addition to its rave review, carried an editorial marveling that this group of white, largely affluent theatregoers had expressed their enthusiastic approval of Walter Lee's decision, and went on to remark that after the show they returned home, probably to continue their battle to keep their neighborhoods free of any such intruders. Implicit in the editorial was an earnest hope that maybe one or two or even three families would act just a bit differently, at home or at their next community meeting, as a result of seeing this play.

Returning now to March 1959: with our production settling into the routine that develops in any play on its way to a long run, the tensions preceding opening night were inevitably being replaced by other backstage crises. Was this to ensure that management did not become too complacent or overconfident? That wasn't likely to happen because in our cast we had a built-in discontent mechanism in the person of the actress who played Mama, Claudia McNeil. I could be fairly certain that few weeks would go by without my getting a call from Lenny Auerbach, our stage manager, to report that Claudia, again involved in a serious dispute with one of our actors, was threatening to quit if the other actor wasn't fired. My staff was usually able to settle these disputes fairly easily, either with our own threats or with other reasonable alternatives, generally followed by much laughter among all the parties involved except Claudia. I was particularly amused when one newspaper critic writing about our play commented on how obvious it was that this company of Negro actors was so extraordinary because they *were* a group of Negroes who were not just actors playing roles as white actors would, but living them, and therefore, unlike a white company, could never get into disputes with each other. I'm sure the writer thought he was paying our company a profound compliment.

Of course Claudia was smart enough not to get into an off-stage dispute with Sidney, and on the rare occasions when something did happen between them onstage, a note from our stage manager would immediately elicit from Claudia a very humble apology. The topper to all these incidents came the day I received a call from Lenny, during a performance, saying very seriously that we now had our most severe crisis: at Claudia's insistence we would have to fire Glynn Turman, who played Sidney's ten-year-old son.

I knew that Glynn was as good a trouper as anyone in the cast. I also knew he was well behaved on or off stage because he had a wonderful relationship with his working mother. As a matter of fact, he would always call her from backstage to say he had arrived safely at the theatre or to discuss any other things they needed to talk about.

It so happens that Glynn's mother knew Claudia McNeil casually as somebody from her neighborhood, and there was no love lost between them. During that day's matinee performance, Glynn was making his usual call to his mother as Claudia came by on her way to her dressing room. Seeing him on the phone she stopped and said in her most imperious voice, "Get off the damn phone." On the other end of the telephone, Glynn's mother, having no problem recognizing that voice, immediately asked, "What did Claudia say to you?" Glynn responded, "She said I should get off the phone." Said Glynn's mother angrily, "Tell her to kiss your ass." Glynn turned and yelled at Claudia's departing figure, "She said to kiss my ass." Fortunately, this encounter took place during an intermission and our stage manager and stagehands were able to prevent the mayhem that might have developed had they not been there to rush Glynn to his dressing room and gently but firmly escort Claudia to hers.

After Lenny and I made a futile attempt to have a serious talk about the situation, I suggested he inform Claudia that in order to fire a contracted actor, we would have to hold a hearing and be judged by Actors' Equity, with Claudia as the star witness against this ten-year-old, very well-behaved boy. Not only might she come off poorly, but other witnesses might be brought in to testify against her. Claudia agreed to settle the dispute with an apology from Glynn for his language, which she magnanimously accepted.

As the run progressed, I continually had to deal with a truly serious matter that I found more and more depressing: my relationship with Sidney Poitier. In the first few days after our opening we were on polite terms with each other. But we seemed unable to move beyond the limited actor-producer relationship that had resulted first from my being in the middle of the script problems between him and Lorraine, and then from what he interpreted as my support of Lorraine's point of view. One day I received a phone call from a mutual friend of ours, Leon Carter. I had met Leon through Sidney some years before. He was a young black man with an ability to keep his balance in dealing with the many problems he had faced in his life, now perhaps made more severe by a physical ailment of some kind. Leon was an extraordinary and, I believe, self-educated man with whom you could have an equally interesting discussion about what to have for dinner or where the world was headed on any particular day. And he could be equally passionate about either.

That Sunday morning, Leon called to invite me to his apartment for a drink and to discuss his health problem. I immediately arranged to meet him at 5:00 P.M. that afternoon, not an unusual hour for us to have a drink together. I knew Leon was aware and deeply disturbed that his very close friend Sidney and I were still estranged, in spite of the huge success of the play. He had freely expressed to me how childishly he thought Sidney and I were acting, and I assumed he had said much the same to Sidney. Leon had also remarked that perhaps he could have understood our attitudes if the play had been a flop; but here we were, both involved not only in a hit play but also, in his view, a truly historic one. So on my way to his apartment to discuss his ailments, I suspected that Sidney's name might come up.

I arrived at Leon's building, rang the downstairs bell, went up to his apartment, and knocked at the door. As he opened it, he oddly stepped out of his doorway and seemed to look down the hallway as if he expected somebody. Then as I walked into the apartment and he closed the door behind me, I heard a key turn in the outside lock. I didn't quite understand that, but I turned toward his living room: there was Sidney sitting on a couch. I turned back to the door to try to open it, and Sidney was quickly at my side doing the same thing. We then realized that we were locked in together for whatever purpose and length of time

Leon had in mind. Because Sidney and I were now only seeing each other when there was some backstage problem, Leon had obviously determined that neither one of us was mature enough to deal with and resolve our bruised feelings, and we both had to be treated as the children we obviously were.

Thoughtfully Leon had, in plain view, provided a bottle of Scotch to lighten the atmosphere, and it didn't take long before Sidney and I were toasting our absent friend. It took no more than a second drink for us to realize what Leon was demanding of us. Very soon we were talking about our families and mutual friends, especially Leon, and all the other social and political issues that were important to both of us. We then began to estimate how long we were to be prisoners in Leon's apartment and how many days he thought we children would need to understand and accept our punishment. Oddly enough, he had greater faith in us than we deserved, for in about an hour we heard a key in the lock. He entered the apartment, walked directly to the Scotch, poured himself a drink, and said he hoped he hadn't kept us waiting too long.

If it is not already apparent, the remaining pages of this memoir will make it indelibly clear that to this day Sidney Poitier has remained one of my closest friends. Our recovery from the brief break in our relationship would have certainly occurred without the inspired aid of our friend Leon, but at the time he helped us to heal a rift that neither of us wanted to continue.

The sad ending to this story is that a short time later Leon Carter came by my apartment to tell me that he was leaving for Boston to undergo heart surgery. Since I was not at home, he expressed to my wife his good wishes for me and the play and his pleasure that things between Sidney and me were fine once again. He also said, it seemed to Doris, more than a fond goodbye. He never returned from Boston, having died during the operating procedure. We still talk about him and miss him a whole lot.

Chapter 16

T he theatrical season of 1958–1959 saw the opening on Broadway of many extraordinary plays, all of which were competing for the support of the theatregoing public. This was a time when Broadway was a discovery and nurturing place for new plays, and playwrights were sought after and competed over by the many independent producers who devoted their lives to and made their living (occasionally) by their theatrical activities. This was before off-Broadway had replaced Broadway as the birthplace of serious plays and long before producers spent time and money doing countless showcases and readings of plays before deciding to produce them. Producers like Kermit Bloomgarden, Robert Whitehead, Cheryl Crawford, Roger Stevens, David Merrick, and many others would read plays, choose the occasional one that impressed them, option it, announce it in the *New York Times*, and then go about the business of raising money and producing it. All of this activity led to theatrical seasons like that of 1958–1959, which included Tennessee Williams' *Sweet Bird of Youth*, Eugene O'Neill's *A Touch of the Poet*, William Faulkner's *Requiem for a Nun*, William Gibson's *Two for the Seasaw*, Archibald Mac-Leish's *J.B.*, Friedrich Duerrenmatt's *The Visit*, and, among many others, *A Raisin in the Sun*. That season was not, however, considered particularly unusual in the number of original plays produced and, indeed, at the time articles were written bemoaning the decline of serious Broadway theatre. It may (or may not) be encouraging to today's struggling young playwrights and surprising to some current producing organizations to learn that all of these plays were written and came to Broadway without an interminable succession of readings or showcases, and without the help or even the presence of a single dramaturg. Playwrights then actually sat in a room by themselves and wrote and rewrote their good or bad plays, and no one thought it unusual. I'm told on good authority that Neil Simon does it to this day and with some success.

During the 1958–1959 season the producer's most desired award for a Broadway play was the Drama Critics Circle's "Best Play." We were pleased to receive four Tony nominations including best play (Lorraine Hansberry), director (Lloyd Richards), leading actor (Sidney Poitier), and supporting actress (Claudia McNeil). However, the Tonys, prizes every Broadway show now dreams about, did not achieve their current influence until 1967, when their commercially sponsored national telecasts began. In the years before, every play that won the Critics Circle Award would take a full page *New York Times* ad to trumpet that fact.

The competition in 1959 was fierce. Lorraine and I knew we were a long shot, given the competition, and particularly because we were certain, based on his reviews, that Brooks Atkinson would be staunchly and convincingly holding out for *J.B.* In fact, Atkinson had followed up his *J.B.* review with several laudatory articles that proclaimed it one of the century's greatest plays.

If we were, nevertheless, somewhat hopeful, it was because overall, our notices were at least comparable to those of the other plays. But we had also noticed something of a recent trend: as *A Raisin in the Sun* became the season's biggest play at the box office, articles were appearing that damned it with faint praise as a very successful "soap opera." Mr. Atkinson himself had pointed out in one piece that *J. B.* was not doing as well as it deserved in ticket sales while *Raisin* was far exceeding expectations.

We knew that we had great fans in Henry Hewes of *The Saturday Review* and Kenneth Tynan of *The New Yorker*. Mr. Tynan had even extolled the so-called "soap opera" aspect of Lorraine Hansberry's work as a tremendous story-telling virtue rather than a fault. But Mr. Tynan was *The New Yorker's* "guest critic" and we couldn't be sure he would be present at the voting session. Fortunately, as it turned out, Henry Hewes was so determinedly in favor of *Raisin* he arranged for Mr. Tynan, if absent, to vote by proxy, a proxy vote he did indeed give Mr. Hewes to cast for *A Raisin in the Sun*, the vote that became the deciding one as *Raisin* beat out *J.B.* by just that margin.

Now *A Raisin in the Sun* was becoming known internationally and production requests came in from all over the world; within a short time the play was being performed in many countries and various languages. I was particularly intrigued that it played in Israel at one of their important repertory theatres, with all the actors except the one white character wearing what we would call "blackface" (without the negative connotation and history that would have had in our country) and, yes, all speaking Hebrew. We also had an interesting debut in Manchester, England, where the actors spoke a language they called English. Incidentally, Walter Lee was played by the fine American actor Earle Hyman, who was brought over from the United States. I was there for the out-of-town opening (prior to London) and read a positive review in which Lorraine was referred to as a talented "Negress." I sent this on to her and received the reply that follows below. The last line about the "manner of a certain lawn" refers to Camp Unity, where, you will recall, Lorraine and I first met and where we would occasionally have political discussions on the lawn.

July 31, 1959
The Colonies,
New World

Dear Little Philip-

    The papers from Manchester arrived this morning -
at 7:30, to be precise. I stayed up to read them, vanity being its
own narcotic.

    I will not pretend that I was not genuinely moved
by them, rather much as a matter of fact, and truly trust that there
will always be an England. I am deeply grateful to the company. Will
you personally extend that fact to them? There is a clear ring of
the recognition of nobility in their work from those who have written
about it. I am deeply proud that such distinguished artists have
graced the European premiere of our play. My most especial congratulations
to Mr. Hyman and Miss Moore. I gather the lady is truly soaring; and that
Walter Lee is being rendered with power. Congratulations, indeed! And
to dear Olga, who has clearly charmed England; and Miss Hamilton and
Mr. Edwards.(To the latter, I would offer an appropiate Welsh salute,
but please explain they only teach "All Through the Night" over here
as the only product of Wales and its culture and "Ayr Hyd Nos" is a
pretty strange way to say thank you.)

    Tell Lloyd Richards that I love him and yourself as well.
Am feeling so mellow about England this morning that I may tell the
"folks" over in Kenya to let them linger a bit. They have their points.

    BUT - what the hell is this _negress_ bit? I am almost
moved to sail tomorrow to discuss the matter on the B.B.C. - ala the
manner of a certain lawn!

    Love to all. Next week, East Lynn...

                    Love,

                    Lorraine

At some point Harold Stern, my attorney, informed me that there was interest in a possible film sale but only from one source. It seemed most of the studios and movie producers weren't yet quite sure that Hollywood was ready for a screen version of this particular play. Oddly enough, the interest expressed came from Columbia Pictures on behalf of David Susskind. As you may remember—I certainly did—Susskind had turned down the opportunity to co-produce the play with me because "it was not commercial." He was also a client of Harold Stern, who told me he rarely let a week go buy without pointing out to David how foolish he had been, often in much more graphic language.

Harold had just negotiated a deal for Susskind to produce three films for Columbia Pictures, the specific projects to be mutually agreed upon. I don't know if the *Raisin* suggestion came from Harold, David, or Columbia, but after advising me of the interest, Harold promised he would get back to Lorraine and me with a concrete offer. I asked if the offer would include Lorraine as the screenwriter and he confirmed that it would. When I mentioned Sidney, whom he also represented, Harold said Marty Baum, Sidney's agent, would be handling those negotiations, but indeed Columbia would not close any deal without signing Sidney Poitier to star in the film. The talks with Columbia continued then for several weeks, during which Lorraine reacted to the flow of information rather calmly. She was amused by the prospect of David Susskind as producer, since she remembered his initial reservations about the play.

At about this same time, Jim Proctor, my press agent, received a call from Arthur Gelb of the *New York Times* asking if Lorraine would be interested in writing an essay for the Sunday *Times* on any subject or opinion of her choosing. Obviously, Mr. Gelb, who was assistant drama critic, assumed that Miss Hansberry would take the opportunity to speak out about her own play and/or theatre in general. Jim Proctor was particularly pleased that Lorraine was offered this opportunity with no restrictions, and he was even more delighted when I assured him soon after that Lorraine had consented to write something.

I was especially excited, because I knew that Lorraine was aware of the resentment that seemed to have emerged from some quarters regarding *Raisin's* enormous success. It was as if Lorraine were entitled to having a commercial hit, but it was too much to accept that she might also have written a very good or even great play, one that critics were occasionally comparing to O'Casey and Chekhov. This point of view led to articles that stated or implied that the play had been overpraised.

Knowing that Lorraine was amused by this strain of negativity, I was looking forward to reading her piece in the *Times*. She finished it in a rather short time and sent it to Arthur Gelb, expecting it would lead to discussion and eventually to agreed-upon revision. She soon received a response from Mr. Gelb which was quite positive and complimentary but held an apology. Mr. Gelb was leaving shortly for a vacation of several weeks, and the *Times* wanted to run Lorraine's piece quite soon, without having to wait for his return for final approval. Actually, he said, the only problem with the article was its length, something both Lorraine and Gelb felt could be easily handled if she were given the approximate length of the required cuts. At that point Mr. Gelb explained that because he was leaving almost immediately, he was turning her essay over to Brooks Atkinson, who would be contacting her shortly to tell her how much space would be assigned to it.

Several days later Lorraine received from Atkinson an edited version of the article she had written, with an accompanying letter saying the *Times* was looking forward to using the piece in *his* edited version.

When I received the call from Lorraine, perhaps fifteen minutes after she finished reading what she now referred to as "Mr. Atkinson's essay," my telephone was almost too hot to handle. It seemed, she informed me, that Mr. Atkinson had decided there was no need either to meet or even to discuss the length of her article since it was now acceptable. In Lorraine's view, by selective editing, the article had been transformed to reflect Mr. Atkinson's interpretation of her play, rather than her own very critical judgment of her playwriting deficiencies. From her summary of what Atkinson had done to distort her point of view, and from the fact that he had edited her piece without calling or consulting her, I knew Lorraine was not going to be easily placated, nor was her anger likely to subside. Personally, I was shocked that Atkinson had proceeded in this fashion, denying her even the courtesy of contacting her. I asked what she would like to do now, and she replied that she would refuse the *Times* permission to print the essay or any part of it, and demand it be returned immediately. I suggested to Lorraine that I call Jim Proctor and have him make the demand (request?), and she agreed to wait until she heard from me.

When I spoke to Jim, his first and expected reaction was just short of hysteria. "You mean that you want me, your press agent, to say to Brooks Atkinson that Lorraine Hansberry is not excited and overwhelmed that her piece has been edited by the most important theatre critic in the world; and that . . .," "Wait, Jim," I interrupted, "you can, if you want to, say she is overwhelmed that a respected professional such as Mr. Atkinson would show such disrespect to Miss Hansberry, but beyond that, inform him that he will be receiving a letter from Miss Hansberry precluding the *Times* from using the article. I'm sure he'll have no trouble understanding the situation." Jim then quietly hung up the phone, Lorraine sent her letter and received a perfunctory letter from Atkinson's office expressing regrets, and presumably the whole incident was over.

But a short time later somebody from the *Village Voice* learned about the existence of the piece and asked to read it. Lorraine sent it on and got an immediate reply offering to print the article in its entirety. Lorraine agreed and it appeared on August 12, 1959.

An Author's Reflections:

Willie Loman, Walter Younger, And He Who Must Live

by Lorraine Hansberry

"A man can't go out the way he came in . . . Ben, that funeral will be massive!" —Willy Loman, 1946

"We have all thought about your offer and we have decided to move into our house." —Walter Lee Younger, 1958

Some of the acute partisanship revolving around "A Raisin in the Sun" is amusing. Those who announce that they find the piece less than fine are regarded in some quarters with dramatic hostility, as though such admission automatically implies the meanest of racist reservations. On the other hand, the ultra-sophisticates have hardly acquitted themselves less ludicrously, gazing cooly down their noses at those who are moved by the play, and going on at length about "melodrama" and/or "soap opera" as if these are not completely definable terms which cannot simply be tacked onto any play and all plays we do not like.

Personally, I find no pain whatever—at least of the traditional ego type—in saying that "Raisin" is a play which contains dramaturgical incompletions. Fine plays tend to utilize one big fat character who runs right through the middle of the structure, by action or implication, with whom we rise or fall. A central character as such is certainly lacking from "Raisin." I should be delighted to pretend that it was *inventiveness*, as some suggest for me, but it is, also, craft inadequacy and creative indecision. The result is that neither Walter Lee nor Ma-

ma Younger loom large enough to monumentally command the play. I consider it an enormous dramatic fault if no one else does. (Nor am I less critical of the production which, by and large, performance and direction alike, is splendid. Yet I should have preferred that the second-act curtain, for instance, had been performed with quiet assertion rather than the apparently popular declamatory opulence which prevails.

All in all, however, I believe that, for the most part, the play has been magnificently understood. In some cases it was not only thematically absorbed but attention was actually paid to the tender treacherousness of its craft-imposed "simplicity." Some, it is true, quite missed that part of the overt intent and went on to harangue the bones of the play with rather useless observations of the terribly clear fact that they are old bones indeed. More meaningful discussions tended to delve into the flesh which hangs from

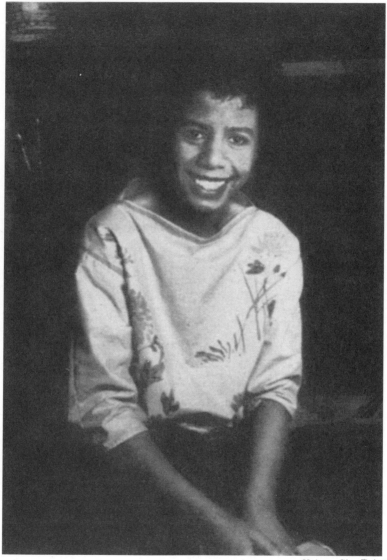

Voice: Gin Briggs

LORRAINE HANSBERRY

those bones and its implications in mid-century American drama and life.

In that connection it is interesting to note that while the names of Chekhov, O'Casey, and the early Odets were introduced for comparative pupuses in some of the reviews, almost no one— with the exception of Gerald **LORRAINE HANSBERRY, author of "A Raisin in the Sun," lives on Bleecker Street in Greenwich Village.**

Weales in Commentary—discovered a simple line of descent between Walter Lee Younger and the last great hero in American drama to also *accept* the values of his culture, Willy Loman. I am sure that the already mentioned primary fault of the play must account in part for this. The family so overwhelms the play that Walter Lee necessarily fails as the true symbol he should be, even though *his* ambitions, *his* frustrations, and *his* decisions are those which decisively drive the play on. But however recognizable he proves to be, he fails to dominate our imagination and finally emerges as a reasonably interesting study, but not, like Arthur Miller's great character—and like Hamlet, of course — a summation of an immense (though not crucial) portion of his culture.

Prior Attitudes

Then too, in fairness to the author and to Sidney Poitier's basically brilliant portrayal of Walter Lee, we must not completely omit reference to some of the prior attitudes which were brought into the theatre from the world outside. For in the minds of many, Walter remains, despite the play, despite performance, what American radical traditions *wish* him to be: an exotic. Some writers have been astonishingly incapable of discussing his purely *class* aspirations and have persistently confounded them with what they consider to be an exotic being's longing to "wheel and deal" in what they further consider to be (and what Walter never can) "the white man's world." Very few people today must consider

the ownership of a liquor store as an expresion of extraordinary affluence, and yet, as joined to a dream of Walter Younger, it takes on, for some, aspects of the fantastic. We have grown accustomed to the dynamics of "Negro" personality as expressed by white authors. Thus, de Emperor, de Lawd, and, of course, Porgy, still haunt our frame of reference when a new character emerges. We have become romantically jealous of the great image of a prototype whom we believe is summarized by the wishfulness of a self-assumed opposite. Presumably there is a quality in human beings that makes us *wish* that we *were* capable of primitive contentments; the *universality* of ambition and its anguish can escape us only if we construct elaborate legends about the rudimentary simplicity of *other* men.

America, for this reason, long ago fell in love with the image of the simple, lovable, and glandular "Negro." We all know that Catfish Row was never intended to slander anyone; it was intended as a mental haven for readers and audiences who could bask in the unleashed passions of those "lucky ones" for whom abandonment was apparently permissible. In an almost paradoxical fashion, it disturbs the soul of man to truly understand what he invariably senses: that *nobody* really finds oppression and/or poverty tolerable. If we ever destroy the image of the black people who supposedly do find those things tolerable in America, then that much-touted "guilt" which allegedly haunts most middle-class white Americans with regard to the Negro question would really become unendurable. It would also mean the death of a dubious literary tradition, but it would undoubtedly and more significantly help toward the more rapid transformation of the status of a people who have never found their imposed misery very charming.

My colleagues and I were reduced to mirth and tears by that gentleman writing his review of our play in a Connecticut paper who remarked of his pleasure at seeing how "our dusky brethren" could "come up with a song and hum their troubles away." It did not disturb the writer in the least that there is no such implication in the entire three acts. He did not need it in the play; he had it in his head.

FOR ALL THESE REASONS then, I imagine that the ordinary impulse to compare Willy Loman and Walter Younger was remote. Walter Lee Younger jumped out at us from a play about a largely unknown world. We knew who Willy Loman was instantaneously; we recognized his milieu. We also knew at once that he represented that curious paradox in what the *English* character in that *English* play could call, though dismally, "The American Age." Willy Loman was a product of a nation of great military strength, indescribable material wealth, and incredible mastery of the physical realm, which nonetheless was unable, in 1946, to produce a *typical* hero who was capable of an affirmative view of life.

I believe it is a testament to Miller's brilliance that it is hard-

ly a misstatement of the case, as some preferred to believe. Something has indeed gone wrong with at least part of the American dream, and Willy Loman is the victim of the detour. Willy had to be overwhelmed on the stage as, in fact, his prototypes are in everyday life. Coming out of his section of our great sprawling middle class, preoccupied with its own restlessness and displaying its obsession for the possession of trivia, Willy was indeed trapped. His predicament in a New World where there just aren't any more forests to clear or virgin railroads to lay or native American empires to first steal and build upon, left him with nothing but some left-over values which had forgotten how to prize industriousness over cunning; usefulness over mere acquisition, and, above all, humanism over "success." The potency of the great tale of a salesman's death was in our familiar recognition of his entrapment which, suicide or no, is *deathly.*

New Typicality

What then of this new figure who appears in American drama in 1958; from what source is he drawn so that, upon inspection, and despite class differences, so much of his encirclement must still remind us of that of Willy Loman? Why, finally, is it possible that when his third-act will is brought to bear, *his* typicality is capable of a choice which *affirms* life? After all, Walter Younger is an American more than he is anything else. His ordeal, give or take his personal expression of it, is not extraordinary but intensely familiar like Willy's. The two of them have virtually no values which have not come out of their culture, and to a significant point, no view of the possible solutions to their problems which do not also come out of the self-same culture. Walter can find no peace with that part of society which seems to permit him and no entry into that which has willfully excluded him. He shares with Willy Loman the acute awareness that *something* is obstructing some abstract progress that he feels he *should* be making; that *something* is in the way of his ascendancy. It does not occur to either of them to question the nature of this desired "ascendancy." Walter accepts, he believes in the "world" as it has been presented to him. When we first meet him, he does not wish to alter *it*; merely to change *his* position in it. His mentors and his associates all take the view that the institutions which frustrate him are somehow impeccable, or, at best, "unfortunate." "Things being as they are," he must look to *himself* as the only source of any rewards he may expect. Within himself, he is encouraged to believe, are the only seeds of defeat or victory within the universe. And Walter believes this and when opportunity, haphazard and rooted in death, prevails, he acts.

Huge Obstacles

But the obstacles which are introduced are gigantic; the weight of the loss of the money is in fact, the weight of death. In Walter Lee Younger's life, somebody *has* to die for ten thousand bucks to pile up—if then. Elsewhere in the world, in the face of catastrophe, he might be tempted to don the saffron robes of acceptance and sit on a mountain top all day contemplating the divine justice of his misery. Or, history being what it is turning out to be, he might wander down to his first Communist Party meeting. But here in the dynamic and confusing post-war years on the Southside of Chicago, his choices of action are equal to those gestures only in symbolic terms. The American ghetto hero may give up and contemplate his misery in rose-colored bars to the melodies of hypnotic saxophones, but revolution seems alien to him in his circumstances (America), and it is easier to dream of personal wealth than of a communal state wherein universal dignity is supposed to be a corollary. Yet his position in time and space does allow for one other alternative: he may take his place on any one of a number of frontiers of challenge. Challenges (such as helping to break down restricted neighborhoods) which are admittedly limited because they most certainly do not threaten the basic social order.

Not So Small

But why is even this final choice possible, considering the ever-present (and ever so popular) vogue of despair? Well, that is where Walter departs from Willy Loman; there is a second pulse in his still dual culture. His people have had "somewhere" they have been trying to get for so long that more sophisticated confusions do not yet bind them. *Thus the weight and power of their current social temperament intrudes and affects him, and it is, at the moment, at least, gloriously and rigidly affirmative. In the course of their brutally dif-*

ficult ascent, they have dismissed the ostrich and still sing, *"Went to the rock, to hide my face, but the rock cried out: 'No hidin' place down here!'"* Walter is, despite his lack of consciousness of it, inextricably as much wedded to his special mass as Willy was to his, and the moods of each are able to decisively determine the dramatic typicality. Furthermore, the very nature of the situation of American Negroes can force their representative hero to recognize that for his *true* ascendancy he must ultimately be at cross-purposes with at least certain of his culture's values. It is to the pathos of Willy Loman that his section of American life seems to have momentarily lost that urgency; that he cannot, like Walter, draw on the strength of an incredible people who, historically, have simply refused to give up.

In other words, the symbolism of moving into the new house is quite as small as it seems and quite as significant. For if there are no waving flags and marching songs at the barricades as Walter marches out with his little battalion, it is not because the battle lacks nobility. On the contrary, he has picked up in his way, still imperfect and wobbly in his small view of human destiny, what I believe Arthur Miller once called "the golden thread of history." He becomes, in spite of those who are too intrigued with despair and hatred of man to see it, King Oedipus refusing to tear out his eyes, but attacking the Oracle instead. He is that last Jewish patriot manning his rifle in the burning ghetto at Warsaw; he is that young girl who swam into sharks to save a friend a few weeks ago; he is Anne Frank, still believing in people; he is the nine small heroes of Little Rock; he is Michelangelo creating David and Beethoven bursting forth with the Ninth Sympony. He is all those things because he has finally reached out in his tiny moment and caught that sweet essence which is human dignity, and it shines like the old star-touched dream that it is in his eyes. We see, in the moment, I think, what becomes, and not for Negroes alone, but for Willy and all of us, entirely an American responsibility.

Out in the darkness where we watch, most of us are not afraid to cry.

While as a producer I certainly regretted losing the *New York Times* space for this essay, I understood and shared Lorraine's position, as I explained to Jim Proctor. But I also felt then, as I do now, that Lorraine's own assessment of the play's—and society's—deficiencies, along with her ability to express it all so publicly and profoundly, was, for a playwright, unique. Her words deserved to be shown to other writers, other critics, as well as to the world in the pages of the *New York Times*.

Now, for all who like happy endings, shortly after Lorraine's article was printed in the *Village Voice*, Brooks Atkinson announced his imminent retirement from the *New York Times* after having served there from 1925 to 1960—thirty-five years as probably the world's most influential theatre critic. Sometime after that announcement, Lorraine and I were attending an off-Broadway opening, and we noticed Atkinson's arrival at his aisle seat just a few rows ahead of us, presumably to review the play.

At the end of the first act, as the lights came up for intermission, Lorraine rose from her seat and, instead of moving towards the rear, she rushed forward. I reversed my direction quickly, following as closely as I could behind her. As she reached Atkinson's aisle seat, she leaned over slightly, and thrust her open hand toward him as she said, "Mr. Atkinson, my name is Lorraine Hansberry." He accepted and held her hand (maybe in self-defense) as she continued, "I have just read and been saddened by your announced retirement. I have admired and respected for years your contribution to and love for the theatre and its playwrights. Your leaving will be a tremendous loss for all of us." She then withdrew her hand and returned to her seat. My guess is that after getting over the shock of what she did at their first and only meeting, Atkinson came to consider that incident a more important event than the play he saw.

In any case, several days later Lorraine received a letter from Atkinson with an apology, deeply regretting what he had done with regard to her essay; while he did not excuse it, he blamed it on some personal problems he was having at the time. He also thanked Lorraine for the magnanimous thoughts about his career that she had so feelingly expressed at their meeting. Mr. Atkinson was, after all, an extraordinary gentleman of the theatre, and I wish he and Lorraine had met again, before she was, too soon, afflicted by ravaging illness.

As I write this today, in 1999, just a few months ago the fortieth anniversary of the Broadway opening of *A Raisin in the Sun* was celebrated. As part of the wide recognition of this event and its impact, the play was recently presented at the Williamstown Theatre Festival. It received not only glowing local notices, but also a beautifully written review by Ben Brantley, the current chief drama critic of the *New York Times*, in which he underscored its historic importance. It is interesting to compare Brantley's critique with Lorraine's self-criticism of fifty years ago. Perhaps the *New York Times* will consider finally printing Lorraine's essay today, forty years later. I will entertain any offers.

Revisiting A Prophecy Of a World Still Forming

By BEN BRANTLEY

Gloria Foster as a matriarch trying to ease frictions large and small.

WILLIAMSTOWN, Mass., July 26 — "You something new, boy."

The words are spoken with wonder, incomprehension and a touch of fear in the Williamstown Theater Festival's production of "A Raisin in the Sun," Lorraine Hansberry's benchmark play of 1959. A mother is talking to her grown son, but at the moment, as far as she's concerned, he might as well be a stranger from another time, another planet. You think of Miranda's line from "The Tempest": "O brave new world, that has such people in't!" But in this instance, the speaker isn't at all sure she wants to cross into that frontier.

As embodied by Gloria Foster and Ruben Santiago-Hudson, in Jack Hofsiss's emotion-

A RAISIN IN THE SUN

ally intense production of Ms. Hansberry's classic about a black family in South Side Chicago, the differences between parent and child have a physical charge that goes beyond the usual generation-gap antagonism. It lies deep in the cadences of these fine actors' movements, in the pitch of their voices, in the pace of their delivery.

Ms. Foster's Lena Younger, the widowed matriarch of a three-generation family crowded into one shabby apartment, moves with unhurried, elegant deliberation, and she speaks so slowly and softly that you wonder if she will always be audible. (She is.)

As her son, Walter Lee, a white man's chauffeur with a wife and child of his own, Mr. Santiago-Hudson is impatiently, explosively animated, and every time he steps onstage he seems to fragment the root calm of his mother's household. You don't doubt

that these two people are from the same family, or even that they love each other. But their very metabolisms seem to be at odds.

This friction, which is given such visceral immediacy here, is the motor of Hansberry's play and what has kept it alive long after many critics would have consigned it to the junk heap of the embarrassingly dated. In a sense, the form and structure of "A Raisin in the Sun" are not unlike Lena herself: old-fashioned, sentimental and so domestic that it is hard to think of a scene in which a dish isn't being washed or some laundry being ironed or folded.

But within the sturdy, kitchen-sink context there are other elements, more combustible and dynamic, that match the anxious, angry temperament of Walter Lee. Windows keep popping open in this ostensibly closed universe, admitting subversive breezes and affording larger views. Mr. Hofsiss's production doesn't always find the natural flow to accommodate the opposing currents of "Raisin," but the production still tugs at the heart.

Part of its enduring power comes from its status as prophecy. The sexual, economic and racial conflicts that shape the Younger family have not begun to subside: from

Walter Lee's frustrated struggles for financial independence and for masculine pride in a world of strong women to the quest for an African, rather than American, heritage by his sister, Beneatha (Kimberly Elise), a college student.

Whispers of the women's liberation movement to come are heard in the gentle bristling of Walter Lee's wife, Ruth (the wonderful Viola Davis), at her husband's brusque domination, and in Beneatha's determined desire to become a doctor and to avoid marriage as an answer to her problems. You can even see glimmers of the contrasting paths of the civil rights movement, passive resistance versus more aggressive action, in the approaches of Lena and Walter Lee to the family's crises.

Most poignantly, and most universally, there is the overwhelming sense of a family under siege trying to hold together in a world that would tear it apart. Yes, the way Hansberry develops the immediate cause of dissension in the family, the question of what to do with the $10,000 insurance payment to Lena after her husband's death, has its contrived aspects. But there is no denying the nonjudgmental clarity and compassion of her gaze as she considers the consequences.

Mr. Hofsiss wisely doesn't mess much with the slice-of-life essence of the play, although I could have done without the intervals of gospel singers performing on a bridge over the central set. Michael McGarty's cozy and claustrophobic take on the apartment has the requisite frayed dignity, and the performers, especially the women, inhabit it by making copious use of every domestic prop in sight.

It's corny, the sort of thing that acting teachers always recommend t. help overcome self-consciousness. (When in doubt, pick up a broom.) But here all the cleaning and straightening takes on another dimension: a sense of women trying to keep the chaos of poverty at bay.

Ms. Davis manages to pack in quite a lot standing over that ironing board, her face an uncanny emotional seismograph registering every tremor in the family upheavals. The actress appeared with Mr. Santiago-Hudson, to splendid effect, in August Wilson's "Seven Guitars," and here they generate a long-married couple's complicated chemistry with remarkable spontaneity.

Ms. Elise. who has the impish prettiness

By Lorraine Hansberry; directed by Jack Hofsiss; sets by Michael McGarty; costumes by Karen Perry; lighting by Rui Rita; sound by Matthew Spiro; choreography by Sandra Burton; stage manager, C. A. Clark; musical director, Charles Alterman; production manager, Stephen Judd. Presented by the Williamstown Theater Festival, Michael Ritchie, producer; Deborah Fehr, general manager; Jenny C. Gersten, associate producer. At Adams Memorial Theater, 1000 Main Street (Route 2 east), Williamstown, Mass.

WITH: Viola Davis (Ruth Younger), James Sneed (Travis Younger), Ruben Santiago-Hudson (Walter Lee Younger), Kimberly Elise (Beneatha Younger), Gloria Foster (Lena Younger), Dion Graham (Joseph Asagai), Donn Swaby (George Murchison), Peter Maloney (Karl Lindner) and Joseph Edward (Bobo).

so loved by television producers, gives a less fully grounded performance, but is excellent in Beneatha's scenes with her two very different suitors, played by Donn Swaby (the preppy, assimilationist one) and the excellent Dion Graham (the Nigerian nationalist). Peter Maloney, as the white man representing a committee to keep the Youngers from moving into his neighborhood avoids the temptations of exaggerated villainy, and James Sneed, Walter Lee's young son, avoids the temptations of exaggerated cuteness.

Ms. Foster is terrific in conveying both shelteredness and stubbornness, and she doesn't shirk from her character's manipulative side, from the passive aggression in Lena's soft-spokennness. Indeed, she falters only when she turns up the volume for an evangelical sermonizing that would be more digestible underplayed.

Mr. Santiago-Hudson, too, can play a big emotional scene too much to center stage and to the audience, as though it were an opera aria. But overall, he is remarkable, finding precise and freshly varied ways for channeling Walter Lee's restlessness and resentment. And it is he who has the production's most resonant moment.

That comes when a drunken Walter Lee returns to the apartment to find his sister dancing in tribal robes to Nigerian music and decides to join in on the ethnic celebration. Mr. Santiago-Hudson plays the scene brilliantly, with the improvisatory clumsiness of a man groping to assume a role he doesn't fully understand yet. Walter Lee is much more than a comic drunk here. Charged with energy in search of an outlet and a bottomless hunger for change, he is the soul of a world in transition.

Chapter 17

During the summer of 1959, I heard that Harold Stern and Marty Baum had completed their negotiations with Columbia for the filming of A Raisin in the Sun. Sidney Poitier had, of course, been included in the deal, and Harold was calling Lorraine to inform her that she would be well paid as both the playwright and the screenwriter. The Broadway producers and investors were to receive a contractual share of the playwright's income.

Just a few minutes after I received the first call, a disturbed Harold Stern was back on the line to tell me we had a slight problem. When Lorraine found out that the sole producer of the film was to be David Susskind, she insisted there would be no deal unless Philip Rose became co-producer. My first reaction was to laugh, since this issue had never come up before and I had not a clue about, or any interest in, the making of a film. But Harold said Lorraine was unequivocal, explaining she had other items on her agenda and it wouldn't matter to her if the film didn't get made. Harold was quite sure we faced a serious stumbling block, so I agreed to call Lorraine.

When I reached her she preempted my arguments by saying there was nothing to talk about. She was not about to turn this play over to Columbia Pictures and David Susskind to do as they liked, with nobody on board who represented her and her point of view. She then allowed me to make three points: first, and rather emphatically, the large amount of money she would be giving up as the original playwright and the screenwriter; second, the embarrassing position I could be in with any investors who assumed I was selfishly a party to a decision that deprived them of their share of income from sale of the film rights; and third, that I knew nothing at all about filmmaking.

Lorraine listened without interruption and then responded: first, she said, her willingness to give up the thousands of dollars she would earn was none of my damn business; second, my possibly embarrassing position with my investors was none of her damn business; and third, my lack of knowledge about making a film, in her view, already put me far ahead of the people I'd be working with.

I told Harold Stern I agreed we had a problem. I suggested he call David Susskind, tell him he might consider asking me to join him as co-producer of the film, and I might then magnanimously agree to work with him. Harold, with no alternative, after a moment of silence began to relish the idea of presenting this to David, and he said he would see to it. I was not party to their conversation, but several days later Harold called me to say that everything was settled. Contracts were being prepared for all the interested parties, including myself, Lorraine, David, and Columbia Pictures. (Incidentally, as I said in an earlier chapter, when Columbia raised the issue that I knew nothing about producing a film, he, Harold, volunteered that I had known even less about producing the play, a testimonial that seemed to remove all their reservations.)

Very soon after that, David Susskind called with warm congratulations on the play's success and to tell me how pleased he was that we would finally be working together. I expressed similar feelings about our coming relationship, and I have no idea which of us was more charming, or the bigger liar. Moving on, David asked if I would arrange a meeting with Lorraine, whom he had not yet met. He also wanted us to meet and to consider Daniel Petrie as a director. Danny, well known in television circles, had worked on several projects for Susskind's company. He had also directed in theatre and film, and had a deserved repu-

155

tation for his sensitivity to writers and actors. I soon arranged for all of us to get together at Lorraine's apartment on Waverly Place in Greenwich Village.

We met on a weekday evening. I arrived deliberately a bit early to tell Lorraine what I had learned about Danny Petrie from David and some other sources and to venture my opinion that he might be a good choice as a director. When David Susskind and Danny Petrie arrived, we exchanged the usual introductions and sat down for a drink and a four-way conversation—or so I thought. But Lorraine pulled her chair closer to Petrie's, directed herself exclusively to him, and mentioned some of her favorite directors and, particularly, some foreign films. Danny was responsive and the two of them were soon engaged in a lively conversation, completely ignoring me, which didn't bother me at all, and David, which annoyed him a whole lot. After several minutes of their informative and entertaining discussion, Lorraine asked Danny to name *his* favorite films and their directors. Danny, to whom David had already promised the job of director, appeared a bit surprised at being auditioned by Lorraine. But he thought about her question carefully, while Lorraine stared at him intently as she sipped her drink, and finally he responded: two French films, *Justice is Done* and *Le Casque D'or*; one American release, *The Bridge on the River Kwai*, and as favorite director, John Ford for almost any film, starting with *The Grapes of Wrath*. He paused and before he could continue, Lorraine turned to David and me, nodded toward Danny and said, "He'll do" as she got up to fix another drink for herself.

I could see and feel the anger rising in David as she was returning to her seat. But he then evidently decided to use his charm and experience as a television talk show host to direct the rest of the evening to where he thought it should go. He began to talk about *Raisin*, which became a fine and lively discussion involving all of us until David, unfortunately, chose to display his erudition by comparing Lorraine's writing to Shakespeare, using as his example a long, esoteric quote from the Bard. David had no reason to suspect that Lorraine was a profound student and lover of Shakespeare, or that she would resent being patronized by David, or that she would go on not only to disagree with him vehemently but to caustically correct his quotation. The evening ended shortly after, as David suddenly remembered a previous engagement and the three of us left Lorraine's apartment.

As David, Danny, and I walked down the street, the silence among us was deafening. Neither Danny nor I knew quite what to say, and David was obviously not in a talkative mood. But as we walked up to Eighth Street and passed by "The Griddle," a well-known coffee shop, David turned into the entrance and we followed him to a table. The first words spoken were to the waiter, who quickly brought us three hot coffees, none of them as steaming as David, who then spoke up. "You know what's wrong with Lorraine Hansberry?" (We didn't volunteer an answer.) "She thinks she's smarter than I am; and I've never met a woman who was smarter than I am." Since neither Danny nor I was prepared to question the number of his female acquaintances, I thought I would lighten the atmosphere by asking, "Well, David, have you ever met a man who was smarter than you?" This brought an immediate response: "Yes, Albert Einstein, Nikita Khruschev, and Albert Schweitzer." There was a pause, and when it became apparent that this list was not going to get any longer, I mumbled something about having to get home, and we all left the restaurant.

Columbia Pictures was anxious to get the picture made and released as soon as possible. Lorraine, surprisingly for a playwright, was prepared to put aside her play and write a wholly new screenplay, obviously retaining her major characters, her story, and her point of view, but using all the possible visual elements to enhance the script. However, having bought the play, Columbia was worried about the direction Lorraine might take it if she started fresh. Therefore, they insisted on going with the devil they knew, and began production in late 1960, Lorraine having given them pretty much the playscript to shoot. There was, however, to be a scene in the film that was not in the play, and that took place in the new white neighborhood to which the Younger family was to move. It would show the entire family, in a joyful mood, coming to look at their new home, exploring each room and the garden, and generally celebrating their new neighborhood.

We had decided to film the scene in a suburb of Chicago, at a site chosen many days before our scheduled filming dates. It was in a very pleasant white lower-middle-class neighborhood with a number of tract houses. The family that lived in the one we selected consisted of a young couple with a child and the wife's mother. The young mother was pregnant, with her new baby due several weeks later. Once we made an agreement to use the particular house, the press began to feature articles about the return of *A Raisin in the Sun* to Chicago, the city that in their view had given birth to the smash hit play. Of course, Sidney Poitier, Ruby Dee, and almost the entire original cast would be appearing in the film and would available for interviews on radio, television, and in the newspapers. So, long before we got to town, all of Chicago was looking forward to our arrival.

On the first scheduled day of filming, trucks filled the street and workmen began emptying rooms of furniture and generally setting up for a couple days of shooting. The people in the neighborhood—adults and children, all of them white, since that was what the script required—crowded the street, hoping to get pictures, and maybe some autographs of Sidney and the rest of our cast.

We began the actual shooting on a lovely warm morning. The actors said hello to the excited family that had to be moved from room to room so that we could create the illusion of an empty house. Everyone was laughing, having a good time, and sharing their sudden celebrity with their neighbors. At a certain point the father in the family told us he had gotten a phone call from somebody asking if Negroes were moving into the neighborhood. He laughed as he said that he had assured the caller that it was just a movie being shot.

Within half an hour of that call, the family's phone began to ring incessantly. These calls were not to ask questions. They were threats to "get those niggers out of our neighborhood, or they'll be bombed out." People from nearby homes who had been enjoying what had seemed like a party were also targets of angry calls and threats. Sad to say, a couple of such calls were answered by the young pregnant mother, who then became frightened to the point of hysteria. Although we had provided lots of security around us, understandably it was not enough to ease the concern of the young father for his wife's emotional and physical condition. As a result, we had to wrap as quickly as possible and cancel our plans to return the following day. Surprisingly enough, it was the young woman's mother, the grandmother of the family, who argued against our giving up and said she would herself "man the barricades" against all the "idiots" who were calling.

So there we were in 1960 doing a film about a black family trying to move into a white neighborhood, and being upstaged by life.

The balance of the shooting resumed on the Columbia lot without any extraordinary incidents. David and I did not grow fonder of each other as the days went by, but he was quite busy with meetings about his plans for future films and with trying to set up his deals. I spent most of my days on the set, presumably to learn something and certainly to get to know and enjoy the crew quite well. One day I was even asked to supervise a second unit that had to film some exteriors of the Youngers' slum neighborhood. We never used any of that footage; I guess everything I shot looked more like a slum than intended.

I did have a meeting one day that once again could have

changed my life completely. Upon first arriving on the Columbia lot, after I was shown to my assigned office and introduced to my secretary, I was invited to meet Sam Briskin, at that time the head of the studio. I expected never to see him again, but one day I was summoned to his office. As I walked over there I was well aware that nothing I was contributing to this film, negative or positive, was important enough for me to be fired. I entered Briskin's office, we shook hands, and he got right to the point, saying, "I know you've had no previous experience in film but I've gotten some positive reports about you from my spies and I understand that you're willing and able to learn quickly. I'd like to offer you a deal as one of our exclusive contract producers to find and develop films for us. Think about it and get back to me." We shook hands again and I left his office.

That evening I returned to the Chateau Marmont, the well-known hotel where Columbia Pictures had chosen to book me and where my wife was currently visiting me. Doris had recently returned to New York from a tour of Paddy Chayevsky's *Middle of the Night*, playing Edward G. Robinson's daughter. Her career as a New York actress was beginning to build and we had very few friends in Los Angeles at that time. On top of that, I still had my music and recording company and I was coming off a smash-hit play and, we hoped, would soon enjoy a film success. There was no reason for me to think I wouldn't go on having one Broadway hit after another. (My next New York production, called *Semi-Detached*, ran on Broadway for three performances.) So I did not accept the offer from Columbia but returned to New York upon the completion of *Raisin*, and never did become the head of a studio.

Chapter 18

I optioned and produced *Semi-Detached* while *Raisin* was still running in New York. The play took place in Montreal and dealt with the deep animosity between Catholic and Protestant families, two of them unwilling neighbors. We opened in Wilmington to mixed notices, and I had my first experience with a playwright who would rewrite the play each night based on the opinions of the critics, the cast members, the ushers, her family, or any member of the audience. We opened in New York at the Martin Beck Theatre with a script that was largely the result of the contributions of all those people, very few of whom were talented writers. Our reviews in New York were appreciably inferior to Wilmington, and quite well deserved.

I do have some fond memories of this production, however. The cast included Jean Muir, who in the 1930s began a Hollywood career as a lovely featured ingenue and became a talented dramatic star, appearing in over thirty films. She then moved on to several notable television guest appearances until 1950. That year, she was contracted to a role on NBC's *The Aldrich Family*, and was fired almost immediately when her name appeared on somebody's blacklist. Playing opposite Ms. Muir was Frank Silvera, a black actor of some reputation, who played the head of one of the two Caucasian families. I was proud to have both these performers in *Semi-Detached*.

I also remember how my manager and I, not surprised by the stinging reviews, had a rather good time at the Saturday night closing after three performances. As we sat in the Martin Beck box office counting the stubs of the few unfortunate audience members who had bought tickets before the reviews appeared, we came across a pair for another show which had preceded ours at the Martin Beck Theatre and had also enjoyed a very brief run. That show was a musical. Obviously, this couple had not read about its precipitous closing and now were sitting in the theatre, half an hour after the curtain went up, still waiting for one of our actors to burst into song or dance. All of us in the box office kept waiting for the couple to come stamping out of the theatre demanding their money back but they never did. We decided afterwards that if we had advertised our play as a musical we might have had a hit.

While *Semi-Detached* was getting completely detached, *A Raisin in the Sun* was still running. Sidney Poitier had left the play in September 1959, after six months of never, to my recollection, having missed a performance. We were fortunate to have available Ossie Davis, who took over the role immediately. He had probably rehearsed it for months at home with his wife, Ruby Dee. In any case it was a smooth progression, and our run continued for almost a year afterwards, until June 1960. During that time I would see Ossie backstage and occasionally he would mumble something to me about a play he was working on. Eventually, it dawned on me that he was actually writing a play. At no time did he tell me anything about this phantom of a play or ask me to read it until I finally questioned him about it. Then our conversations got more specific, to the point where he asked if I would like to read a play. Assuming he meant his play, I said yes. But then conversations about the play seemed to end and I put it out of my mind and figured it had been turned over to someone like David Merrick. One day, again weeks later, Ossie called to ask if I would like to see his play. We got past my response of "What play?" and I received a copy of *Purlie Victorious* a very few days later.

I should add here that I had known Ossie Davis and Ruby Dee for years, long before *A Raisin in the Sun* existed. My admiration for them and their family and lifestyle preceded my professional involvement in theatre by many years. With Ossie's play in hand, I had mixed feelings of anticipation and trepidation. What if I thought it was terrible? I remember Ossie once telling me he'd gone to see an actor friend of his in a play that was awful and a performance not much better. Since he had to go backstage and say something to his friend, what he chose was "Man, you were *on* that stage." Well, I certainly couldn't say that to Ossie after just reading his play, but what would I say? The dilemma disappeared somewhere around the fifteenth page of the script. After finishing it I was certain that this was one of the funniest plays ever written about a very serious subject. I remembered Zero Mostel, that wonderful performer, saying to me, "If you're going to write a very serious piece about anything, you'd better be very, very funny." While that may not necessarily be true, *Purlie Victorious* certainly emphasized his point. I called Ossie immediately and invited him to my office.

When he arrived I wasted no time in telling him I wanted to produce his play. He seemed so stunned to hear this that I almost thought he was looking forward to my rejecting it. But I made my position clear. I would not take no for an answer. And so we began the pleasant task of talking about the play.

While Ossie did not admit at the time that he had shown the play to other Broadway producers and received no offers, he did say that he would like Howard Da Silva to direct. This was in response to my suggestion that Lloyd Richards, just coming off *Raisin*, was an obvious choice and that his being black was presumably an asset. Ossie then explained that his inspiration to turn *Purlie Victorious,* a play he had begun as a very angry attack on this country's racism, into a comedy, came from *The World of Sholom Aleichem*, which substantially treated the life of Jews in the "old country" in similar fashion. *Sholom Aleichem* was an off-Broadway hit, directed by Howard Da Silva and stage managed by Ossie Davis, with Ruby Dee in a leading role.

I knew Howard Da Silva quite well, respected him as an actor and artist, and admired him especially for waging a fierce and honorable fight against the blacklisting of himself and others. My reservations about him stemmed from his treatment of actors he had directed, some of whom I knew very well. Reportedly, he would often go after the most sensitive and vulnerable member of the company, usually a young woman, and verbally attack her. I've previously mentioned his abuse of Diana Sands, as observed by my wife, during the run of *Sholom Aleichem*.

Ossie admitted he knew of Howard's reputation and had even witnessed some of the reasons for it, but he asked if I would at least meet with Howard privately and allow him to make his case to me. Besides, he said, he believed Howard understood *Purlie Victorious* better than any other director would.

So here we were, Ossie Davis, a black playwright, arguing for a white director, and I a white producer, arguing for a black director. But at Ossie's fervent requests, I finally agreed to meet with Howard, a meeting which Howard himself had requested. At home the evening after I made this decision, I mentioned it to Doris and asked if she would have any qualms about my possibly hiring Howard as director. She told me that it was no problem at all for *her*, but added that I'd better have my bags packed if and when I made up my mind in Howard's favor.

Howard came to my office two days later. It was a rather extraordinary meeting, beginning easily enough with his congratulations for *A Raisin in the Sun* and his praise for my production and Lloyd Richards's direction. Conversation then proceeded to a very stimulating and, for me, enlightening discussion about *Purlie Victorious*. Needless to say, I was certain he fully understood the play, and in that regard we enjoyed a wonderful rapport. Then, after a pause, he moved on to the next topic. "Phil," he said, "I know that you've heard some terrible things about the way I've sometimes conducted myself in the theatre as an actor and director. I would like you to know that most of them are true. But I've now been in analysis for some time and I've accepted and regretted all of that. I want to ask you, even plead with you, to believe that I've changed completely and none of this will ever happen again. But I hope you agree that I can do complete justice to Ossie's play, and if you do, I promise to give you no cause to complain about my demeanor as a director."

My reaction to this confession was first discomfort and then embarrassment. Here was this very talented and respected actor, much older than I, with the most courageous anti-blacklist credentials, and with a theatre background far superior to mine, pleading with me for a job. Again there was a pause, and then Howard wisely chose to tell me a completely unrelated funny story about himself and his father, an elderly Jewish gentleman. After Howard had been nominated for the best supporting actor Oscar for his portrayal of the bartender in *The Lost Weekend*, his father began to follow the film around to various movie houses to see his son's performance again and again. On one particular day Howard received a phone call from him in which he said: "Hello, Howard. I saw your movie again last night at the Loew's Pitkin. You weren't so good last night. What happened?" I've wondered how far in advance Howard had planned to close our meeting with this story. It certainly served to relax the atmosphere between us, and as Howard left I promised to get back to him quickly with my decision.

When I returned home that evening and told Doris that as a result of our meeting I was giving Howard some serious thought, I received a blank stare which seemed at least a bit less threatening than her initial reaction. I also called Ossie to tell him I had more or less enjoyed my meeting with Howard and was "thinking about it."

I spent most of that sleepless night considering all my options. The next day I called Howard's agent, who knew about our meeting and was awaiting my call, to tell him that I was ready to make an offer for Howard to direct the play; we could proceed to negotiate with one caveat: I would want a letter separate from our contract giving me the right to fire Howard during rehearsal without showing cause. I promised not to show this additional document to anyone and to destroy it on opening night. His agent went berserk, saying he would never insult Howard by even mentioning this. Nevertheless, I knew Howard must have given his agent a substantial account of our meeting, making him aware of the problem, and, indeed, the agent got back to me within an hour with a subdued OK, and we started negotiating our contract that same day.

During rehearsals of *Purlie* I spent a great deal of time in the theatre, observing that most of the time Howard was a pussycat, losing his temper pretty much only with Ossie, who I knew could take care of himself. One day, when he started to lose it with Ruby, he suddenly turned around, saw me, and walked out of the theatre, only to return moments later fully composed and ready to continue rehearsals. Howard did a beautiful job directing *Purlie Victorious*, our side letter never saw the light of day and was never discussed again.

The cast included Ossie Davis and Ruby Dee as the leads and in a supporting role, Alan Alda, making his Broadway debut. Also in the supporting group cast was Beah Richards (recently deceased), a wonderful actress, classically trained, who later became familiar to film audiences from many roles, including Sidney Poitier's mother in *Guess Who's Coming to Dinner*. She was also Claudia McNeil's stunning understudy in *A Raisin in the Sun*. Ms. Richards once told me a great casting story. When she was a very young actress, she decided to audition for a major new production of *The Merchant of Venice*. She arrived at the theatre along with many other actors and, after being ignored for a while by the stage manager, she received a number for her audition. She was, of course, the only black actor to show up at this event. When her number was passed by she remained there, quietly waiting to be called. It was obvious to Beah that the stage manager had informed the producers, director, and others out front that they had "a problem," and he hoped the "problem" would get weary and disappear. Finally, when she was the last person left, the stage manager, with no apology, called her number. She walked on stage proudly and in her rich voice and beautiful speech announced to the assemblage, "My name is Beah Richards and I shall do 'The Quality of Mercy' speech from *The Merchant of Venice*." She proceeded to perform Shakespeare's poetry, word perfect, in the thickest Southern Negro dialect, from beginning to end, with nobody daring to interrupt her. After saying "Thank you, gentlemen" in her own beautiful diction, she walked off the stage. Of course, I have no idea what actually took place after Ms. Richards left, but I like to imagine the stunned and (if there was any intelligence out there at all) embarrassed reaction.

Purlie Victorious opened on Broadway at the Cort Theatre in September 1961. It received largely enthusiastic reviews from the important theatre critics, with Howard Taubman of the *New York Times* raving about the play and the performances, and closing his comments with the lovely sentence, "It won't let you wipe that grin off your face." Walter Kerr at the *Herald Tribune* was equally enthusiastic, also emphasizing how funny the play was. It was not a very expensive show to produce, coming in at under $100,000. The sets by Ben Edwards were imaginative rather than literal, with old newspapers lining the walls of the family shack to keep out the cold. After opening night we thought we had a hit but, surprisingly, we found instead we were having trouble selling tickets.

This certainly was a very disappointing development. After all, I had put together, in my view, a superb production, praised by the most respected critics as a wonderful comedy, and yet we were attracting only small audiences. Gradually, the reasons began to come clear. For the regular—that is, white—theatergoers, the show had no star, and this was an obstacle for any play to overcome. Nor were we were getting many requests for interviews. Ossie and Ruby did not yet have the star quality they would acquire in time. Most shocking, I began to get phone calls from some progressive white organizations and individuals vehemently berating me for putting on a show which not only made fun of Negroes but also portrayed an "Uncle Tom" character. This meant that the very organizations I was depending on for theatre parties were, in effect, boycotting us. I did my best, and met with these groups, most of whom had not seen the play but were hearing rumors.

Then came the next blow. Many members of the black community were reacting in the same way. Even at our first preview, when we had a large benefit house from CORE, an important, then militant group that embraced blacks and whites, we discovered that the audience was not quite sure it was OK to laugh at the obviously funny things happening onstage.

It was hard for me to hold fast to my absolute certainty that Ossie had written a marvelous satire on our country's race relations, and I knew that Ossie had been devastated by some of the response. When we talked, I assured him that I was not going to give up. It was helpful to our resolve that among the people who had seen and enjoyed the play were Roy Wilkins of the NAACP, Dr. W.E.B. Du Bois (perhaps this country's most brilliant philosopher on black issues of the 19th and 20th centuries, who came to the opening night at the age of 93), and later on, Martin Luther King, Jr. and Malcolm X. That all these men were enthusiastic about the play was more than encouraging.

At some point Ossie introduced me to Sylvester Leaks, a young black man who had access to many of the black organizations and church groups in the five boroughs. After we talked, I immediately and gratefully put him on our staff to promote group sales in the black community. Sylvester not only made a difference at the box office; he also became a friend, and later we worked together on other shows. But as things were improving, I received notice from the Shuberts that they had booked another play into the Cort Theatre. We would have to leave because we were selling too few tickets, and thereby not grossing enough to make it worth their while to allow us to remain.

This was my chance to close the show honorably, cut our losses, and bask in the praise for my courage in having produced this play as well as *A Raisin in the Sun*. For whatever reason, acquiring that reputation for courage was not sufficiently appealing to me, and I decided also to begin building my image as the most stubborn, and, to some, the dumbest producer on Broadway. I requested a meeting with the Shuberts, at which it was made clear to me that their decision was unalterable, and that that they had already signed contracts for another show to move into the Cort. When I asked if they had another theatre available, I was told that the Longacre would be dark for a while but they wondered why I would spend the money to move an obvious financial loser. I responded that if they would guarantee I could stay on at the Longacre for a reasonable length of time, I would nevertheless make the move.

When I then informed the cast we were not closing as anticipated but were moving instead, there was rejoicing among the company, and particularly from my stage manager, Lenny Auerbach, who still remembers the *Victorious* days as the most satisfying of his long career and our cast as the most enjoyable to work with.

Moving to the Longacre meant working with a new box office crew. Ordinarily, this would just be a matter of form: I would introduce myself to them and they would go about their usual jobs expecting no interference from me. But, under changing circumstances, I was anticipating a problem. As a result of the work of Sylvester Leaks and our advertising in some black publications, we were now reaching out to and attracting black patrons, many of whom had never been to a Broadway show. This was long before the automation of ticket selling; and anyone wanting to buy tickets had to come to the theatre in person. The old-timers at the Longacre box office had little experience dealing with inexperienced theatergoers who ask a lot of innocent questions. The possibility that a ticket buyer might face a very impatient box office employee seemed very real. So I decided to ask the head treasurer to lunch to explain what concerned me.

After a couple of drinks, he told me how excited he was that we were coming to his theatre and repeated all the good things he had heard about the play. As he loosened up I broached my subject, explaining that we were trying to expand the theatre audience, and how we were doing it. He listened for a while and then spoke up: "Listen, you don't have to worry about anything. I've been around colored all my life. I know how to get along with them. And I'll make sure all my staff does." I wondered then whether I should just say thank you and leave, but not quite finished, he continued, "Now there's just one thing. I know you want me to make sure they're all sitting in the back of the theatre."

At this point, I was tempted to get up and go, leaving him to pay the check, but instead, as reasonably as I could, I explained that what I wanted was actually the exact opposite of what he thought I wanted. He accepted this as easily as he had proudly assumed the opposite, but I left with a sinking feeling that he didn't realize he had been contradicted. I later made a point of talking to all the other box office assistants, and they all assured me that our ticket buyers would have no problem with their seat selections or their purchasing. And in fact, we stayed on at our new theatre for some months with very few complaints.

From left:
Bea Richards, Helen Martin, Godfrey Cambridge, Ruby Dee,
Ossie Davis, Ci Herzog, Roger Carmel, Sorrel Booke, and Alan Alda

For me, however, it remained a frustrating defeat that *Purlie Victorious* never received the recognition it deserved. I consoled myself with the reasoning that it was ahead of its time both for the usual theatre audience and to a significant degree for the black community, which was neither accustomed to Broadway theatregoing culturally nor able to afford it financially. But for a long time afterwards, *Purlie Victorious* would be in my thoughts. I kept searching my mind for what I might have done differently. After some years of fruitless self-questioning, the play for me became not a consideration of the past but of the future: I decided that one day *Purlie* would come alive again and truly be "Victorious."

To further illuminate the times and attitudes of the 1960s: during the run of the play David Susskind and I were invited to a meeting to discuss the publicity plans for the now completed film of *A Raisin in the Sun*. I remember attending the very first advertising session at the Columbia Pictures office in New York. After we had received the congratulations of the entire assemblage, one of them, obviously the man in charge, got up and opened the discussion by saying, "Now this is our problem. We've got to get the white audience to come see this wonderful film, and the only way we can do it is by not letting them know in advance that it's about Negroes." After a short pause without comment from anybody, he continued, "Well, we all know that our star Sidney Poitier is a Negro, but we don't have to emphasize that it's *all* about Negroes."

I tried to point out that our play and our black family had been seen not only on Broadway for almost two years, but also by now throughout the country and indeed the world. But I got the feeling that I was making no impression and David and I left the meeting shortly afterwards.

Regardless of that meeting, *A Raisin in the Sun*, the movie, has been seen by millions around the globe, has gone on to be shown repeatedly, to this day, on network and cable television with great fanfare, and to audiences not even born at the time of its initial release. And if I may be allowed a completely objective comment, in Sidney Poitier's acting it contains one of the finest performances ever given by an American actor. If you don't agree with me, ask any actor.

Chapter 19

While I was occupied with *Purlie Victorious* during 1961 and 1962, I was also busy preparing two other productions: one a musical, *Bravo Giovanni*, and the other a play called *Nobody Loves an Albatross*. *Giovanni*, with music by Milton Schafer and lyrics by Ronnie Graham, opened in May 1962. It was warmly received in Philadelphia and Detroit and coldly in New York. However, I have two fond memories of this musical. One was that I was able to persuade Cesare Siepi, then the world's most famous bass-baritone, to star in a Broadway show. I would show up at each morning's rehearsal just to listen to the beautiful Siepi voice singing his warm-up scales. I lived vicariously through those rehearsals, imagining that if we became a hit I might become his understudy. Realistically, I had to accept that at five feet five inches tall, and not growing very rapidly, I would not have fit his six feet two inch costumes.

After the opening night in New York, we had a small party with Cesare and his wife and a few friends at my apartment. The first review we saw came from Walter Kerr and it was unforgivingly negative. My press agent stopped reading it in the middle, and then the first voice heard was Mr. Siepi's magnificent bass asking plaintively, "Did he at least like my singing?"

The other vivid memory of *Giovanni* relates to our casting sessions. The director of *Bravo Giovanni* was an old friend of mine, Stanley Prager, who had been a Broadway performer but had recently turned to directing with Neil Simon's first play, *Come Blow Your Horn*. Stanley had been in many Broadway musicals, including *The Pajama Game*, and had worked for the

great George Abbott. After we had signed Mr. Siepi as our leading man, we were concentrating on finding a young woman to
co-star with him, preferably an actress in her late twenties or
even thirties since Mr. Siepi was a "mature" leading man.

One day my assistant, Lynda Watson, who, having been with
me for three years, now knew I would see anybody if I was not
seriously occupied, buzzed me to say there was a young woman
who would like to see me. "She says she's an actress, but she can
also sing." "Send her in," I said.

The door opened and in walked this person dressed in what
looked like secondhand clothes even if they had never previously
been worn. She was obviously a teenager. As we shook hands, I
introduced myself and invited her to sit by my desk, which she
did. There was a pause during which I was waiting for her to say
something. Finally, she spoke her first words: "You think I'm
ugly, don't you?" I realized quickly that this was a person who
was not nervous or frightened at meeting a Broadway producer
and I did not have to try to put her at ease. The reverse might
well be true. So I answered, "No, I don't think you're ugly, but
would you tell me your name?" "Barbra" she answered, "Barbra
Streisand." (She didn't spell it for me at the time, but I've
learned to spell it since then.) I then remembered that a friend
of mine had seen her perform in a little off-off-Broadway show,
Another Evening with Harry Stoones. The cast consisted of Miss
Streisand and another young actress named Diana Sands, and as
I recall, they closed after one performance with a *New York
Times* reviewer not even mentioning Barbra.

We talked for a while and then I asked her to wait while I
went to my other office to ask Stanley Prager to come and
meet her. He came in and stayed briefly, and I could see that
he was not impressed. But I asked Barbra if she would come
back and sing for us, and she agreed to learn one of the songs
from our show. When she left, Mr. Prager confided that I was
crazy to even consider her.

Several days later, at the large Broadway Theatre, Barbra Streisand sang "Steady Steady" from *Bravo Giovanni*. I ask that you imagine listening to that talent coming off the stage, emanating from a completely unknown performer. Stanley Prager sat next to me in the theatre, and his words to me, which I never let him forget, were, "Well, I'll give you that she can sing, but with those looks she'll never be a star. Besides, she's much too young for Siepi; we'd be arrested." So we didn't cast her. We finally cast Michelle Lee in the role, and this became an important debut for *her* career.

I soon became a Streisand fan, and got to know her and her manager, Marty Erlichman. My wife and I saw her at her first appearances at the Bon Soir and the Blue Angel. At the Angel, where she was the opening act for Fat Jack Leonard, a borscht belt comic, she did something amazing. The audience, which had of course come to see Leonard, paid no attention to the loudspeaker announcement, "We now present Barbra Streisand." She came on, sat down on a stool, and her pianist Peter Daniels played an introductory arpeggio to her first song. The audience continued drinking, talking, paying no attention, obviously prepared to be bored until Leonard would appear. While the pianist repeated the arpeggio, Barbra kept staring at the audience. Some of them turned toward the stage wondering why no sound was being heard, but Barbra continued to wait. Only when most of the audience was finally looking at her, did she nod to the pianist and begin her opening number, a quiet Harold Arlen song. During that performance she also sang her incredible version of "Happy Days Are Here Again." By the end, the audience wouldn't have cared if Jack E. Leonard had never come on.

A short time later, as Barbra was beginning to get attention, she and Marty requested a meeting at my office. They informed me that Barbra had just been offered a small role, Miss Marmelstein, in a new Broadway musical called *I Can Get It for You Wholesale*. Since things were beginning to happen for Barbra, they asked my opinion about her being stuck in a play for a while in a less-than-starring role. They mentioned that the role included a song written especially for Barbra, and I told them that even if Barbra sang only one song, hers would then become a starring role. Of course, Barbra did do the show and "Miss Marmelstein" was the highlight of the evening. Her next job on Broadway was the title role in *Funny Girl*.

In 1963, I was trying to cast the lead in a play called *Nobody Loves an Albatross*, written by Ronald Alexander. It was a funny, satiric, and, I thought, appropriately vicious play about the Hollywood television industry, particularly its sitcoms. My first choice for the lead was Robert Preston, whom I had never met. I did, however, know his agent, Charlie Baker of the William Morris Agency. I called Charlie, got the script to him, and was promised a swift reply. As good as his word—in retrospect, perhaps not the most accurate phrase—a few days later he called me to say that Preston did not really like the play and would pass.

I moved on to approaching other people and got a positive reaction from Alan King but no final commitment. Some weeks later, Ronnie Alexander was at a party in Hollywood when Robert Preston appeared. Ronnie, never the bashful type, walked up to him and asked, "Why didn't you like my play?" Preston, always a gentleman, didn't say, "Who the hell are you!" but instead asked, "What play?" Ronnie replied, accusingly, "*Nobody Loves An Albatross.*" Said Preston, now equally aggressive, "I guarantee I never read that play, but so far I sure do hate the title. Is the play just as bad?"

This friendly exchange led to a promise by Preston to read the play, of which Ronnie just happened to have a copy in his car. Within one week I received a not-at-all embarrassed phone call from my friend Charlie Baker, and we quickly negotiated a deal for Preston to play the lead. Charlie confessed to never having shown the script to Preston because he thought Bob was on the verge of a film comeback as a result of *The Music Man*. There was, obviously, a fatter commission for the William Morris agency in a film than a play.

I was then able to hire Gene Saks to direct *Albatross*. Gene was not only a talented actor but had directed a previous Broadway success, *Enter Laughing*, with Alan Arkin. I was also joined by Elliot Martin as co-producer on *Albatross*. We opened in Boston to mixed notices, and for a short time Elliot wanted to either close the show or resign his position. I'm happy to say he reconsidered, and together we brought a hit show to the Lyceum Theatre.

My experience with Charlie Baker on *Albatross* also added something to my limited knowledge of how show business works. Agents do not always tell the complete truth. They have even been known to lie on occasion. My awareness of this has served me well from time to time.

I very much enjoyed working with Robert Preston and became one of his enormous list of admirers and friends. His unlimited energy on and off stage never failed to amaze me. In Boston during the tryout period, he had a heavy rehearsal schedule in addition to his regular performances. One night, a group of us were partying in his hotel room after the show. It got to be way past midnight, and Bob was scheduled for a morning interview as well as matinee and evening performances. As I was about to leave, he began to tell me about a musical called *We Take the Town* in which he had starred as Pancho Villa and which had closed out of town. It remained one of his favorite shows and he was disappointed and shocked by its fate. But my expression of sympathy was not enough. Insisting that I sit back down, he proceeded to give a one-man performance of the show, telling us the story and singing all of his songs. We left his room after three. He did his interview the next morning, followed by matinee and evening performances, with enough energy left over to power the entire cast. Truly an extraordinary man and performer.

Chapter 20

I now have to delve into an area that I find extremely difficult to write or even talk about: incidents of the early 1960s that deeply affected my relationship with Lorraine Hansberry. Actually, I have to begin by going as far back as the mid-1950s. But before I do, I want to emphasize again how important our friendship had been to me and how dramatically it had changed my life, as indeed it had changed hers.

During the early 1950s I achieved some success with my own recording and music publishing company. With its concentration on "rhythm and blues," I was discovering new young black artists and reaching a large audience of discriminating record buyers. It was then that I recorded the album *Poetry of the Negro*, for which Lorraine had written the liner notes (which appear in Chapter five), my first realization that she might truly be a fine writer.

Some time after the release of the poetry album, Lorraine asked me if I had room in my office for another employee. For a moment I was startled, thinking she was applying for a job, but she immediately made it clear she had in mind her husband, Robert Nemiroff. Obviously, I knew Bobby through Lorraine and I was aware that he was usually unemployed. And though he often spoke of himself as a writer, I had never seen any evidence of that. I had no idea what he could possibly do in my office, but I knew that getting him a job was very important to Lorraine or she would never have asked. I decided to add him to my small staff, which then consisted of a secretary, Shaindy Rubenstein, and my publishing partner Lou Sprung. So in 1957, Bob Nemiroff began reporting to my office: occasionally he sat in on auditions, and he did show interest in the process of recording and publishing.

One day a young man carrying a guitar came to my office and asked to sing for me. While he was white, I saw no reason to turn him away and, indeed, I thought his performance had a lovely folksong quality. His name was Vince Martin and I was sufficiently impressed to say that I'd call him back in a week or two.

A few weeks before, I had received a call from Burt D'Lugoff and his brother Art. Burt, an old friend of mine and Bobby Nemiroff's, was at the original reading of *A Raisin in the Sun* at Lorraine's apartment. His brother Art was at that time a talent manager and he wanted to introduce me to a singing group he was promoting that was, obviously, looking for a recording contract. I arranged an audition, and though the performers were clearly talented, I didn't know what to do with them. The trio, called "The Tarriers," included a white banjo player named Erik Darling, a black guitarist named Bob Carey, and another white guitarist named Alan Arkin, who, I later heard, also thought of himself as an actor.

One day Bobby Nemiroff arrived at the office with our mutual friend, Burt D'Lugoff, hoping to perform a song for me. Too late for me to plead a previous engagement, I reluctantly sat down to listen. Before they began, they volunteered that this was a song they had written, which I accepted as a further warning to prepare myself accordingly. They then sang a chorus of a song, the original melody of which was immediately familiar. Their title was "Cindy Oh Cindy," but the folk melody came from a song about landlords and tenants called "Pay Me My Money Down." Their lyrics had turned it into a simple but pleasant "pop" song.

After listening to them I first had to make it clear that performing in public was probably not indicated in their future. What did they have in mind? Their very excited reply: "We want you to publish and record this song. It'll be a big hit." I asked if they knew if the melody was in the public domain and they assured me that they had checked it out and it was. I pointed out that this was not the kind of music I usually recorded, but as I spoke I suddenly thought of the Tarriers and that young man Vince Martin who had impressed me. I then cut the meeting short, asking them to give me copies of "Cindy Oh Cindy."

I subsequently talked with Vince Martin and the Tarriers, and within two weeks we went into a studio and recorded "Cindy Oh Cindy." I rushed it out to the disc jockeys and within another two weeks we not only had a hit record but "Cindy Oh Cindy" reigned as number one on the "Hit Parade" for weeks afterwards. Vince Martin and the Tarriers made personal appearances around the country but split up when Alan Arkin left to begin his acting career. By then, Bob Nemiroff and Burt D'Lugoff had made a great deal of money as the writers of "Cindy Oh Cindy," and Lorraine was very pleased at the change in her husband's financial status.

By now we were in the year 1958 and I was intent upon producing *A Raisin in the Sun*. I assumed that Bob would now stop coming to the office. As a matter of fact, I looked forward to our complete separation, because I had heard complaints from Lou Sprung about things Bobby was doing and saying when I was not there. But Bobby did not quit his job. Meanwhile, I was devoting more and more of my time to *Raisin* and less and less to the music business. I now assumed tension between Lou Sprung and Bobby Nemiroff was due to personality problems which they could work out. As time moved forward, *Raisin* went into rehearsal, opened out of town, and arrived in New York on March 10th, 1959, changing my life and Lorraine's dramatically. Some months later Shaindy Rubenstein married and left New York, and I acquired a new secretary, Lynda Watson, an eighteen-year-old, just out of high school, whose life would also be very much affected by the sweeping change in mine. She came from a cloistered family background, and had had no previous contact with the "wild, uninhibited world of show business." I wasn't sure she would be able to adjust, and since this was her first job, it began with a tryout period for her and for our relationship. (You might conclude it didn't really work out because some thirty-five years later she left me and accepted another position.) Matters weren't helped when a few weeks after Lynda arrived Lou Sprung left my office, no longer willing to work with Mr. Nemiroff. At that point, Lynda Watson really began her lengthy service as my invaluable left and right hands, and Bobby officially retired.

During the years of 1961 and 1962, Lorraine would occasionally mention to me a play she was working on that she hoped to have ready to show to me soon. Of course, she assumed, as did I, that I would love it and make immediate plans to produce it. Also in 1961 Burt D'Lugoff and Bobby Nemiroff, who, while no longer on my staff would still occasionally appear at my office, approached me about a musical they had found. It was called *Kicks & Co.* and was written by Oscar Brown, Jr. They were interested in my joining them as co-producer of a Broadway presentation. They described the material as a contemporary version of the Faust legend, about a black man who sells his soul to the Devil. I was intrigued for two reasons. First, because it would be an interracial musical and second, because Oscar Brown was from Chicago which in my mind held such fond associations with *Raisin*. I was willing to read the script and listen to the music, but they were so excited about the possibility of our working together that they insisted I also go to Chicago, at their expense, to hear Oscar Brown perform the show in his living room. I agreed to do this, and arrived at Oscar's home several days later, having by then read the script, of course.

Oscar Brown, Jr. did a fine job of performing the show for me and a few guests, who comprised a very receptive audience. After the usual congratulations, Bobby, Burt, and I met privately and I expressed my opinion. I thought the musical numbers were quite good and the legend itself had proved successful many times before, especially in *Faust*, the famous Gounod opera which also had a pretty good score. My problem was with Oscar's book; I thought it needed a great deal of work, perhaps even the services of a co-author. I was willing to get involved if we could agree on the choice of another writer. It even occurred to me to talk to Lorraine about rewriting the book, a possibility that would have created a great deal of anticipation and would have been as close to an insurance policy for a hit show as anyone could want. But almost before I finished expressing my thoughts, Bobby Nemiroff jumped in to say that I didn't understand what Oscar had written, that it was better and more profound than anything I was accustomed to reading. I never did find out what Burt's opinion was, but it was evident that Bobby would be very happy if I were to bow out, which I did immediately. I offered help in any way I could, including the continued use of my office for a period of time. Bobby did indeed occupy space for several weeks afterwards, until it became apparent to me that the situation was untenable. With Lou Sprung having already left me, I was not about to have Lynda Watson follow suit. So I told Bobby I no longer had any room to spare.

While it was going on, I never discussed any of this with Lorraine, and I still have no idea whether she knew anything about my near involvement with *Kicks & Co*. My conversations with her continued to be about *Raisin*, or politics, or when I would get her next play. But I most assuredly did continue to hear from Bobby and Burt D'Lugoff, whose constant questions I would answer to the best of my ability. For example, they asked if I could suggest a director for *Kicks & Co*. I was surprised that they didn't already have a director, but I thought about it for a few days and then recommended Vinnette Carroll, a talented woman and friend of mine. Vinnette had directed, among other shows, an all-black *Dark of the Moon* and the Langston Hughes play *Black Nativity*. I was pleased to learn very soon afterwards that Vinnette had signed to direct *Kicks*, and she and the producers graciously called to thank me for bringing them together.

After *Kicks & Co.* went into rehearsal, I would occasionally get reports or hear rumors of difficulties, but not necessarily more than any show engenders. Burgess Meredith had been engaged to play Satan, and that certainly sounded positive. But when the company traveled to Chicago, I began to hear news that was more disturbing. One rumor soon became a fact: Vinnette Carroll had been fired and Burgess Meredith was now directing. Immediately after that bulletin, I received a call from Lorraine. She told me that Bobby had just called her and asked that she come to Chicago to take over as director of *Kicks & Co.* She sounded very distressed as she asked me what to do. When I suggested we meet and talk about it, she said Bobby had demanded that she leave New York immediately because he needed her to save the show. Having just produced *Bravo Giovanni*, I knew, unfortunately, that directing a big musical is a most difficult theatre challenge. Taking over that job on a show already in trouble only compounds the problems faced by a director. So, forced as I was to respond immediately, I told Lorraine emphatically that to return now to Chicago, where she had triumphed over all the odds with *Raisin*, where she had become an idol, almost an icon, where she could return with a new play of her own and no longer be afraid of Claudia Cassidy—all of this she would be casting aside without the possibility of enjoying even a glorious failure. I also privately thought she would be making the wrong decision in response to an incredibly unthinking and selfish demand from her husband, but did not express this to her. She heard me out without offering any opinion, which in itself was an indication of how emotionally distressed she was, and then quietly said goodbye. The next announcement I heard was from Chicago: Lorraine was the new director. *Kicks & Co.* opened on August 12, 1962, and Claudia Cassidy's review was pretty much like what Lorraine had originally feared and written for *A Raisin in the Sun,* only this time it was real and not a parody. With all negative reviews, the show closed in Chicago, losing its entire investment.

For a while, I didn't hear from Bobby or Lorraine, and when I did it was with an invitation to attend a one-time performance of *Kicks & Co.* at a New York theatre. Bobby Nemiroff's purpose was to raise the money to reopen *Kicks & Co.* in New York, and he was trumpeting to the entire theatrical community the direction of Lorraine Hansberry, author of *A Raisin in the Sun.* Invitations were received by top producers, theatre owners, and investors, almost all of whom, my wife and I certainly included, responded affirmatively, in all likelihood because of their interest in Lorraine.

It turned out to be one of the most unusual afternoons Doris and I had ever spent in a theatre, not because of the show performed, but because of the one that followed the final curtain. While some in the audience had left immediately, many stayed on out of respect for Lorraine. At the curtain Bob Nemiroff came out onto the stage, held up his hand to stop the applause (which was not difficult) and then, with Lorraine sitting silently on a chair placed behind him, he addressed the audience.

He began by first thanking us for coming, and then applauded us for recognizing that we had just seen an extraordinary, wonderful, and daring musical, which unfortunately had been reviewed in Chicago by a group of critics who not only failed to understand the work, but were, obviously, all racists. This, of course, explained the vehemence of the negative reviews which they would have written, he said, even if they *had* understood the show.

Bobby Nemiroff was never one to use a few words when he could make long speeches to a captive audience. So these remarks, as I have compressed them, went on for some time. Many in the audience who were sitting in the rear took advantage of their location to leave as unobtrusively as possible.

Nearing the end of his remarks, Bobby extolled—and asked us to applaud—the brilliant directing job Lorraine had done, which the racist critics couldn't have begun to appreciate. Those of us who were still there obediently applauded Lorraine, though Doris and I wondered what she now might say about, and how she might perhaps humorously forgive, those same "racist critics" who had given her rave reviews not so long ago at the original Chicago opening of *A Raisin in the Sun*. But, in fact, Lorraine stayed in her seat and said not a word while Bob finished his address with a plea for our help, financial and otherwise, so that he could bring *Kicks & Co.* to Broadway for a triumphant resurrection and personal vindication.

Only Doris and I plus some other friends of the host's stayed to the very end, when Bobby Nemiroff moved to the back of the theatre, with Lorraine at his side, to greet and be congratulated by all of us as we were leaving. We all tried to find words as innocuous and kind as we could to hide our embarrassment as we left the theatre.

Until the day of this presentation, neither Doris nor I had had any contact with Lorraine since she had called weeks before to ask my advice about taking over the direction of *Kicks & Co.* I had then given her my opinion in a warm and friendly way, and while I was surprised when she turned up in Chicago, I expected that she would call from time to time to discuss her progress just as we so often had talked on many other issues. But the silence between us wasn't broken until the New York presentation and, under the circumstances, very little was said on that occasion. I did hope and expect that with the disappearance of *Kicks & Co.* from the theatrical scene, Lorraine and I would be getting together to talk and even enjoy some laughs about her experiences in her first directing job.

But I heard nothing for a while longer, until we had a brief meeting which Lorraine requested to inform me that she had decided that Bobby was going to produce her next play. The

reason for her decision, as she expressed it, was that I was a better musical producer than a play producer. In addition, she
voiced her resentment at my "attack" on her for directing *Kicks
& Co.* Though I was very disturbed by what she was saying and
doing, my reply merely reminded her that she had called me for
my opinion about going to Chicago and I had merely responded to what I considered a call for help. She then said
something about her right to direct, sing, produce, or dance in
the theatre if she chose to, and I cut the meeting short, accepting her decision and wishing her well. I still had hope that all of
this would blow over and that, in spite of Bobby, we might resume the friendship we once had.

In all the years I had known Lorraine, the one subject we had
never discussed was her relationship with her husband. Knowing more and more about Bobby as I did through the years, I
was often curious about it, but I respected Lorraine's privacy
and realized this subject was strictly off-limits. I knew Lorraine
to hold strong opinions about other people's writings—even
her friends'—opinions, positive or negative, she was never reluctant to express to me. But at no time during the development of *Kicks & Co.* and until this last meeting had she ever
said a word to me about the show or any aspect of its production. This reticence caused me to speculate further about her
relationship with her husband.

A few days later, Burt D'Lugoff called to ask me to meet with
him and Bobby. I reluctantly agreed, telling Burt to be prepared
to hear a blunt statement on my feelings about Bobby. We did
meet, and it was then I learned Bobby had one quality that was
indisputable. There was no way to insult him. In Burt's presence, I presented a long, dirty laundry list of things Bobby Nemiroff had done and lies he had told to and about me and my
staff, all while using my office for his own purposes, and always
depending on my feelings for Lorraine to protect him. And
though I even cited disparaging remarks he had made about

Burt, through it all, Bobby sat with a smile on his face, as if I were showering him with compliments. He made no attempt to refute or deny anything, and when I was finished, he thanked me quite graciously, at which point the meeting was over.

Soon after, Doris had a conversation with Lorraine in which she expressed her disappointment at what had happened between Lorraine and myself. Lorraine's response came in the form of a letter to Doris saying that my wife was just "one more woman on Phil's plantation" whose feelings were being forced upon her. Doris was so upset by the letter that it made me, in turn, angry enough to respond in writing.

August 27, 1963

Dear Lorraine,

Having been given by Doris the opportunity to read your letter (I should add at once that as one more woman on my plantation, she didn't dare withhold it), I thought I might set down some of my thoughts, deciding later whether or not to mail them to you. The choice I made should be obvious.

I believe your attitude towards me ever since Kicks & Co. has been ill-advised and harmful to both of us, I need use no stronger language than that because in only one instance do I feel you have been dishonest with me. That case is specifically the unsolicited promise you made to me some months ago when I called you for the 'Off Broadway' rights to Raisin. It was you who volunteered and led me to believe that I would be producing your next play. I quote "What do you want to bother with that old stuff for? You'll have my new play in 2 weeks." In many subsequent phone

conversations, you referred to this specifically. However before you made that offer, I had long since put
out of my mind such a possibility, being well aware, I
thought, that Bobby and Burt would have prior claim.
Let me reiterate, the choice of the offering was yours
and the reneging on that promise was yours.

However, I can even accept calmly your about-face
on this, knowing as I do your feelings about my
miserable deportment in regard to Kicks & Co. But let
us at least be able to share a sense of humor about
your saying to me that your reason for not giving me
your play is that I am a good musical comedy producer
but a bad serious play producer. That sense of humor,
restored to both of us, might even let us enjoy the fact
that so far I've produced one musical, Bravo Giovanni,
which was a distinguished failure, and two plays, A
Raisin in the Sun and Purlie Victorious, both of which
might be considered fairly successful.

Having mentioned Kicks & Co. above, let me set the
record straight on the incident of the New York run-
thru. We did speak to you, in spite of our embarrassment. It was neither a lengthy nor an easy conversation, but it never is under such circumstances. What
Doris and I thought was an unfortunate afternoon,
however, had already been compounded by many
feelings regarding Bobby and myself which were now
ineradicable. More on that later.

In our last meeting you berated me for my attitude
towards your directing Kicks & Co. You made a speech
about your right to direct, sing, produce or dance in
the theatre. If I didn't make my feelings clear then,
let me do so now. You are hereby released from the
plantation and can do anything you like in the theatre.
I will merely assume that I have the right to think that

as a director, you may be no better than Lillian
Hellman, as a singer, no better than Doris Belack,
as a producer, no better than Bob Nemiroff and as
a dancer, no better than Lorraine Hansberry.

My last paragraph, I devote to Bobby. I catch on
slowly in some areas. Even all through the Kicks
production, when he was using me for all sorts of
advice and information, finally using Burt to perform
these chores; even when I discovered through many
sources that he was simultaneously maligning me and
Bravo Giovanni and Purlie, I still somehow held to the
belief that the open faced wonderment that is Bobby
could not be guilty of these things. I had one last
meeting with Bobby and Burt at their request after <u>our</u>
last meeting. I will repeat to you what I said to him
then. He has been deceitful, devious and has lied to me
for a long time now; and I believe he has done the
same to Burt and to you, all for his own personal
gains. Fortunately, he is no longer my problem, but he
is still yours.

Phil

Three months later, in November 1963, when *Albatross*
opened in Boston, I began to hear rumors that Lorraine was not
feeling well. I had no idea it was anything serious until some
time later, after I was back in New York and heard that Lorraine's new play, *The Sign in Sidney Brustein's Window,* was
about to go into rehearsal as a production of Bob Nemiroff's.
Since Lorraine would be needed for casting and rewriting, I just
assumed she was not gravely ill. I also heard that Lorraine and
Bobby had separated, but I was getting involved with a play
called *The Owl and the Pussycat* and was not especially attentive
to rumors. As that year wound down, however, rumors became

fact and it became generally known that Lorraine was quite ill, probably with cancer. She was in and out of hospitals for treatment but didn't seem to be improving. Doris and I had one brief hospital visit with her, and saw her again at a preview of *Sidney Brustein's Window*, I believe in late 1964. She was warm and friendly but disease had already severely enfeebled her, both physically and mentally. She died on January 12th 1965.

After her death it was revealed that she and Bobby had been divorced some months before, a fact Bobby had kept secret for a long time.

I have never forgiven Bobby Nemiroff for his role in denying me two more years of friendship and caring for Lorraine Hansberry. I hope I have fully expressed what she meant to me. But, that aside, I must convey my feeling—no, my conviction—that when we lost Lorraine Hansberry to cancer at the age of thirty-four, we lost not only a brilliant playwright, but a woman who if she had lived would have had even greater impact on our culture and politics for generations to come. In my view, it is impossible to overestimate what she could have meant to our country as an artist, an educator, a political activist—or, indeed, anything else she might have chosen to do.

Chapter 21

In late 1963 or early 1964, Alexander Cohen announced his intention to produce *The Owl and the Pussycat*, a new two-character play that was to star one of the brightest lights of the theatre, Kim Stanley. The playwright was a Hollywood sitcom writer, Bill Manhoff, the director was to be my old friend Stanley Prager, and the theatre had already been booked, the Booth in Shubert Alley. I congratulated Stanley, and he offered to let me read the script, which he was very enthusiastic about. I did read it, and thought Alex might well have a winner.

Several weeks later I received a phone call from a very depressed Stanley Prager, telling me that he had just lost his job. "How could that be?" I asked. "You haven't even gone into rehearsal. Did you try to do something indecent to Kim Stanley?" "I never even had the chance," he responded. "Alex Cohen has just canceled the production and given up his option because we—the writer, the producer, the star, and I—could not agree on an actor to co-star with Kim Stanley." I asked Stanley if he had any objections to my trying to option the play and he wished me luck, adding there was no way Manhoff would again agree to him as director since, in fact, they had not gotten along well.

As soon as I hung up the phone, I called Harold Cohn, the agent who represented Bill Manhoff, and asked him to corroborate that Alex Cohen was no longer interested in the play. When he did, I made an on-the-spot offer to option it. He was obviously very pleased; having just finished a depressing phone conversation with his client the writer, he could now call him back to prove what a great agent he was by already coming up with a new producer. In answer to Harold's question about my production time frame, I said I planned to begin work as soon as I had a written agreement. He promised to get that to me within a few days (and he did). He also provided a phone introduction to his client, who seemed very pleased with my enthusiasm and my intention to move swiftly.

I began by making several phone calls. One was to Pat Fowler, a young actress friend of mine who had recently given up that career in hope of becoming a producer. I told her I'd send her the script. I then called Gene Saks, who had so successfully directed *Albatross* the year before, and offered the play to him as well. I then made the two most important phone calls of all.

When Stanley had first sent me the play and I was reading it, I envisioned it with two actors who had previously worked for me, both of whom, I thought, could under the right circumstances become stars. One was Diana Sands, the black actress who had played Beneatha in *A Raisin in the Sun*, and the other was Alan Alda who had made his Broadway debut in *Purlie Victorious*. The circumstances seemed ideal because, in my view, the play's two characters could have been written for them. Of course, the playwright might have seen Felix, the male character, as perhaps not as tall as Alan Alda, and the female, Doris, with a somewhat lighter complexion than Diana's, but there was nothing in the play to indicate that. So the next two calls were to Diana Sands and Alan Alda. I told them I had a play for them and to please read it quickly because I wanted to proceed with production plans.

I received enthusiastic responses to the play from all of the above, although Gene Saks expressed a slight reservation about my casting choice of Diana Sands. As a result of our conversation, I decided to have a reading of the play at Pat Fowler's large West End Avenue apartment. It took place on a Sunday afternoon, with an audience that consisted of some friends of Pat Fowler's,

Philip Rose

some of mine (including Sidney Poitier), plus Gene Saks and, of course, Diana Sands and Alan Alda to do the reading. I would point out that the invited audience had no advance knowledge of the content of the play or the nature of the casting.

While Diana and Alan had not rehearsed for this reading, after a few pages they were holding nothing back, working brilliantly with and off of each other (no surprise to me), and demonstrating to all of us how funny the play was. When the reading was over, and the applause had subsided, I asked for specific comments from the audience. These were generally approving, with praise for both the play and the actors. Finally, someone mentioned how pleasantly surprising it was that the dialogue contained no mention of the actress's being black, and this set off a discussion in which Saks expressed his opinion that major changes would have to be made in the script for the audience to accept the relationship between the characters.

What followed was a spirited conversation between Sidney and Gene—indeed a no-holds-barred disagreement between those two artists—with the audience looking on in fascination. Of course, I couldn't have had a more eloquent and emotional spokesman for my point of view than Sidney. But when it seemed things were getting a bit too hot, I interrupted to ask Diana Sands and Alan Alda if they had felt any discomfort as artists playing these characters as written. The response from both was a resounding and even incredulous "No." Gene Saks then said that because of his limited experience with mixed-race relationships, he was probably the wrong person to direct this cast. Thereupon, he thanked me for considering him and proceeded to bow out.

That afternoon was enough to convince me that I had a good comedy and an extraordinary cast, a view that was wholeheartedly confirmed by Alan and Diana. She, however, had a problem: a previous commitment to appear in a play which she could not ignore, and therefore we might have to wait for her. But just starting to put this project together, I was sure we could overcome that obstacle. I did have to contend with some reservations from our hostess Pat Fowler, who thought it would be harder to raise money if we didn't have at least a female star.

I now began to face the challenge this play presented. I had already received and signed the option agreement, but I had not yet met the playwright, Bill Manhoff, and it was time for me to inform him of my somewhat unorthodox plans. I called and first told him about our very successful reading of the play (I had invited him to attend but he had not been available), and I then informed him that I had committed to a cast. He was more than a bit stunned, since contractually the playwright had approval rights to casting. But he wasn't about to create an issue over casting after his horrendous experience with the Alex Cohen production. He was, in fact, very pleased to learn I was moving so quickly, and naturally curious about the actors I'd chosen. I first mentioned Alan Alda. He did not know him but was reassured when I gave him Alan's credits, including *Purlie Victorious*. When he asked, "Who's the girl," and I said "Diana Sands," there was a long pause and then the question: "Isn't she a Negro?" "Yes," I answered. Another long pause. "Well, how much rewriting will I have to do?" "None." He said, "I don't understand." I knew I then had to convey my thoughts about casting as persuasively as I possibly could.

So for the first time I tried to put my point of view into words. When I had first read *The Owl and the Pussycat*, two actresses came to mind immediately. One was Anne Bancroft, the other Diana Sands. I had seen Anne Bancroft in *Two for the Seesaw* and when Diana had appeared in *Raisin*, I remember thinking that these two great actresses had very similar gifts for both comedy and tragedy. Later, after watching Ms. Bancroft's wonderful performance in *The Miracle Worker*, I wondered whether anyone would ever give Diana Sands a chance at a comparable starring role. Now I had the opportunity to do that, and there was no excuse for me to consider any other course.

I also argued that I thought that Kim Stanley, a great actress, would have been all wrong for the part except for the fact of her being Caucasian. I don't know whether it was my words, my vehemence, or the implicit threat that I might not go forward with his play, but Manhoff finally consented to Diana Sands, with one condition—that he choose the director. He had met Arthur Storch at a party in New York and liked him. Would I talk with him? I agreed, we met, and we made an agreement.

I proceeded to take the other first steps toward production, beginning with the announcement in the *New York Times* that *The Owl and the Pussycat,* formerly to be produced by Alexander Cohen, was now to be a Philip Rose production, and that the role originally to be performed by Kim Stanley would be played by Diana Sands, with Alan Alda as her co-star. Among the first phone calls I received was one from Alex Cohen, an old friend then and until his death. His first question was about the rewriting he assumed we had done to accommodate the casting of Diana. After I assured him that there had been no rewriting and I didn't think the play required any, he said, "Oh, now I fully understand the explanation. You've lost your mind, you're nuts." All of this was said in a very compassionate friendly fashion.

I very quickly became aware of several unwelcome reactions to the *Times* announcement. First, the Booth Theatre, originally booked for the Alex Cohen production, was no longer available. Second, money was not going to be pouring in. Third, due to her previous commitment, I could not get the immediate services of Diana Sands. Nevertheless, I began to gather money in small amounts while also pursuing alternative means of financing.

One day I received a call from David Biegelman, then an important agent at ICM. "Phil," he began, "how would you like to have Judy Garland as the star of *Owl and the Pussycat*? She's read the play and is dying to play the part." Evidently, Ms. Garland had received a copy of the script, perhaps from the playwright, and decided she had to do it. I pointed out to David that since Judy Garland, even when shooting a film, was no longer trusted to show up on the movie set, how could she possibly be expected to be at the theatre eight times a week? David Biegelman assured me this was the one play she wanted to do and would do. I asked him facetiously if he would legally guarantee this, and in reply he promised to get me an insurance policy from Lloyds of London. I said, "David, you get me the policy and then we'll talk." I then returned to the real world and continued my production meetings.

About a week later, my assistant Lynda answered our phone, then turned to me with an incredulous expression and said, "There's a Miss Garland on the phone who would like to speak to you." I said hello and heard the unmistakable voice (even when not singing) saying, "Mr. Rose, I'm so excited! David, my agent has told me we're going to be working together. I'm looking forward to meeting you. I've got to run now, but I would like to talk to your costume designer as soon as possible so we can discuss my wardrobe. So would you please have him or her call me." Apparently, David had told Judy Garland, "Of course they want you." I never heard from her again, nor did David Biegelman ever mention her again.

When it became apparent that the usual ways to raise money for this production were not going to work, I began to look for other options. I made a call to a theatre in Paramus, New Jersey, across the George Washington Bridge. I was acquainted with the producer who, for years, faced with constant financial deficits, had struggled to keep the theatre alive. He would generally do revivals of well-known plays but occasionally a tryout of a new one. In curtain speeches to the audience he would ask for contributions to help keep the theatre going. It was said that he was also an unpublished novelist who by regularly sending his manuscripts to publishers had accumulated an impressive file of rejection letters. His name was, and still is, Robert Ludlum, and after I got to know him, he occasionally would say his writing was going to change his life one day. (It certainly did.) He read and liked *The Owl and the Pussycat* and agreed to have me put it on at his theatre, with some financial assistance from me. At about that time Diana Sands's previous commitment was completed and we went into rehearsal shortly afterwards for a debut production in Paramus, New Jersey.

The rehearsals were relatively uneventful with few of the problems which usually occur within a company. As a matter of fact, our entire cast got along quite well. While there were some disagreements between them and the director. Diana and Alan were working together beautifully, improvising bits of business and even some dialogue that then became part of the script. This did not always please Manhoff or Storch, and after the first preview performance they requested a meeting with me, which was held in the lobby of the Paramus Theatre. Right off, the playwright told me they were dissatisfied with Diana Sands and would like me to replace her—that is, to fire her! The meeting was brief: I just pointed out to them that I might consider firing the director, or the writer, or even the producer, but not Diana Sands. The meeting was over.

Evidently it had become unhappily apparent to Mr. Manhoff that the audience was reacting enthusiastically to the performances of Diana and Alan but perhaps less so to the play. This inevitably created a conflict between the writer's ego and his bank account. But through the many years following as *The Owl and the Pussycat* became a virtual money machine for Bill Manhoff, that conflict disappeared.

Soon after our first preview, I received a call from Max Gordon, who wanted to go to Paramus to see our show. He had been one of Broadway's most distinguished producers, whose credits included the classic hit *Born Yesterday* starring a newcomer named Judy Holliday. That was in 1946, and while Gordon continued his producing activities for some time after, he was now, in 1964, partially retired. Currently he was working as an advisor for Columbia Pictures to alert them to new Broadway projects with film potential. I not only invited him to the play as my guest but offered to drive him to and from the theatre the following evening. On the way out I enjoyed hearing his stories about Judy Holliday, *Born Yesterday,* and other legendary events Gordon had been part of.

On the drive back from New Jersey after the play, the atmosphere in the car changed somewhat. While Gordon once again reminded me of how important and prescient he had been in his career and his production choices, he now offered me the benefit of his expert advice, to wit: "Phil, I admire what you've done in theatre. *Raisin in the Sun* was wonderful, but now I have to warn you. Don't even think about bringing *Owl* to New York. Not only will you have a disaster, but you'll be too embarrassed to even produce again. And it's not just the play, which is terrible, but those two actors—you'll be laughed out of the theatre. I'm telling you all this as a friend."

I don't quite recall the exact words with which he continued but they were not quite as complimentary. I wondered what he would have said if he were my enemy. We somehow made it to New York and I reluctantly delivered Mr. Gordon safely, to his apartment.

We received generally favorable reviews from the local New Jersey newspapers, particularly for the performances, and some money began to flow in for the New York production, some of it through Pat Fowler. More importantly, I received a surprising phone call from Ray Stark, then the head of the film company Seven Arts Productions. He was also the producer of *Funny Girl,* which was not only an enormous hit but confirmed that Barbra Streisand was the theatre's newest musical star. Mr. Stark offered $25,000 to become a one-third investor in *Owl* and to buy the film rights from Mr. Manhoff and the production. He wanted the property as a vehicle for Barbra to star in, which she did six years later.

With the budget fully financed, I was offered a theatre, the ANTA on West 52nd Street (now renamed the Virginia). I would have preferred a more intimate venue, but I had no other immediate choice, and it did allow me to bring the show directly to New York after the New Jersey closing, thereby saving lots of money and holding on to the cast. We did have to do an immediate search for two understudies, not required in the New Jersey contract but obligatory in New York. Storch and Manhoff quickly chose and I agreed to Rose Gregorio and Robert Moore, two very fine actors, both white.

We opened in New York in November of 1964 with no advance sale, and to a set of mixed notices for the play but reviews for the performances that varied from good to ecstatic. Walter Kerr wrote the most enthusiastic one in the *Herald Tribune*, saying that to see these two actors onstage together would be worth the admission even if they were interpreting the telephone book. The excitement he communicated and the weekly income from the film sale kept us going for the first few weeks until the play really caught on.

One of the most gratifying calls I then received came from Alex Cohen. He was more than gracious in expressing how wrong he had been about the casting of Diana Sands and how significant and instructive he considered the successful result. In making that call he had to rise above the regret and envy he might naturally feel given his own one-time involvement. Incidentally, Alex also made a point of interviewing Diana Sands on his weekly radio program, where he once again discussed the wonderful piece of casting.

During the course of our run in New York an incident occurred which has become an often-quoted theatre story. Diana Sands developed a very bad cold and even ran a fever but she insisted on performing anyway. At the height of her illness, she made her entrance one night, but with each line of dialogue her voice became increasingly feeble. The audience soon noticed this and became increasingly uncomfortable. Normally, just about eight minutes into the play, the two characters engage in a noisy argument, after which Alan Alda goes off stage left to his bedroom. Diana Sands turns on her radio then goes up center stage to the bathroom to change into her nightgown. The stage is empty for about two minutes while we listen to a funny soap opera parody before Diana's character returns. Well, this particular evening, when the bathroom door reopened, out stepped Rose Gregorio, Diana's Caucasian understudy. There then occurred maybe the longest sustained laugh that has ever been heard in a theatre, followed by thunderous applause. When it finally subsided, the play went on as usual, with no announcement made or necessary. Of course at the curtain call, Rose Gregorio received proper recognition in the form of a tumultous ovation as she took her bow.

What had happened backstage was that Lenny Auerbach had started to prepare Rose as soon as he heard Diana's voice begin to fade. He wisely chose to make the change without stopping the show or making an announcement, probably breaking many Equity rules in the process but giving the audience one of their most memorable theatre experiences.

The box office treasurer at the ANTA theatre was Rod McMahon. He and I had become known as the odd couple on the street. He was a tall (six feet four) Irishman and I was a short (five feet five) Jew. I'm not quite that tall anymore and he, sadly, has been gone for many years. For whatever reason, we loved each other's company. We used to meet at Gallagher's, the restaurant bar directly across from the theatre, almost every day to drink our lunch. He would cheerfully volunteer to anyone at the bar that I, his short Jewish friend, had turned him, this tall Irishman, into a drunkard.

Rod loved *Owl* and worked very hard at promoting it. He was a wonderfully kind man. I remember him here in order to relive the hugely enjoyable times we shared. I was not alone in my appreciation of Rod's goodness. The line often quoted about him by friends and acquaintances was that if he were a woman he would always be pregnant, because he couldn't say no to anyone. Since he never walked past a panhandler without making a donation, many street people knew him by name—and also knew his schedule. I once asked him about his generosity and he explained it by telling me a story about his mother.

Rod and his brother were for a while wrestling impresarios. They would present wrestling matches at the Uline Arena in Washington, D.C. Each morning as their mother served them breakfast, they would plan the match for that evening, discussing the choreography and theatrics and, of course, deciding which wrestler would win. Their mother, a real wrestling fan, would listen attentively to their conversation, knowing all the wrestlers by name and some of them as friends. One morning the boys were discussing the loser of the night before and how well he had performed. Their mother broke into their conversation, saying sadly, "Yes, I lost five dollars betting him." Rod said, "What do you mean? You heard us planning the match. You knew he was going to lose." "Yes I know," she answered, "but I like that boy." Rod McMahon was his mother's son all the way, and I loved that boy.

Many years after the closing of *Owl*, in the year 1992, as an observance of Black History Month, a joint celebration was planned by the three theatrical unions, Equity, AFTRA, and SAG. The Equity portion was to be produced by my assistant at that time, Cooki Winborn, and sponsored by Equity's Committee for Racial Equality. Equity had chosen to make the evening a tribute to Diana Sands, who had died at the age of thirty-nine. Ms. Winborn and Equity first asked, then cajoled, and finally bludgeoned me into directing the Equity portion of the evening. What I decided to do was an abridged (one-hour) version of *The Owl and the Pussycat*. We did four major scenes from the play with two casts. The male actors were Michael Tolan (white) and Hinton Battle (black). The females were Phylicia Rashad (black) and Mia Dillon (white). I alternated the possible combinations with each scene and the audience enjoyed the fun not only as theatre but as an expression of the essence of the evening.

One area in which I was completely ineffectual in promoting my point of view was in the casting of the film version of *Owl*. Ray Stark, a major investor in the play, had acquired all the film rights and, as I knew, he always had Barbra Streisand in mind for the leading role. I certainly shared his enthusiasm for that choice. What I wondered about was how he would cast the leading man. From what I had heard, Alan Alda was not being considered. I had by then achieved at least a telephone and mail relationship with Stark through the monthly checks I signed for him as his part of the profits from the play. So I decided to ask for a meeting at his office.

It turned out to be a pleasant encounter, with Stark repeating his appreciation for what my production had accomplished, artistically as well as financially. After emphasizing how excited I was by the idea of Barbra as the female lead, I got to the heart of my agenda: to suggest Sidney Poitier for the co-starring role. His response was complete astonishment and I confess to having been almost as surprised by his reaction. I had assumed he was aware of my past and continuing relationship with Sidney, and that should have at least hinted at the reason for my visit. In any case, he gave me the courtesy of listening to my opinion that Mr. Poitier and Ms. Streisand together would produce a wonderful chemistry on and off the screen. He then dismissed the idea politely and quickly, saying that Sidney Poitier was not a big enough star. Our meeting ended on that peculiar note.

I have never mentioned this meeting to Sidney so, assuming he reads this far into my book, he'll probably be learning about it for the first time. *Owl* was finally filmed with Barbra Streisand and George Segal, and proved a major disappointment. I still think Sidney and Barbra would have made it a smash hit, but who knows? Sidney might have turned it down because Barbra wasn't important enough.

During the many years since *Raisin* and particularly after *The Owl and the Pussycat*, I have been involved in many discussions, both friendly and confrontational, about "nontraditional" casting. I presume, by now, it is quite evident that I am a strong advocate of affirmative action in that area. I would like now to explain and support my position.

Let me say that I believe casting calls should generally be open to any actor who might express to some degree both the internal and external requirements of a character. The external is easy to fulfill if the playwright has given us such specifics as: the character needs to be short or tall, attractive or unattractive, athletic or disabled, old or young, etc. This list can go on and on, and in some cases may include, according to the playwright's description, black or white. Presumably, what you see is what you get. But it doesn't always work out that way, because the internal qualities that derive from talent, given a chance, may sometimes overcome the writer's or director's original external view of the character. One great playwright, Arthur Miller, has written that Willie Loman was originally envisioned as a small man. However, the part was finally cast, superbly, with the large Lee J. Cobb. But it was also played by a smaller Dustin Hoffman, and just recently by an almost giant Brian Dennehy. One-armed characters have been played by actors with one arm hidden; height can come from built-up shoes, fatness from pillows, old age from lots of makeup. But blacks as whites or whites as blacks, never. Wait a minute—didn't that fellow Shakespeare write something called *Othello*, and wasn't that character played for centuries by white actors wearing black makeup? In the 1800s Ira Aldridge, an American black actor, had to leave his country and go to Europe to play Othello. He became world-famous as the greatest Othello of his time. During his career he also played Richard III, King Lear, Macbeth, and Romeo to equal acclaim. He died in 1867 near the age of sixty without having the opportunity to play Othello in his own country.

It was literally a century later when Paul Robeson was acclaimed for the same role on Broadway and throughout the United States. And of course, on tour he could not stay in the same hotel as his co-star Uta Hagen. Meanwhile, white actors have continued to play Othello in makeup for the last century and to this day they've had no problem staying at the same hotels as their co-stars.

But can we accept a black actor playing a white character? Well, there is that thing that actors use called makeup. Yes, but would that sufficiently hide a black face to fool the audience? Does anyone think seeing Laurence Olivier play Othello made the audience blind to a white man in makeup? Some years ago a wonderful black actor, Canada Lee, appeared on Broadway wearing white makeup. Because he was a fine actor, the audience suspended belief just as they did for Olivier.

Let me move on to the larger and more realistic problem. Most of the time what the black actor is facing is not that he wants a role that is expressly described as white or black, but that if there is *no* description of the character, he will not be allowed to audition unless he *is* white. To state it another way: each actor presents himself as a personality to be taken into consideration in all its parts. There is no need to emphasize that for centuries white people made no attempt to consider a black man or a woman as possibly a many-faceted personality. And the failure to see black people as individuals leads even today to racial profiling "accidents" or tragedies like the shooting of innocents in black communities. It has taken a long time for the entertainment industry to even try to overcome this.

Now there are times when so-called nontraditional casting is more difficult to accept. Consider the family story, which so many great plays are. How do we introduce a black son into a white family? For instance, how can we explain Willie Loman having a black son in *Death of a Salesman*? Or Willie Loman himself being played by a black actor as he once was by the wonderful Frank Silvera. The point is that the *son* would *not* be black, only the actor would, and Frank Silvera was *not* playing a *black* father, he was playing Willie Loman. Does the audience sit there for two hours and wonder: why does he have a black son, or why doesn't Willie Loman have a black family? *Not if the play and the actor are truly good.*

Nowadays there has been a controversy over whether black artists should even want to play in anything but black plays or to be involved in anything except black theatre companies. While I wholeheartedly support and appreciate black theatre's importance and contributions to our culture, I do not agree that black actors should not compete equally as artists for the best roles in the best plays ever or still to be written.

I'm pleased that there has recently been considerable progress on Broadway in this area. We have therefore been privileged to enjoy the extraordinary talents of Audra McDonald as Carrie in Carousel and Brian Stokes Mitchell as Fred Graham in Kiss Me Kate. They both received Tony Awards for their performances.

*Diana Sands
and Alan Alda*

ANNUAL ROSETTA LENOIRE AWARD
PRESENTED TO PHILIP ROSE

Philip Rose (l) is joined by (l to r) Sidney Poitier, Rosetta LeNoire and Andre De Shields following his acceptance of Equity's Rosetta LeNoire Award.

Producer/Director Philip Rose received Equity's seventh annual Rosetta LeNoire Award at the Eastern Regional membership meeting on April 7, 1995. The award recognizes outstanding achievements in non-traditional or affirmative casting.

Rosetta LeNoire, who had received the first award in 1989, was on hand for the occasion, along with Sidney Poitier, a long-time friend, who starred in Mr. Rose's landmark production of *A Raisin in the Sun* in 1959.

André De Shields, Chair of the Committee for Racial Equality, made the presentation, "a long overdue tribute to a gentleman whose entire career as both a theatrical producer and a director perfectly personifies the precept of the Award." He thanked Mr. Rose "for being an innovator in the theatre," for sharing his "exceptional insight with us," for showcasing through his talents as a director and a producer "a vast and rich array of actors and playwrights and for exposing Broadway audiences to a world of diversity."

Mr. De Shields went on to say that "years before these terms, 'non-traditional casting,' 'multi-culturalism,' 'ethnic diversity,' had entered the theatrical vernacular," Mr. Rose "had already done it, by casting the exceptionally talented actress, Diana Sands, who just happened to be African-American, in the non-racially specific lead role in *The Owl and the Pussycat* opposite Alan Alda. That was in 1964.

"It is now 1995," he said, "and one would be hard pressed to find another producer working in the commercial theatre who could lay claim to a similar accessibility and openness in casting.

"This gentleman is also responsible, for having produced the first play on Broadway written by an African-American female, and we all know that female to have been the marvelous Lorraine Hansberry. The director was Lloyd Richards, the play was *A Raisin in the Sun*, a production which is now legendary, a production that ushered in a host of talented actors that have since continued to dominate the stage and the screen," including Sidney Poitier, Ruby Dee, Claudia McNeil, Ivan Dixon, Douglas Turner and Ossie Davis.

"Both the 1961 play, *Purlie Victorious,* and the 1970 musical, *Purlie,* are other examples of the fact that this outstanding producer has consistently provided the American theatre with a diverse array of voices and acting talent," Mr. De Shields continued. Mr. Rose also brought Denzel Washington to Broadway in *Checkmate,* Al Pacino in *Does A Tiger Wear A Necktie?,* Ossie Davis and Alan Alda in *Purlie Victorious,* Sherman Helmsley and Melba Moore in *Purlie,* and others too numerous to mention. Mr. Rose received three Tony nominations for *Purlie,* as director, producer and co-author, and *Shenandoah* received six Tony nominations and won two, including Best Book for Mr. Rose.

MORE ACCOLADES

The program continued with Michael Tolan reading a letter of congratulations from Ruby Dee and Ossie Davis who were unable to attend. Sidney Poitier called the award "an affirmation of a great humanitarian instinct in the personality of this man." He recalled the opening performance of *A Raisin in the Sun,* "a miraculous journey engineered, directed and sculpted by Philip Rose. It was the beginning of a change of attitude in the American theatre," Mr. Poitier said. "He husbanded that play from the point it was a first draft from the pen of a very gifted writer and actress. And he brought it to be a presentation of landmark importance at the Barrymore Theatre that particular night.

"Today it is appropriate," he concluded, that we "gather to pay tribute to him for that and for all the illustrious accomplishments in his most distinguished career."

DEE & DAVIS
Post Office Box 1318
New Rochelle, New York 10802

April 7, 1995

Phillip Rose
137 West 78th Street
New York, NY 10024

Re: The "Rosetta Lenoire Award

Dearest Phil,

We cannot be with you in person today, but wish to express our congratulations old friend!

How much so many of us are indebted to you for your vision and dedication. It's been a pleasure and an inspiration knowing you. We can think of no one for whom this award could be more deserving. You are forever and ever in our hearts.

Love,

Ossie Davis   Ruby Dee

Chapter 22

During the year 1966, *The Owl and the Pussycat*, in addition to our own road company starring Eartha Kitt, and a London production in which Diana Sands repeated her role, became one of the most performed plays throughout the country. I had given a Los Angeles producer, Ted Thorpe, a brief period of exclusivity to present it at the La Cienega Theatre, and had approved the casting of Bill Bixby, a current television star, along with a young black actress named Carol Cole. I had never met Ms. Cole but I was assured by Thorpe that she was not only very talented but her résumé included the fact that she was the not-very-well-known daughter of Nat "King" Cole. I assumed that some of her father's considerable talent must be in her genes, and if it didn't carry over into acting, we could always ask her to play the piano and sing. Thorpe was also excited about having signed as director Danny Simon, brother of Neil Simon. So, if necessary, we could get some new lines that Neil might have thrown away.

A few days after going into rehearsal, Thorpe called me sounding very desperate. His production was about to fall apart. My first thought was maybe Carol Cole was too inexperienced, but in fact the problem was with the director. The "entire" cast wanted him fired and was refusing to work with him any longer. They threatened to resign unless he was removed within 48 hours, and demanded a meeting with and prior approval of any replacement. My advice first was to tell Ted to forget it, but he pleaded that he could not afford the loss of his already considerable investment. I couldn't see any other alternative, but he asked me to please fly to Los Angeles at his expense for a meeting with Mr. Bixby and Ms. Cole. He said he had already proposed this to the cast and they had agreed to continue rehearsing their lines for two more days if I would come out. I said I didn't know what I could accomplish but that if he would find another director in the interim, I would meet with everybody and perhaps prove to be of some help. He thanked me profusely and I left for California the following day.

I arrived at the theatre and was introduced by Mr. Thorpe to Bill Bixby, recognizable from many television performances, and to Carol Cole, a very attractive young woman. In a few minutes we were all having a good time, laughing and talking about everything except the play. But I was much impressed with the chemistry between the two actors. When I finally asked what the problem was with the director, I was informed that Mr. Simon had already resigned. They then said they would like to do a scene for me. Without even waiting for a response, they proceeded, and when they were finished I explained I was thoroughly convinced they must not desert this show, for they would have a great time and a successful opening. "All you need to do," I said, "is find a new director that you're all happy with and forget whatever problems you've had before." There was a short pause and then a look that passed between Carol, Bill and their producer. Then they all said simultaneously, "We already have found him and the problem is solved." "So what did I come all the way cross-country for?" I asked. "Because you're the new director," they said. "We've all just voted on it."

I stayed on for the next three weeks not only to steer *Owl* to the successful opening I'd predicted but to another curve in my serendipitous career. I had thoroughly enjoyed directing and I knew I wanted to continue to do it. I also, under Bill Bixby's tutelage, became an enthusiastic pool player at the bar next door. This was an entirely new venture for me, and while it hasn't much improved my financial status, it has earned me the increased respect of many people who are not avid theatergoers.

When I returned to New York, I spent many months casting and directing different stock productions of *Owl* with stars of varied ethnic backgrounds. I particularly enjoyed working with Pat Suzuki, a Broadway star of Japanese descent who had appeared in Rodgers and Hammerstein's *Flower Drum Song*.

During the next few months, in addition to my work on the many productions of *Owl*, I was searching for a new play that I might produce and direct, preferably a serious one that allowed me to make what I hoped would be an important and impressive Broadway directing debut. After reading many scripts, I finally settled on one which was not particularly serious or important and, as it turned out, not very impressive. But at the time I thought it would be funny and at the very least entertaining. It also gave me the opportunity for the first time to direct my wife, Doris Belack, in a role on Broadway, a position I was not necessarily able to assume in my role at home. The play was *The Ninety-Day Mistress* by J. J. Coyle. I was happy to be joined by James Nederlander and George Steinbrenner as co-producers, along with a friend of mine, David Wilde. Having these gentlemen on board immediately provided the production with financing and the theatre booking.

For the star of the play I was looking for an ingenue as provocative as the title, and while conducting the search itself was quite enjoyable, I had trouble finding someone who met the acting requirements. Many months before, Bradford Dillman, a very good-looking, talented young actor and a friend of Doris and mine for many years, had invited us to the opening of a new Broadway play called *The Fun Couple*. Brad was appearing with two relatively unknown ingenues who were starring in the show. The play unfortunately did not run for very long and, in truth, it was not very exciting, except for two memorable elements: the two young stars who spent most of their time onstage in a beach setting, wearing bikinis. They were both obviously extraordinarily talented and quite comfortable in their costumes, which fit very well. The names of the actresses were Jane Fonda and Dyan Cannon. A long time after *The Fun Couple* had come and gone, Dyan Cannon's name, or something about her, popped into my mind. I located her agent, whom I knew very well, and asked if I could contact her about *Ninety-Day Mistress*. He asked for a copy of the play and after reading it, forwarded it to her. Several days later he called to give me Dyan's phone number in L.A., where I was auditioning other actors.

When I called the number, the phone was answered by a man whose voice I had known all my life. I had no trouble recognizing Cary Grant, but it wasn't easy to remain poised while I asked for Dyan. Though I knew they had recently married, I hadn't expected he would be answering the phone and taking messages. Dyan returned my call and we soon met, got along well, and she signed on to play the lead. In addition to Dyan and Doris, I cast Martin Milner, Ruth Ford, and Walter Abel—all theatre veterans—and a young Tony Lo Bianco.

We opened on Broadway in November of 1967 after a relatively calm rehearsal period. One of the most talked-about developments at that time was the legal separation of Mr. Grant and Dyan. Doris and Dyan had by now become backstage pals, with Doris probably enjoying her "girl talk" gossip sessions with Dyan more than the play. Meanwhile, we received mixed reviews, with many saying that the play was amusing but a piece of fluff, which was certainly valid. Our smallish audiences, however, were having a good time, while we fought to stay alive.

One evening I was at the theatre box office an hour before curtain time and my stage manager came to tell me Ms. Cannon wanted to see me in her dressing room. I soon walked through the theatre to the backstage area to find a crowd of people in her dressing room. As soon as I entered Dyan broke through the group to grab me and bring me to the center where stood Cary Grant. I remember my first reaction, after my surprise, was that I was looking at one of the most beautiful men I had ever seen.

I know men are supposed to be called handsome, and he certainly was onscreen, but up close in person he was more like a stunning photograph. Dyan introduced me as her director and producer. We were surrounded by some friends of his who were all, I gathered, there to see the play. Mr. Grant shook my hand and seemed to turn on a charm switch as he concentrated on me, saying something to the effect that he was glad to see me again. I was about to deny any previous meeting but he continued, "Yes Phil, we've met before! Let me see—was it at something in L.A.?" I just quietly shook my head while the entire group watched and listened to this little scene between us. Growing ever more charming and insistent, he suddenly said, "Oh yes, now I know, of course, it was at Cannes at the film festival we met, wasn't it?" Since this was a direct question, I jumped in and said, "No, Mr. Grant, I think I would have remembered you." That brought some laughter from the group, but then Dyan ushered us out of her dressing room. As we left, Grant told me he might be coming around from time to time, and he hoped I wouldn't mind. I told him he was welcome at any time backstage or in the theatre. I didn't have the guts to ask if he would let me know in advance so I could publicize it and fill the house.

A few days later there arrived backstage a large package for Dyan Cannon, and minutes later Doris was summoned to her dressing room. There was Dyan standing in a brand new sable coat that extended almost from the floor to the ceiling. It was a gift from Grant and evidently the sort of expenditure which didn't occur very often. That evening Doris gave me all the gossip before it hit the papers. Dyan and Cary had reached some sort of understanding and had decided to try again. Sure enough, Grant began to turn up backstage regularly. He would go to Dyan's dressing room, always asking if Mr. Rose was in the theatre, and if I was we would have long chats and I would hear great stories. He gave me his personal New York telephone number to call at any time. He now called me Phil, and I had no trouble remembering his first name. He also became aware that we could use some additional funds to keep our show alive.

Unfortunately, the rapprochement between Cary and Dyan did not last very long. A few days after the delivery of the sable coat, Doris was again summoned to Dyan's dressing room to find a very disturbed actress almost in tears. There had been a call from the furrier who had sold Mr. Grant the coat, which, they said, they now needed to retrieve briefly in order to do some required minor alterations. They were arranging to pick it up that evening and would return it promptly. Dyan asked Doris what she should do. Doris replied wisely and reasonably, "Just give the coat to me. I'll take it home and you can borrow it whenever you want to. Or you can return it and I'll kill you."

Our closing notice went up on a Monday, the show to close after the following Saturday evening performance. I arrived at the theatre that Saturday at about 1:00 P.M. for the matinee and found a message waiting for me from Mr. Grant to please call him. I did, and he asked me two very direct questions. First: "How much money would it take to keep your show going?" I answered, "About $30,000 would get us through two or three more weeks and we would then catch on." (This was 1967.) His second question: "If I give you the money today, would you fire Dyan and put in her understudy?" As soon as I realized he was serious, I just said no and hung up the phone. I never heard from him again. Dyan, as far as I know, kept the coat.

Chapter 23

In 1968, I heard about a play being performed at Stockbridge, Massachusetts, entitled *Does a Tiger Wear a Necktie?* I was invited to come see it but I was busy at the time and requested a script instead. It was sent to me by the playwright, Don Petersen, and was intriguing enough to prompt me to meet with him, whereupon I optioned the play for a Broadway production.

Don and I made a quick decision to hire Michael Schultz, a very talented young black director who has since become quite prominent in film (*Car Wash*, for example). For the leading roles, we signed two well-known actors, Hal Holbrook and David Opatoshu. Moving on to the supporting roles and guided by Don's experience, we reached out to actors who had done well in the Stockbridge production, including William Devane, who had played the important supporting role of Bickham. Michael Schultz and I quickly agreed on Devane as our first choice. However, he was considering an offer, to do the leading role in another show soon to open on Broadway. While waiting for his decision, we saw other actors, among them Jon Voight, and others who one day would also achieve stardom. But we kept waiting for a decision from Devane.

We asked another young actor to recreate his role in the original production and received word from his new agent at the Creative Management Agency that he was not available. But the following day the actor himself telephoned to say that while he would not consider the small role he had originally played, he wanted to audition for the role of Bickham. Since we were still in limbo with Mr. Devane, I set up an appointment for him the following day. Having been in the original production, he was of course familiar with the role, and he said he didn't think he'd require much preparation. The next day, as scheduled, Al Pacino appeared to audition for the role of Bickham—and almost frightened us out of the theatre with his intensity.

Some years ago, in a book he wrote, the great English director Tyrone Guthrie explained how he managed to get brilliant performances from his actors. "Well," he said, "I try to bring them back to what they achieved in the first reading." While Guthrie may have been a bit too modest in describing his own role, I can only say of Al Pacino's first reading that I would have gratefully settled for that performance on opening night. I told Mr. Pacino that we were interested if he was, and his answer was an unqualified yes!

I called Devane that evening and told him we needed his final yes or no within 24 hours. He got back to me the following day to decline, permitting me to diplomatically express my regret at his withdrawal. I immediately called Pacino's agent at CMA and was told, this time unequivocally, that Pacino was signed to do the film *Catch 22* for Mike Nichols, and he was in no way going to give that up for a play. I hung up the phone and called Pacino. He was as direct as his agent was. He asked, "Are you offering me the role of Bickham?" "Yes," I answered. "Then go ahead and negotiate with my agent," he said. I called his agent again and this time she was as insistent as he was, saying, "If you try to sign Mr. Pacino we will sue you *and* Mr. Pacino and so will Mike Nichols." I quickly reported this conversation to Al. He then hung up the phone without saying a word. Within approximately ten minutes, I received a call from his agent offering to make a deal. I suspect that Pacino may have done his Bickham-type performance over the telephone and given her an order she couldn't refuse.

I began to move rapidly toward production and was able to find an associate producer, Jay Weston, who was also a friend and neighbor of mine. Equally important, particularly for money, some weeks before I had met a gentleman named Huntington Hartford, one of the wealthiest young men in the country, heir to the A & P supermarket fortune. I convinced him to come on board and he wrote a check for a good portion of the budget, thereby becoming my co-producer.

The play *Does a Tiger Wear a Necktie?* takes place in a center for recovering drug addicts, and it deals not with the graphic depiction of what the addicts go through (as was shown in Jack Gelber's off-Broadway play *The Connection*) but with who these characters are—including their needs, struggles, desires, talents, which they all possessed in varying degrees. They were people of different ages, colors, ethnicity groups, and education. In short, they interested me, and playwright Don Petersen, who had for a while taught at such an institution, knew them well.

We opened on February 25th 1969. The entire cast was at its best and we were all optimistically anticipating the reviews. When they arrived, the adjective "mixed" more or less accurately described them, and we knew we'd have to fight to survive. But the critics' reservations were about the play. The performances were almost unanimously praised and Al Pacino in his supporting role received stunning superlatives. Unfortunately, Clive Barnes of the *New York Times* seemed disappointed that the play dealt with the characters as complex human beings rather than as stereotypical drug addicts.

I knew we would have to raise money to promote the show. My obvious major source was Huntington Hartford, but for him the timing was not propitious. Hartford had not seen the play because he had recently left for his home in the Bahamas. The problem was not the distance. It was, rather, that he was involved in one of his many divorce cases, this one with a wife who was determined to put him in jail the moment he again stepped foot on his native soil. According to the newspapers, she was claiming he had illegally tapped her phones, and she couldn't wait to have him arrested so that she could more easily pursue her financial demands. When I contacted him, he suggested that

Foreground, from left:
Roger Robinson, Hal Holbrook, and Al Pacino

I come to the Bahamas. I did, and after spending a mostly fruitless two days trying to separate him from the many teenyboppers always surrounding him, I finally extracted a promise that he would see the show when he returned. Since that return didn't occur until months later, our major investor never saw what he had co-produced, and we received no additional money.

Several other more felicitous events occurred. First, within two months of our opening Al Pacino received his well-deserved Best Supporting Actor Tony Award for his Broadway debut; he also received front-page coverage in the *New York Times* theatre section, and his performance drew the attention of the entire theatre and film industries.

But soon after our opening and on the heels of Clive Barnes', mixed notice, there had appeared in the *New York Times* another review of *Tiger* under a headline called "A Black View." It was written by Peter Bailey, and for the first time ever I felt angered enough to write a letter to the newspaper. The reason for my rage was not that Mr. Bailey's piece criticized or could even hurt the play. It was that he attacked a young black actress, Lauren Jones, for accepting a role in it (her performance earned her a Tony nomination for Best Supporting Actress), and in passing also attacked Diana Sands for having played her role in *Owl and the Pussycat* five years earlier. But the real object of my anger was not so much Mr. Bailey as the *New York Times.* Just a short time before, the paper had printed a vicious article by Clifford Mason (another black writer) ridiculing Sidney Poitier for *his* choices of roles. In my view these were not judgments on the quality of the performances. Instead, they were personal assaults on three artists (particularly Mr. Poitier), who through their acting were probably making more important contributions toward reducing our society's delinquencies and deficiencies than they could in any other way.

I was pleasantly surprised that the *Times* published my letter in its entirety. I was not so pleased that our show closed on Saturday, March 29th, one day before the following letter appeared.

Drama Mailbag

Yes, Some Addicts May Be Poets

To the Editor:

AS THE producer of such plays as "A Raisin in the Sun," "Purlie Victorious," "The Owl and the Pussycat" and "Does a Tiger Wear a Necktie?", I am pleased to see that The New York Times has finally decided to appoint a Black man as a play reviewer. We can now, of course, look forward to Peter Bailey's review of "40 Carats," "Hadrian VII," "The Man in the Glass Booth" and other plays currently running on Broadway. We could all be enlightened by a Black view of these plays, and I for one welcome it. I certainly don't expect The New York Times to segregate its new reviewer to plays that deal with Black people or narcotics addicts.

I also want to congratulate The Times on its choice of Mr. Bailey over such people as, perhaps, Ossie Davis, Douglas Turner Ward, Ruby Dee, Vinette Carroll or anybody else who has spent the last 25 years struggling to work as an actor, writer, director, etc., in our commercial and non-commercial theater. It is refreshing to read a man like Bailey who is obviously not burdened by any such background, knowledge or experience. In any case,

now that The Times has taken this brave step forward, may I say a few words about Mr. Bailey and his review of "Does a Tiger Wear a Necktie"?

*

Mr. Bailey reminds me of the man who, upon seeing "Death of a Salesman," remarked, "That New England territory never was any good." If all Mr. Bailey got from the magnificent and moving portrayal by Miss Lauren Jones in "Tiger" and the brilliant comedy performance of Miss Diana Sands in "Owl and Pussycat" was that they were playing Black whores, he should be reviewing a much simpler form of entertainment. I don't think I need apologize for the casting, nor do Miss Jones and Miss Sands for their performances. It might, perhaps, have been interesting . and pertinant for The Times and/or Mr. Bailey to question both these artists about their feelings about playing these characters and their experiences in doing so. In any case, it may enlighten Mr. Bailey to learn that Miss Sands in "Owl and Pussycat" was not cast as a Black whore, but rather as a Polish girl named Doris Wilgus who was desperately lonely and therefore slept with men who occasionally gave her money. When "Owl" was scheduled to be done originally by another producer, Kim Stanley was to play the part. When I undertook to produce it and decided that Miss Sands was my first choice over many more prominent actresses, it related to my feelings that Miss Sands was the best actress for the part. Of course, I am somewhat prejudiced toward Diana Sands. She would also have been my first choice as Annie Sullivan in "The Miracle Worker," Gittel in "Two for the Seesaw," and many other plays if I had been producing them.

Mr. Bailey seems to be tired of seeing so many Black actresses, on Broadway and in films, playing whores. "This trend needs to be broken," he says. I have a feeling the avalanche has not yet overwhelmed our young Black actresses, and they may want to give it another month or two. Parenthetically, I think many Black actresses on both coasts are going to be surprised to learn that they have been waging a pointless struggle for years against being cast exclusively as domestics, when all the time they were being constantly sought to play important roles on Broadway and in films as Black whores. We all remember particularly fondly Scarlett O'Hara's favorite Black whore played by Hattie McDaniel and all the wonderful whores played by Butterfly McQueen, and so on. They always got those challenging roles.

∗

I will not discuss Mr. Bailey's remarks about the level of writing talent in "Tiger." I will leave that to more objective responses. I would like to point out to The Times readers that I would not concern myself with a play about addict withdrawal symptoms or anything else vaguely related to "The Connection" or plays of that genre. I am concerned, rather, because I am sick of reading and hearing about cleaning up neighborhoods by getting the addicts off the streets. I am sick of the recurring campaigns to get the Black whores out of the Broadway area. These people are not garbage, to be swept into another neighborhood or into the nearest incinerator. They are human beings with needs to love and be loved and, yes, some of them may even be poets. And they are being expended by our society as easily as the casualties in Vietnam. When do we start attacking the criminals and not the victims? When do we begin expressing our horror at the wasting of children? This is what "Tiger" is about.

I recommend to Mr. Bailey and The Times that they talk to one of the local groups of former drug addicts, such as Phoenix House, who have been attending performances regularly. They might find it enlightening to discover that these former addicts do not think they have been treated as "Our Gang," or kids withdrawing from cigarette smoking, but, rather, for the first time, investigated as whole human beings.

My last point: Has The New York Times decided that in the present struggle any Black actor, writer or director who makes it big in the commercial theater or films is fair game to be attacked by anyone with the excuse of "A Black View"? Are we to be subjected, following a gratuitous attack on Sidney Poitier of some months ago, to one on Diana Sands if she makes it big, on Ossie Davis if he does, on Lauren Jones if she does, etc.? And how is The Times arriving at its choice for "A Black View"? Did it canvas all prominent Blacks involved in the theater for a point of view towards "Tiger"? Would The Times have printed this review if it had been laudatory? Or is it now to be that one way to get an article in The New York Times is to attack a "commercial" Black artist or any "commercial" play dealing with Black subjects? I am looking forward to "Another Black View of 'Tiger,'" which I assume will follow next week.

PHILIP ROSE

A few more words about Sidney Poitier, my final ones, which I'm sure will be a relief to him if he's read this far.

In all the years I was producing and/or directing, every black actor, young or old, who came through my office door and saw Sidney's picture on my wall, would volunteer something like, "If not for Mr. Poitier I wouldn't be here." Many of them could quote lines from his films, especially, from *In the Heat of the Night*, his rendering of "They call me *Mr.* Tibbs." That line, I was often told, was repeated and delivered proudly at many black dinner tables by and for young children, underscoring its significance far beyond a line in a film.

Very much aware of Sidney's profound engagement in the struggle for civil rights and true freedom for black citizens, I was also fortunate enough to witness a slow but dramatic transition in the response of the white world towards this black man. In the black community the reaction was not slow, but instant and appreciative in recognition of his impact and his accessibility. Somehow black people knew that when they joyfully greeted Sidney on any street, his response would be equally warm and friendly. No matter the occasional criticism of his choice of roles as a "Black Superman," the black community knew better. One incident, which exemplified both their respect and love for him, occurred when I was doing a play called *Checkmates*. It starred Paul Winfield, Ruby Dee, Marsha Jackson, *and* Denzel Washington, and I'll be writing more about it later. While it had not been warmly received by some critics, both its cast and its subject matter attracted a large black audience, including such well-known performers as Eddie Murphy and, finally, at one matinee, Sidney Poitier. When Sidney arrived and took his seat in the theatre, there was the inevitable buzz throughout the house. As the lights came up at the end of the first act, instead of the usual mad dash for the restrooms or the street, the entire audience seemed to be rushing, forward or backward depending on their seat locations, toward Sidney. They came with programs in hand for his autograph, somehow knowing that they would be treated with warmth and respect. Our usual ten-minute intermission became twenty when the house manager finally came down the aisle with his crew of ushers to get people to return to their seats so that the performance could resume. All of the many who were fortunate enough to have reached him, white or black, felt, I am certain, they had met a friend. This was Sidney's effect, on screen and off, on the millions of people in this country whose eyes and minds he opened to help them at last understand "Black can be beautiful."

Chapter 24

Through much of the 1960s while I worked on other shows, my mind would return to my disappointment that *Purlie Victorious* had not achieved the success that Ossie Davis and I felt it deserved. Though we'd had a fine cast starring Ossie and Ruby, well directed by Howard Da Silva, and garnered some very good reviews, we had never managed to attract a large audience, white or black. The memory of this haunted me, and by the end of the decade it became an obsession.

I had always thought Ossie's play had a poetic element, almost musical at times, that was particularly evident in Purlie's final sermon about his imagined victory over his enemy, the "Old Captain," which he now regarded totally as reality. When one day I mentioned to Ossie my idea of reviving the play as a Broadway musical, he gave me his immediate approval. His enthusiasm, however, was restrained, because implicit in it was his expectation that this project would never see the light of day. I was too grateful to him for his complete trust to remind him that both he and Ruby had never fully believed *Purlie Victorious* or even *Raisin* would ever make it to Broadway. Further, part of Ossie's restrained feelings, then and much later, stemmed from the fact that he didn't really like or respond to musicals to begin with. In effect, then, he was saying, "Go ahead, but just don't bother me."

I knew that my first and most important challenge was to find the right lyricist, someone who could preserve Ossie's wonderful language but move it to another plane. To begin, I let it be known in the theatre community that I was looking for

a lyricist and composer. But I then spread the word outside industry circles that I would be willing to consider aspirants
without any professional credits. I was pleasantly surprised to
hear from people in both ranks.

One of the first calls came from Burton Lane, the renowned
composer whose work includes the scores for *Finian's Rainbow*,
On a Clear Day You Can See Forever, and a long list of hit songs.
When I sent him a copy of Ossie's play I received an immediate
and excited positive response. He asked if I had a lyricist and of
course I replied that I would immediately call Yip Harburg,
Lane's equally famous collaborator on *Finian's Rainbow*. There
was a slight pause before Burton said he would also make some
inquiries. I didn't understand this until I spoke to Harburg who
said emphatically of Lane, "Not if he was the only composer on
earth." Yip Harburg was not a reticent man. I found out soon
afterwards that on their last collaboration they had had many violent disagreements and would never work together again.

I called Sheldon Harnick, who was too busy to take *Purlie* on
but was very encouraging about its possibilities. One day I heard
from Frank Loesser, who invited me to lunch to tell me he was
taken by the idea and would read the play. He also cautioned me
that if he were to take it on he would do it all himself—book,
music, and lyrics. I countered this by offering him sets, costumes, and checkroom concessions if he agreed to write *Purlie*.
He promised to get back to me quickly. Loesser, for anyone who
doesn't recall, wrote words and music for, among other hits,
Guys and Dolls, one of the greatest musicals ever.

Loesser called me a few days later and said he had written an
abbreviated structure for the book and some song ideas that he
would send to me. He also said he would like to meet Ossie
Davis so I set up a lunch date for the three of us. I had to assure
Ossie that this did not mean he would have to be very involved;
it was just a courtesy. Meanwhile, I read through what Loesser
had done and found it intriguing but frustrating in its brevity.

While the three of us did have our lunch at the Russian Tea Room, I believe its only purpose was for Frank Loesser to socialize and to express his admiration for Ossie's play. About two weeks later, when I again had lunch with Frank, this time alone, he told me that he was reluctantly bowing out of the project, for an interesting reason. He thought the play was too funny to be interrupted by the performance of songs, and in fact, didn't think it could be enhanced in that way. Also at that point in his career he said he was searching for a more serious libretto.

Soon after this rejection a Mr. Peter Udell called me. He had heard about my search for a lyricist through Frank Loesser's attorney. Mr. Udell arrived at my office with a track record of several rhythm and blues and early rock songs. I enjoyed reading through his book of lyrics and was especially impressed with "First Thing Monday Morning," a presumably innocuous song about going shopping, which I could envision onstage having the serious implications of a threat. As I began to think I might have found my lyricist, Peter told me he had worked as a stock-boy in Mr. Loesser's publishing company, Frank Music. It was there that he first thought about writing lyrics and showed one of his efforts to an associate of Mr. Loesser. That gentleman chose to show it to Frank, who fired Mr. Udell from his stock-boy job immediately and hired him as a songwriter for Frank Music. Mr. Loesser proceeded to teach Peter a lot about the technique of songwriting, and indeed became Peter's mentor.

This fortunate development, following so soon after Frank's reluctant exit, was too much for me to ignore, and I decided right then that if I couldn't get the master I would employ his star student. I told Peter, "Get me an acceptable composer and the job is yours." Peter said he already had somebody in mind and would get back to me. I asked if they had written together and he mentioned a hit song called "Sealed with a Kiss." I knew the song well, as did most of the young people in the country and even a few of us older ones.

Peter called me in a few days and said I could now talk to his partner, Gary Geld. When I asked if we could meet the following day, I learned that Gary was in California and had no plans to return, but he would like to talk to me. I called him and he assured me that we could start work immediately; as Peter and I wrote the script and lyrics, we could send the material to him and he would then write the music and play it for us over the telephone.

I was now undertaking not only to raise money for and produce *Purlie* as a musical but also to direct it and work closely with Peter Udell on the book and lyrics. I suspected that working long distance with our composer was not the ideal way to collaborate. When Peter and I talked about this, he suggested that we get to work and send some lyrics to Gary. If I was unhappy with what Gary then sang and played for us over the telephone, we could look for another composer. Of course, we would have to allow for busy telephone lines, static, or perhaps even wrong numbers.

So our labors began. There were two elements we quickly agreed upon. We wanted a large opening number, a celebration of Purlie really being victorious. In other words, the end of the play would be the opening of our show, and we would then flash back to tell the story of his struggle to win back his church from Ol' Cap'n, the plantation owner, our villain. We wanted this to be a gospel number that included the entire company in an explosion of song and dance. We also decided that the scene would encompass Ol' Cap'n's funeral service, with his coffin upright on the stage, because he was "the only man who ever died standin' up" and was therefore going to be buried vertically.

Very soon Peter came to me with his opening lyric, "Walk Him up the Stairs," a funny and satiric comment on Ol' Cap'n on his way to heaven but not likely to get there. I thought the title and the image were perfect as were all the words. However, as Peter recited them to me several times, I realized that the rhythm of the repeating phrase, "Walk Him up the Stairs," was exactly that of a famous gospel hymn called "Bringing in the Sheaves." I told Peter, "If we send this to Gary we'll be giving him an almost impossible problem." Peter announced, "Well, let's do it anyway and see what he comes up with."

Gary Geld must have called me within five minutes after he received the lyric in the mail. His first line was, "Are you guys nuts? You've just sent me 'Bringing in the Sheaves.' What am I supposed to do with that?" He didn't wait for my answer and hung up the phone. Well, I thought, this is going to be the shortest collaboration ever. But within a day, Gary called to play and sing us our opening number. What he had done was to take "Walk Him up the Stairs" and shorten it to "Walk Him Up," repeating this through several bars of music to which at the end he added the words, "the Stairs." Changing the rhythmic structure, he had made the problem disappear. He wrote a lovely melody for the song, one which provided a churchly opening as the curtain went up and then became our rousing uptempo gospel celebration. Peter and I were left with the almost insurmountable task of trying to maintain the excitement and joy of that ten-minute opening number for the next two hours. We came close to doing that some of the time and, fortunately, we could justify returning to the song at the end of the show by reprising it as our concluding funeral celebration. After hearing what Gary had written, I recognized that our long distance collaboration had officially begun, though I insisted on and received a commitment from Gary to come to New York when we approached actual production.

In consultation with Peter and Gary, I chose as orchestrator for our show a man they had worked with many years before who also had a background of rhythm and blues and early rock music. His last name was Sherman, his first (unfortunately) was also Gary, but since he was an extraordinarily talented musician, initially I wasn't bothered by that flaw. As it turned out, we then hired an orchestra contractor and percussionist whose last name was Chester but who also had a first name of Gary. Consequently, during our rehearsals with orchestra, when I heard something that bothered me and yelled for Gary, I was always sure of an immediate response, though not necessarily from the person I wanted. By then I resolved that the next appointment to the music department would go to the first applicant who wasn't called Gary. That man turned out to be Luther Henderson; he not only filled the name requirement but was a brilliant orchestrator who worked with Gary Sherman to create wonderful song and dance charts.

The next principal to be chosen for our musical staff was the conductor, who would be crucial to putting the orchestra together and holding it together, we hoped, for many months to come. I was well aware that in the orchestra pits of Broadway shows there were very few female musicians, and almost a complete absence of black musicians, male or female. The excuse usually given was that while there were undoubtedly many talented black musicians, most of them could not read music. Well, I made it clear to our contractor, Gary Chester, that I wanted a number of black musicians in the orchestra, though I of course did not give him a quota. And then I thought how nice it would be to have a black woman as our conductor: someone who would not be hidden below in the orchestra pit but would stand on her podium to be seen from the beginning of the show to the end.

We found that woman in the person of Joyce Brown; not only was she always in view of the audience, she turned out to be a highly kinetic, almost dancing figure, a conductor as charismatic in her way as Leonard Bernstein or Leopold Stokowski. Reviewers almost always cited her as an exciting performer and, believe it or not, she could also read music. Soon after Ms. Brown was signed I met a young choreographer, Louis Johnson, and asked him to join our staff. Now, with our musical department in place, we were ready to take on the tasks of casting the play and raising the money.

As I began making the usual phone calls for money, I realized that I again had a project that was not going to be easily financed. I explained to Gary Geld that we had to accelerate our long distance phone meetings and soon bring them to an end, because I needed a composer in New York to play the score for potential investors and theatre owners and to help in casting everyone from leading actors to chorus members. We agreed on a date when Gary would arrive, and meanwhile I began to see and in some cases audition actors and singers in my office.

Purlie Victorious, which had opened on Broadway in 1961, was easily high on my list of favorite plays. And while I retained vivid memories of the performances of the wonderful cast headed by Ossie Davis and Ruby Dee, I knew I now had to be responsive to all the additional and different talents a musical requires, singing and dancing only the most obvious ones. Among the performers who first auditioned for the role of Purlie were Cleavon Little, Lou Gossett Jr., and Moses Gunn, all of them very fine actors. I definitely decided to have Gossett and Gunn return for a second audition that included singing. I had already worked with Lou Gossett in *Raisin* and we were friends. Moses Gunn I knew only casually but admired greatly. I had seen Cleavon Little perform off-Broadway and been very impressed. But Cleavon, in his reading for me, strangely read Purlie as a very defeated man right from the outset. When we discussed this and I asked that he consider Purlie as someone who would never accept defeat as final, he disagreed and would not try a new approach. I asked him to think about it but he refused again and left my office. I then asked his agent if he could possibly convince Cleavon to come back and discuss the role further, only to be told later that Cleavon's answer was no.

While I disagreed with Cleavon's choices, I was impressed with his reading, and well aware that his ego had been bruised by my rejection of his interpretation. I sensed that if I could break through the armor that every actor wears to deal with rejection, Cleavon could be a brilliant Purlie. So I didn't put him out of my mind.

One day my assistant Lynda said there was a very young man in her office, with no appointment, who would very much like to see me. He came in, this rather shy, short, and not particularly impressive-looking young man, and said he would like to audition for the role of Gitlow in *Purlie*. We talked a bit and then I said Lynda would set up an appointment for him when I planned my general auditions. He replied that he might not be able to come back at another time. It seemed he had come to my office all the way from Philadelphia, without an appointment and unaware that it might be impossible even to get into the office of a Broadway producer, much less get an audition. It also became apparent that not only would he not be able to come back at a later date but that he barely had the money to return to Philadelphia. As we continued our conversation, he informed me that he had once done the role of Gitlow in a school production of *Purlie Victorious* and had come to New York certain he would get the part: could he possibly audition for me "right now." I hesitated briefly, then found two scripts, offered him one, and chose a particular scene. He said he wouldn't need the script and I began to read with him, amazed that he knew the role so well. And soon I was so impressed by how beautifully he performed it that I didn't let him finish the scene. I talked to him a while longer, then persuaded him to accept my money, go out for a sandwich, and return an hour later.

When he left I asked Lynda if she had ever seen or heard from him before and she assured me he had just walked in off the street. I told her that unless I had imagined the whole thing, he was possibly coming back, and if he read anywhere near as well, I would hire him that very day. When he returned I had Lynda join me in my office to hear his reading. Afterwards, I told him he had a job, his first professional role ever, in a Broadway play. He seemed to hold back tears as he thanked me, but then he almost casually accompanied Lynda to her desk to give her all the important details we needed—including his name, which was Sherman Hemsley. Sherman's first reading of Gitlow was to be repeated over several hundred performances of *Purlie,* including the video. He was incredibly consistent, even, some people thought, to the point of later becoming a star by recreating a very similar character in the hit television series, *The Jeffersons.*

I knew and respected actress Novella Nelson for her active role in the civil rights struggle. An accomplished and serious actor-singer, I thought she would be right for the role of Gitlow's wife. She could bring to the part the kind of dignity I wanted to counter the cartoon quality of the Gitlow character. However, when I contacted her agent, I was soon told Novella was not interested. I was quite surprised because though Novella had achieved a glowing reputation as a singing actor, there weren't many such roles being offered on Broadway, so I followed up with a phone call and spoke to Novella directly. After thanking me for my interest, she said she would never consider participating in an "Uncle Tom" play. I was shocked. I assumed she had seen the original *Purlie Victorious,* but she had not. When I then asked if she had read the play, the answer again was no. She had to admit her strong opposition was based solely on what she had heard about the subject matter of the 1961 production. After further conversation, I persuaded her to come to my office for a chat.

Novella's opinion, based as it was on neither firsthand involvement in or knowledge of the play, reminded me of why we had had such difficulty attracting both black and white audiences to our original production, and strengthened my resolve to correct some false perceptions of *Purlie Victorious* as an "Uncle Tom" play or, worse, as a denigration of the civil rights struggle.

When Novella arrived, I explained my feelings about the play and emphasized that by reaching a negative view without even having seen it, she was doing an injustice to herself as well as to the play. To refuse to even read a script that held a major role for her exhibited further shortsightedness. But I finally used my most potent argument when I said, "Novella, forget me and my life in and out of the theatre. Do you really think—or can you allow yourself to imagine—that Ossie Davis and Ruby Dee could have written and performed any piece that degraded black people?" Novella took the script out of my hand, walked out of my office, and came on board a few weeks later. She was wonderful in the part, much better than she was as a bridge player, as my wife and I discovered many weeks later.

At about this time, Gary Geld arrived in New York to complete writing the music and to begin the process of working with the orchestrators, helping with casting the chorus members, and generally overseeing the music department. Gary and I first met at the apartment he was renting and there I had my first personal disorienting encounter with a musical genius. After I arrived at his temporary abode, I went from room to room looking for a piano I could not find. When I asked when the piano would be arriving, he answered with a question: "Why would I need a piano?" In my ignorance I reminded him that lots of music was still to be written, to which he replied, gently and comfortingly, "Yes, and when you need to hear it I can play it on your piano or at a studio. I don't need to hear it." That turned out to be true. Gary Geld heard complete arrangements in his head, which never ceased to surprise me. His first name wasn't even Wolfgang or Amadeus. And he finally did get a piano, just to satisfy me.

I was having a hard time coming up with Lutibelle, the costarring role, played so spectacularly by Ruby Dee in 1961. In my office I was seeing well-known professionals as well as newcomers, and I was probably unfairly comparing all of them to her. Then I received a call from a young woman who was appearing on Broadway in the musical *Hair*. Someone in that show had already auditioned for us and told her about *Purlie* and the role of Lutibelle. When, invited, she arrived at my office and we began to talk, something began to happen for me very quickly, and to this moment I'm not sure why but I asked her to come back and read for me. She returned soon afterwards, and I was stunned not only by the quality of her reading, but by her complete grasp of the character, because as far as I knew she'd had no training as an actor. Just recently Melba reminded me that after the reading I took her to lunch at the Russian Tea Room and she told me that until the age of ten she was raised in New York by a woman, not her mother, after whom she had patterned her character. That may not have been a Stanislavsky approach, but it was enough for me, and I told Melba Moore she had the part.

We were now getting close to having to choose our Purlie, and I was about to ask Moses Gunn and Lou Gossett Jr. to return for final acting and singing auditions. I decided to take one more shot at Cleavon, who no doubt by now would have heard through the Broadway grapevine that we had made casting progress and that actors of such stature as Moses Gunn and Lou Gossett were being considered for the role. The third time around, Cleavon was slightly more receptive and agreed to come to my office for another reading. He arrived with an open mind about the character, and as we talked and read he became more animated and ready to try different things. I was soon able to see what he could do with the role, and I asked if he would come to a final audition in a theatre where, I told him frankly, his competition would be Moses Gunn and Lou Gossett Jr. This challenge was enough to turn the key, and he left assuring me he would not only audition but would land the part and *be* Purlie.

For these crucial auditions I had rented the Winter Garden Theatre for three hours, wanting to be sure there would be at least one hour for each of these fine actors to read and sing. Present in the theatre were of course Peter Udell, Gary Geld, and, briefly, Ossie Davis. Because I had not yet told Gary and Peter that I had found my own choice for Lutibelle, I had called Melba Moore and asked her if she would join us at the theatre for the men's auditions. I made it clear that this was nothing to be concerned or nervous about, just a favor to help us select our Purlie. She agreed and also came to the theatre that day.

We read Lou Gossett first. Of course he was very good, as was Melba, who read with him. We then had Moses Gunn read, and as I expected, it was a brilliant reading. What was astonishing was how Melba was able to adjust to a quite different reading and be even more captivating than the first time. As Peter Udell remembers, I then leaned over to him and said, "That's our Lutibelle!" When, his reading over, Gunn talked with us before he left, he seemed more interested in discussing Melba than himself, marveling and wondering where she came from. Since we had some time before Cleavon's scheduled arrival and our accompanist standing by, I asked Melba if she would like to sing something for us. She agreed, stepped up on stage, took just a brief moment at the piano, and sang a song from *Hair*. We were stunned, all of us. Nobody would quite believe that until that moment I had never heard her sing a note. I remember turning to Peter and saying, "We don't have enough for Lutibelle to sing in the show."

Cleavon arrived shortly afterwards and I was very pleased to see that he had come full circle. He now portrayed Purlie as this energetic, passionate young man who did not have the word defeat in his vocabulary. He was Purlie. I was very impressed with Moses Gunn, as well we all were, but finally Gary Geld made, I believe, the most perceptive comment to me. He agreed that in Moses Gunn we would have a fine actor who would give all the realistic qualities of the role in a straight play, but in Cleavon Little we would see the elusive personality elements that allowed us to accept or even expect his singing under the most serious circumstances. I also felt there was a chemistry and a look between Cleavon and Melba which was youthful and right. At last we had our leads.

We soon were holding auditions for singers and dancers. There, too, we were fortunate to find the superb talents who became our chorus, all performing as though they deserved to be stars, which indeed many of them became. Among our chorus was Linda Hopkins, whose voice opened the show. Linda went on to present her one-woman Bessie Smith show on Broadway to rave notices. We had a young dancer who almost stopped the show just by arriving late at church during the opening number and walking (dancing) across the stage, thereby unsettling Reverend Purlie. Her name was Debbie Allen. We had a tall young dancer, George Faison, who went on to do his own choreography for Broadway shows like *The Wiz*. Two other important nonsinging roles were filled by Helen Martin and John Heffernan, who was our villain, Cap'n Cotchipee.

We were coming close to assembling a complete company. Peter and Gary were working hard and fast to complete the score. I had hired Ben Edwards, Tom Skelton, and Ann Roth for sets, lighting, and costumes respectively. Everything was falling into place except those two perennial small items, the money and the theatre. Unexpectedly, a call came from the Shuberts offering us the Broadway Theatre, one of their largest, if I would make a commitment. I did, and now that I had a theatre and the cast, money began to come in to add to what I had already raised.

Some time before, through Peter Udell I had met Joe Abend, who was in the music and recording business. He had learned about *Purlie* through Peter and Gary Geld and was so enthusiastic about it, he arranged for me to meet a Mr. Don Hall, who was then CEO of a company called Ampex, the company manufacturing most of the equipment used in recording studios. Mr.

Hall, with whom I became quite friendly, was considering having Ampex start its own record label. After hearing our score, he decided to option the exclusive rights to record our show by investing in it. We arrived at an agreement that brought us some immediate funding. It allowed Ampex to proceed with the original cast album after opening night by making a further investment at that time; if they then decided against this, we would be free to try other record companies.

We set a rehearsal date in late January, shooting for an opening in mid-March of 1970, dates carefully chosen to ensure we would be eligible for that year's Tony Awards. As a general rule, the chorus of a new musical goes into rehearsal about a week before the principal actors. This was true in our case as Louis Johnson began to work with the dancers while the singers worked in another room with our conductor. The following week I started rehearsing with all the principals in a third room. The idea is to have each department move forward individually and then, as the days by, to see if everything could come together. To help coordinate the various needs, our stage managers would report back to the producers and of course keep the director informed of the progress being made in each room. At the same time, meetings were required with the composer, the lyricist, the book writers, costume people, orchestrator, et al., all of which were arranged by our very efficient stage managers. The only problem was that the crazy producer Philip Rose was often not available for meetings because he was directing the show or collaborating with Peter Udell on book or lyrics or observing the dance routines; and, at every break, he was on the telephone raising money for the show.

Nevertheless, as best as I could tell, each department was doing fairly well, though I did have some reservations about an elaborate ballet Louis Johnson was doing based on an idea of Peter Udell's. After about two weeks, we began to put the various pieces together so I could get a sense of the whole. In general, I was quite pleased by our progress, but with previews fast approaching, I was growing concerned about whether we could possibly meet our deadlines. I was always aware that we didn't have any out-of-town time to fix what wouldn't be ready.

But what was most increasingly worrisome was the shortage of money. We were approaching our third payroll week. By Equity rules, actors must be paid by Thursday evening. Otherwise Equity would take the money out of our bond, which would automatically close the show. Peter Udell and I, who had over the past few months gotten to know each other almost too well and therefore had very few secrets, had a meeting at which I told him I saw no way to raise the payroll of $15,000 that I would need by Thursday evening. Peter, who at that time was married to a woman whose father was a very successful doctor, called his mother-in-law. He may have had a better relationship with her than with his wife. She told us to meet her at her bank Thursday morning and to bring a large brown bag. Later that morning Peter and I deposited in the *Purlie* account $15,000 in ten and twenty-dollar bills. It took quite a while for the very suspicious teller to count it, but as far as I could tell we were not followed by the FBI. Obviously, Peter's mother-in-law became another investor.

During our third week we moved from the rehearsal space to the Broadway, the theatre that would be our home. This enabled us to use both the upstairs and downstairs lobbies as well as the stage for rehearsals. After our first run-through on stage, I realized we would not be ready to begin previews on the date scheduled. Though it would be costly, I considered postponing the first preview for a few days. That created a new problem: we then would not meet the eligibility date for the Tony Awards. I called my friend Alex Cohen, asked if we could get a one-week extension, and was told, with regrets, that the date was fixed and inalterable. I informed my associates that we had no choice but to move quickly to solve all our artistic problems and make whatever additional changes we could within the specified time. I remained concerned about the long ballet number, but was assured by Louis Johnson and Peter Udell that once I saw it with costumes and all the scenic effects, I would love it. And, in fact, at the first orchestra rehearsal I was indeed impressed by the beautiful score Luther Henderson had written for the ballet.

We played our first preview on February 25th, 1970. Not having gone out of town, I was prepared for the chaos of that first night. However, at our after-the-show meeting everybody agreed that with some time and money, we would be in very good shape. I had invited some friends and potential investors to that preview and was pleasantly surprised by the reaction from John Kelly, an executive at my local Chase Bank who handled my theatre accounts (and was always invited to my opening nights). The next day Mr. Kelly called to tell me that because he was absolutely certain I had another hit (I did not argue the point), any shortage in our account for the payroll checks would be temporarily covered by the bank. He was confident that the bank would be completely reimbursed right after opening night. Once again I chose not to argue with him. He remained my friend for years afterward.

Just a few days later I was stunned by a not-so-welcome piece of news about a musical called *Applause,* starring Lauren Bacall, a musical scheduled for the Palace Theatre some time after our opening and therefore not eligible for the Tonys. Suddenly it was announced that the eligibility date was being postponed to allow *Applause* to be considered. I called my friend Alex Cohen and received a not very satisfactory explanation from him as to why what was impossible just a few days ago for *Purlie* had suddenly become possible for *Applause.*

Meanwhile, the creative team worked all day and night to improve what was on the stage. It was now unavoidably evident to me, and reflected by audience reaction, that our ballet, the longest musical piece, was not working. I had persuaded

Johnson at least to reduce its length, which he was gradually doing, but somehow the more it was shortened, the longer it seemed. By now people in the audience, including those who sounded very positive on the way out, were heard making remarks like, "What was that thing in the middle?" A few days before opening night I had a private conference with Louis Johnson to tell him I was going to try the show that evening without the ballet. He was not pleased. We had our conversation in the downstairs lobby of the theatre, but I was told that our voices at times carried well into the theatre and even to the balcony, with no amplification necessary.

Because the ballet was a set piece in the show, with no particular relationship to the story line, all we had to do to strike it was to so inform the cast, the crew, and the orchestra. And at that night's performance it became obvious to all of us that we had made a major improvement, and I announced that the ballet was gone forever. This was not an easy decision for me to make: it meant discarding our most expensive set, over twenty of our most expensive costumes, over ten minutes of orchestrations for twenty-six musicians, and some of our most beautiful music. On top of that, we were eliminating a great opportunity for our dancing chorus to shine and were replacing it for them with two hours of boredom as they sat in their dressing rooms.

Therefore, it was no surprise when the next day I was invited to a meeting requested by the dancers to express their unhappiness to the producer, director, and co-author of *Purlie*. My stage manager made it clear that all three of us had better attend. I did, of course, and expressed my sympathy and understanding that of all the artists who work in musical theatre, the dancers more than anyone need and love to work hard. Perhaps I should have foreseen the problem early in rehearsal and replaced the ballet with something more effective. Now, four days before our official opening, there was nothing I could do. I did, however, offer to accept two weeks' notice from any dancer who wanted to leave after the opening. The meeting ended on a quiet and somber note.

Afterwards, as I went down to the lobby with Peter Udell and Gary Geld, I pointed out, and they agreed, that while the show was unquestionably better without the ballet, we now had two long dialogue scenes back to back, with no music in between to remind everyone that they were, after all, at a musical. While we recognized that the audience was adoring Melba Moore, we hadn't added anything to enhance her singing contribution. I told Peter and Gary, "Now's our chance! Write a song for her to put between those two scenes." Peter was at first somewhat resistant to writing a song with no other purpose than to give Melba another number but he promised to think about it. He thought so long that within hours he and Gary were playing a new song for me in the downstairs lobby of the theatre. We immediately had Melba break from rehearsal and come down to hear the song. Within minutes she memorized it, and Gary Geld called for our orchestrator, Gary Sherman, to come hear her sing it. I staged the number with Melba starting to sing the verse quietly in a rocking chair and exploding from it at the start of the chorus; at the following performance, two nights before our official opening, Melba Moore sang "I Got Love" for the first time and received an ovation. We had a hit song from *Purlie*. On opening night "I Got Love," and Melba Moore, were even more breathtaking.

On that opening night of March 15th, 1970, I was still short $100,000 of the money I was committed to raising. If we had opened and closed that week I would have had to come up with that amount personally to fulfill all our legal and ethical commitments. When the curtain came down, the first person to grab my hand and congratulate me was Don Hall of Ampex, who had that option for the album rights in return for a further investment. When I opened my hand after shaking his, I discovered a check for $100,000, the further investment that completed our deal.

We then, as usual, had to wait for the morning paper notices and, by that year, even some late-night television critics. We were quite pleased with most of them but probably most intrigued by the review of Walter Kerr, who had been one of the strongest supporters of *Purlie Victorious.* Mr. Kerr's reservations about the musical version, with specific reference to the song "First Thing Monday Morning," boiled down to his feeling that we had deliberately departed from the lighthearted, almost cartoon approach of the straight play to become more militant and serious about our country's racism in the musical. On the one hand, Peter and I, who had collaborated very closely in adapting Ossie's play, were grateful that Kerr had recognized what we had so intentionally done in both book and lyrics. On the other hand, I was shocked to read that he would have preferred laughing through the show without having to take it seriously. But I was particularly pleased that he had singled out "First Thing Monday Morning," which, as I mentioned earlier, Peter had written years before as an innocuous pop song. We used it to open our second act, when the audience no doubt expected to resume the laughter they had enjoyed at the first act curtain. Instead, they were greeted by a group of powerful black men singing about an implicit threat: come Monday morning, things might be different on the plantation called the U.S.

As time went on, I learned that for years some of our most prestigious theatre owners resisted bringing *Purlie* to their cities because, as one put it to me, "It's an attack on white people." Obviously, our musical had struck a defensive chord. However, we were reaching audiences both black and white, and I was happy to see more than the usual number of college and high school students in the theatre. Then, shortly after our opening, came the Tony Award musical nominations with several for *Purlie,* including Best Actor for Cleavon Little, Best Supporting Actress for Melba Moore, Best Director, and, most important from a business standpoint, Best Musical. I had already been contacted by Alex Cohen some time before to discuss the probability that we would receive some nominations and to choose what single number we would like to have performed on the Tony television show. I asked if we could possibly have two numbers and was told there would be no time for that. I tentatively settled for one.

There is a tradition that all the winners of Tony nominations attend an afternoon cocktail party at Sardi's, where they can be interviewed and photographed by the media. I escorted Cleavon and Melba to their assigned table while I moved to another table to make room for all the press then gathered around Lauren Bacall. I then watched and waited for the representatives of the Tony committee to bring the cameras and the interviewers to Cleavon and Melba. Time went by, and I grew angrier with each sip of my second drink. I finally got up, went back to the *Purlie* table, and said to Cleavon and Melba, "Let's get out of here." They followed me to the elevator quite depressed, if not quite as angry as I was. As we arrived there, somebody from the Tony staff came running up to ask us what was wrong and where we were going. I told him nothing was wrong but I was planning our own meeting with the press later on and had to rush off. In a fraction of a second Alex Cohen came to apologize and say that everybody was now ready and anxious to meet Cleavon and Melba and to ask if we would come back. I looked at Melba and Cleavon and since I could tell they really wanted to meet the press, I agreed.

As we were escorted back by Alex, I found a moment to tell him we would not do the Tony television show. When the next morning he asked me to reconsider, I reminded him how after our request for a few days' postponement of the Tony deadline had been turned down, it was then granted to *Applause*. He asked what he could do to satisfy us, and I said I wanted two spots on the television show instead of one. He first said there was no time, then said he would get back to me, which he did.

So it came about that our two best numbers were performed on the Tony show, to tremendous response. Of course, *Applause* won the most important award, Best Musical, which seemed preordained, but Cleavon Little and Melba Moore did win the awards for best performances in a musical.

When Ampex released the album of *Purlie* (which Gary Geld produced), it was hailed by the critic of the *New York Times* as the best album of a musical since *My Fair Lady*. Some years later a staged performance of *Purlie* was filmed by Fox Television with many of the original cast returning to their roles. This unfortunately has become a collector's item, since Fox later ceased distribution of the video. But it was shown extensively on PBS as one of their most successful fund-raisers. In the last few years *Purlie* has earned recognition as an often-performed classic in professional and amateur theatres and also, I'm pleased to say, in schools everywhere. It even led Ossie Davis to admit in his autobiography that while he still dislikes all musicals he has come to enjoy the continuing residuals this one provides. And, like it or not, Ossie still deserves a large portion of the credit, because *Purlie Victorious* was his child, born in 1961, who came to maturity as *Purlie* in 1970.

*Philip Rose
and Melba Moore*

PLAYBILL
The Broadway Theatre
the national magazine for theatregoers

PURLIE

Cleavon Little

From left:
Novella Nelson, Melba Moore,
Sherman Hemsley, and Cleavon Little

Carol Jean Lewis, Patti Joe,
Sherman Helmsley,
and Cleavon Little

Entire
company
of "Purlie"

Novella Nelson

Zodiac

Moore, Little: Beautiful

Down Home

The rarest commodity on Broadway is simple human intelligence. Congratulations are therefore due to Philip Rose, who produced, co-authored the book, and directed **PURLIE,** for the intelligence and taste he demonstrates in all of his roles. A Broadway musical is a cooperative affair, and Rose has ingeniously managed to use only good people. Composer Gary Geld and lyricist Peter Udell have produced a clean, bright, varied score in a country-gospel-folk-rock vein. The arrangements, by Garry Sherman and Luther Henderson, are unusually good; choreographer Louis Johnson seems to have touched everything with cadence and grace; Joyce Brown, the first black woman ever to conduct the opening of a Broadway musical, does the best job in the pit I have ever seen, infecting the entire show with her musicianship, vitality and upbeat emotion.

Cleavon Little has always been a terrific actor, mostly saddled with dog shows; as Purlie he stretches out in his spacious, sharp, savory style. Melba Moore is sweet, cleverly funny, brilliant in her touching, trumpeting, rousingly theatrical soul singing. Novella Nelson is dramatic and strong in presence and voice; her duet with Little, "Down Home," is the best Broadway number in a long time. The book, based on Ossie Davis's 1961 play "Purlie Victorious," about a black Georgia preacher who outwits ole massa, is dated in the context of today's racial situation. But why shouldn't we be reminded, as a reactionary Administration turns back the clock, of the prideful, morally simple beginnings of the black man's revolution? There is something beautiful about "Purlie," and it's all black.

—JACK KROLL

Newsweek, March 30, 1970

Chapter 25

During the early 1970s the entire country was torn by the continuing and controversial Vietnam War. I believed that it was an unjust war, so the argument that we had no choice but to continue our tragic deadly involvement had no validity for me. However, I was also aware of, and wondered about, the position held by some that there was never any just war. Accepting that, I would have to include the war against Nazi Germany, which I could not, for a moment, even consider. But I often pondered my own feelings about the use of violence in a good cause.

Peter Udell and I had for some time been searching for another musical project to work on together. Of course, we had also discussed the Vietnam War and my somewhat ambivalent position about violence. One day he asked if I had ever seen the Jimmy Stewart movie *Shenandoah*. Peter had just seen it on television and been impressed. I vaguely remembered it and was equally enthusiastic. Peter agreed to try to come up with at least one conceptual song that would point him in the right direction toward a full score.

The story of *Shenandoah* centers on the Andersons, a Southern family during the Civil War, the father raising six sons and a daughter, his wife having died at the birth of his youngest son. Charlie Anderson refused to permit any of his sons to join the Confederate army, not because he was pro-North, or on either side, but because he was fervently opposed to any war.

Within a relatively short time, Peter came up with ideas and partial lyrics for two songs, one Anderson's personal antiwar anthem, "I've Heard It All Before," the other his "Meditation" on his farm and his family and how his love for them outweighed all other responsibilities, including fighting a war. Peter and I knew immediately that we had our conflict and point of view outlined, and we proceeded to begin writing the book and lyrics, once again with Gary Geld composing the music. But this time Gary would join us in New York immediately, and he would be the only Gary I would hire. I contacted James Lee Barrett, the writer of the original screenplay, and, after some negotiations with him and Universal Pictures, secured the rights to do the stage adaptation.

The writing progressed quite rapidly for both the score and the book, with Peter and I again working very hard to make book and lyrics as seamless and complementary as we could, with our disagreements lasting until one of us won the argument. In much less time than expected, we had enough material to begin holding backers' auditions and to think about the casting. The early reactions to our story and music tended to confirm our own feelings that we had a strong story enriched with beautiful, melodic music. The trio of Gary Geld, Peter Udell, and myself performing in my living room contributed to the enjoyable and relaxed atmosphere. It didn't hurt that Gary was a brilliant pianist who could bring out the eclecticism of the score.

It soon became obvious that we were creating an enormously demanding leading role, one that would require an exceptionally talented actor-singer. Not too many people would write checks without knowing who that actor was. So as I began to search for him, I first went after the most obvious choice: well, why not Jimmy Stewart? He had been a stage actor first, returning to Broadway from time to time. He would certainly ensure loads of theatre parties, bring us all our investors, and get us a theatre. Furthermore, we had the movie as his audition. I sent him the script and a music tape, and received the following letter in reply.

JAMES STEWART
9201 WILSHIRE BOULEVARD
BEVERLY HILLS, CALIFORNIA 90210

May 9, 1972

Mr. Philip Rose
157 West 57th Street
New York, New York 10019

Dear Mr. Rose:

I have just finished reading the new musical
version of "SHENANDOAH" which Jim Barrett gave
to me yesterday. I was tremendously moved by
the story in this form, even more so I believe
than I was when I read the first draft that Jim
gave me of the original movie script. The music
seems to strengthen the original concept in a
very dramatic and exciting way.

As I told Jim, I only wish I was ten years
younger and had a voice. I don't know exactly
what kind of a voice, but some kind of a voice.
However, this is not the case so I guess we'll
have to leave it at that.

I can see that this will be a very demanding and
large project for you and I hope that you will
have tremendous success with it.

Sincerely,

James Stewart

mb

My second choice was Robert Ryan, whom I knew as a fine actor with a stage background and some singing ability. Moreover, I was certain that he would respond to the subject matter of *Shenandoah* and the issues it raised. I sent him a script and he responded almost at once that we should meet immediately. I went up to his apartment and spent a lovely afternoon of Ryan trying to persuade me that he and only he should play this part. I did not protest too much, and we went on to discuss his schedule, all the political issues of the day, and *Shenandoah*. We found very little room for disagreement. I left his apartment with instructions to contact his agent and to send him the available songs from the show, which he was eager to learn. Peter and Gary were as excited as I that we now had an image of Charlie Anderson to write for, an image that for all of us looked exactly like Robert Ryan. I was able to seriously begin raising money and getting a theatre.

After a few months, while I did not yet have a theatre, with the promise of Ryan's participation the money had started coming in and we were moving ahead nicely in other areas. We tentatively planned to open in late 1973. Gary and I were able to hire as orchestrator Don Walker, whose previous shows included *Carousel, The Pajama Game, The Music Man* and *Fiddler on the Roof*, and chose Robert Tucker to be our choreographer. Meanwhile, Robert Ryan had been working hard with a singing coach and learning all the songs. Then, suddenly, one day everything came to a halt. I was shocked and devastated to receive a cable from his agent informing me that Mr. Ryan had just died of cancer. What a terrible loss to us, to his family, and to his many friends and associates. The date was July 11, 1973.

I now had to start over again, and also to return most of the money that I had raised on the strength of Robert Ryan's name. A deep depression descended on my creative team, who seemed to share an unspoken acceptance that *Shenandoah* was finished. Gary Geld returned to California. Work came to an abrupt halt. Some sleepless nights later, as often occurs, I had an inspiration. I jumped out of bed to write down "Gregory Peck!!!" and the following morning I began my attempts to reach him. I was finally assured by his agent that if sent, my script would be forwarded to Mr. Peck. I did send the script, and was pleased and surprised to receive a phone call soon afterwards from Gregory Peck himself. He was very much impressed by the book and lyrics and looked forward to hearing the music at our mutual convenience; I said that any time or place, including the ends of the earth, was agreeable to me, and we set a date for a Tuesday about three weeks away, when I would be in L.A. working with Gary Geld. Peck later told me one of the reasons for his quick response was that he had originally been offered the movie of *Shenandoah* and had turned it down. He didn't want to make the same mistake again.

I called Peter and Gary immediately and, needless to say, their excitement was equal to mine. We knew that bringing Gregory Peck to Broadway would pretty much guarantee sold-out houses for as long as he chose to play the part of Charlie Anderson. I made reservations for Peter and me at a "reasonable" hotel, since I was already deeply in debt from advances and expenses, as well as the investments I was forced to return after Mr. Ryan's death. But when Gary heard where we were planning to stay he went berserk, saying, "There is only one place to entertain Gregory Peck and audition for him, and that's at the Beverly Hills Hotel."

Back in the 1970s that hotel, with its "cottages," its Polo Lounge, and its swimming pool, was still known as the place all the important deals got made. Peter and I might have settled for the YMCA, but Gary, a long-time resident of California, was imbued with L.A. culture. At the insistence of Gary, I agreed to let him use his influence to get me a room for two nights at the Beverly Hills. He also promised to ensure that the hotel would provide my room with a piano for the audition. Peter booked himself into the middle-range Sunset Marquis hotel.

I arrived in L.A. on a Monday. Peter and Gary were waiting for me in the Beverly Hills lobby, and we were escorted to my "room." It turned out to be an enormous suite that included a living room with three large couches and enough chairs for three separate seating areas. It also contained (moved in at Gary's instructions) a large grand piano which, in the space, was hardly noticeable. I didn't count the bathrooms, but I did notice two enormous beds for use in the bedroom if I were planning to entertain there.

I was flabbergasted. I asked Gary if he had any idea what this would cost, and he said he didn't want to embarrass me by asking. But he added, "It's only two nights and if we get Greg, you can legitimately charge it to the company. Besides, we've already told him where we will be tomorrow, so it's too late to change." I had no choice but to agree, and we arranged to run through our planned audition the following morning, just before Peck was due to arrive at 11:00 A.M.

Tuesday morning, Gary and Peter turned up at my suite and just as we began rehearsing, the phone rang. It was Gregory Peck's secretary, informing me he had been delayed out of town and would like to reschedule the audition for Wednesday or Thursday. I swallowed once and then spoke the obligatory "No problem" as I hung up the phone. I related the happy news to my associates, then wondered aloud if Gary, with his contacts, could possibly invite Bing Crosby or somebody like that to the brunch we had ordered for Mr. Peck—anybody we could just sing a few songs for. Or maybe there was a dance company in town that needed rehearsal space.

I received my next call on Thursday morning, when I learned that Mr. Peck was now in Washington, D.C., on some important political business (with, I suspected, the President), but he was looking forward to seeing us on the weekend. By now I had grown accustomed to my accommodations, and realized this was not a bad way to live, having so far not paid out a dime. I was spending the time seeing friends and coming and going to my suite as though I belonged there. We set a new date for Saturday, with assurances from Greg (we were now on a first-name basis) that he would definitely be back in town by then.

When I returned to my suite on Friday afternoon, there was a note indicating that the hotel manager would like to see me. I wondered whether the hotel had now checked my bank account, but in fact I found the manager to be courteous and apologetic, as he explained I would have to be moved to a different suite. He had waited for my return so that this could be done in my presence. When I asked the reason for the move, I was told my suite had been booked months before for a wedding party. When I then asked why the wedding party couldn't be put in the other suite, he answered that the party was for 150 people and my suite was the only one large enough to accommodate them. He did emphasize that since I had originally been booked for two nights, he hadn't expected I would still be there on Saturday, and he volunteered that I would be given one day's credit on the new suite for any inconvenience caused me. Of course, they also had to move the piano.

The following morning, Saturday, when Gary and Peter arrived at my new suite, Peter immediately commented on how crowded we were. Then the phone rang. Peter and Gary were already laughing when I answered it. I will now, as closely as I can remember, quote Greg: "Philip, as you know I've had a very busy time and been away from my family all week, so I wondered if you fellows would mind coming over to my house tomorrow? We can relax, have coffee, get to know each other, and I can hear the score. I have a wonderful piano. What do you say?" I of course said "yes," enthusiastically, and resisted asking if there would be any charge for use of the space. Gregory Peck never saw my suite at the Beverly Hills. I could have stayed at the YMCA and left California with several thousand more dollars to invest in *Shenandoah*.

We did, indeed, do our audition the next day and enjoyed a wonderful afternoon with Gregory Peck, a warm, friendly, and charming man who reacted quite favorably to our presentation. We admired his beautiful home and were introduced to his lovely wife, who was as hospitable as our host. Peck did express some doubt as to whether he was up to the demands of the score, but Gary hastened to assure him that we were flexible in that area, making the obvious reference to Rex Harrison's performance in *My Fair Lady*. When we left, Peter and I knew we had tempted him but nonetheless were facing long odds. As I'd expected him to be, Peck was considerate and called me within just a few days. Unfortunately, he was forced to say no to coming to Broadway, not because of any reservations about our project, which he loved, but because some important personal and scheduling considerations made it impossible.

Of course, our disappointment was almost palpable, but I was pleased that through the many months that followed, up to and including opening night, we had unstinting support from Gregory Peck. Not only that, but he would call me when he was in New York to invite me to his suite at the Waldorf where we would chat about things he was involved in, particularly a film he was producing. Later I was invited to its opening. I lost a great star, but gained a great acquaintance.

After returning to New York, Peter Udell related to me an incident that had occurred while he was at the Sunset Marquis in L.A. Sitting at the swimming pool one day he recognized Zero Mostel as a fellow guest. They got into a conversation inevitably about theatre and Peter mentioned that he was working with me on a new project. Zero, who knew me and my background quite well, exploded in his inimitable fashion, "Enough already you guys with your shows about blacks! When are you going to write a show for a talented Jew like me?" Peter, no more shy than Zero, responded, "We've just written one. It's about this Southern Jewish landowner during the Civil War. Would you like to audition?" As a result of this conversation and, I suspect, swimming while swallowing something more potent than water, Peter promised to have me set up an audition for Zero upon our mutual return to New York.

When we arrived home I spoke to Zero and sent him a script including some music from *Shenandoah*. Shortly afterwards, with the approval of Sam Cohn, Zero's very prominent agent, we arranged a meeting at Zero's Central Park West apartment.

On our way to that apartment, Peter and I were making all the obvious jokes about Tevye becoming the head of our Southern family, and the fun continued when we arrived at Zero's home with Gary, our composer, and Merle Debuskey, our press agent. Finally the moment came when Gary went to the piano and Zero read the lines leading into "The Pickers Are Comin'." Zero then proceeded to do a very moving performance of that song from *Shenandoah*. Afterwards we sat around a table and had some lunch while enjoying a lovely afternoon.

When we left the apartment, Peter, Gary, and I were seriously considering committing ourselves to this unusual casting decision, but whatever reservations we had became moot when several days later Sam Cohn called to say that Zero would not be available for our show. I have always felt it was Sam's decision rather than Zero's but I might be wrong.

From left: Philip Rose,
Gary Gold, Peter Udell, and Zero Mostel

From left:
Philip Rose, Gary Gold,
and Zero Mostel

Several days later I heard from an agent representing Jack Palance, then one of Hollywood's most charismatic and scary villains, who wanted to see the script and be considered for the lead in *Shenandoah*. To demonstrate how serious his interest was, I was sent a résumé of Mr. Palance's stage career, which was impressive, plus an album of songs, recorded and released, that displayed his singing ability and musicianship. I immediately sent out the script and soon after was asked to set up a meeting with Mr. Palance at my office. With some trepidation, my assistant Lynda complied. She wasn't sure, however, that she wanted to be in her office when he arrived. I told her I would protect her, and if that didn't work she could protect me.

Mr. Palance's arrival at my office was an event. We heard about it later from the elevator operator and other people who shared that ride with him. He was an enormous presence, his height (my guess, six foot five) being only part of that. His features up close were a unique mixture of strangeness and attractiveness. He was not a man who could under any circumstances be ignored. As we shook hands and I invited him to sit on my couch, I found it a bit disconcerting that even as he sat down and I stood beside him he was still much taller than I was. I imagined that if I were directing him, I would have to do so from a specially constructed high chair. But our meeting was quite interesting and rewarding. He was eloquent about the script and the role. The one concern I raised was about his way of speaking: that his whispery voice, which was so effective in frightening people could be problematic on stage. He admitted to the same concern and promised to work with a voice coach if he were hired. As he was leaving my office, Lynda summoned enough courage to shake his hand, with hers just slightly trembling. I wasn't sure whether she was scared or aroused.

We were now moving into the fall of 1973 and Gary and Peter warned that if we didn't get going quickly, we might as well drop this project and move on. When I suggested taking our chances with Jack Palance, they only made one demand of me. I would have to be the one who handled any artistic confrontation with him, and they would have the right to photograph it. I signed a contract with Palance on October 1, 1973, planning to go into rehearsals in early 1974. I had approximately six months in which to raise the money and find a theatre. I thought that with Palance as the star, neither would be too difficult. What I began to discover was that while some of my investors were pleased, just as many or more were hesitant or even opposed to the idea of this "scary" man playing our very sympathetic role. As a result, at the beginning of 1974 I was still far from being sufficiently financed to begin production.

One day I received a call from Michael Price, who ran the Goodspeed Opera House in East Haddam, Connecticut. He said he had an opening during his forthcoming summer season, and had heard good things about *Shenandoah*. Would I consider bringing it to Goodspeed? This meant I could reduce my investment needs, since Goodspeed would provide the theatre, the sets, costumes, orchestra, etc. Michael read the script and a few days later heard the score in my office. He immediately agreed to present the show at Goodspeed, with me as the director and Jack Palance as the star. Because I had to get an extension of Palance's contract in order to go into rehearsal in July and open at Goodspeed in August, I immediately called him and his agent. They both agreed to my request, saying it would give Palance more time to get into shape vocally. Of course, the Goodspeed theatre, being very small, paid a top salary of only $750 per week. When we moved to Broadway, his salary would revert to his Equity contract of $5000 per week and a percentage of the gross.

We began choosing the rest of the cast for the Goodspeed production, but sometime in March I received calls from Palance's California agents and attorneys. They said he could not do the Goodspeed production unless he received his Broadway salary. I pointed out the obvious: the Goodspeed Opera House was not a Broadway theatre, but a small regional theatre—they might not be able to gross $5000 per week, much less pay that to one actor. Mr. Palance would be getting their top salary, and his engagement could be considered a rehearsal period for Broadway. In reply they simply repeated their demands. When I called Palance, in Pennsylvania, he said, "Don't worry. I want to do Goodspeed. It's no problem." More weeks went by. Michael Price reminded me that he had to have a signed contract to start his publicity, and we were approaching Goodspeed's deadline. But I kept receiving mixed signals from Palance and his representatives, and no agreement.

One day when I discussed my dilemma with Morty Halpern, my dear friend and great stage manager, he said, "You know, you ought to meet this actor who's working for me out at Jones Beach. He's not a big star, but he's very good. His name is John Cullum." I had vaguely heard of John and knew he had appeared in many musical revivals in stock or regional theatres. I told Morty to give him a script and have him call me. A few days later John called, and I invited him to my office.

When he walked in, with his *Hamlet* haircut and looking thirty years old, his first words to me were "I'm much too young for this part," as indeed he was. Then he began to offer me his suggestions for the actors I should consider: Alfred Drake, Richard Kiley, Robert Preston (all of whom had turned me down). As John demonstrated how these fine actors could do the role, he used dialogue from the script to prove his points. I soon realized he was auditioning for me, and doing it very well, growing older before my eyes. When he had reached the age of forty-five, I stopped him, expressed my gratitude for his suggestions, and asked if he would consider learning a song from the show. He did a good job of acting surprised as he took the sheet music, and we set a date for his return.

I immediately called Peter and Gary and told them I thought

we had a new Charlie Anderson. When John returned and sang, we were all convinced. I gave Palance's representatives a final chance to have him do the show at Goodspeed but received no reply. I told John's agent I could not offer him anything but Goodspeed for now. He accepted this, and Michael Price, though disappointed about not having a big star at Goodspeed, agreed to go along. Once John's contract was signed, all my efforts were concentrated on the Goodspeed production. My money-raising efforts for Broadway were put on hold.

We went into rehearsal on July 22nd, 1974, with a total of three weeks to put on a brand new musical with a cast of thirty-five. John had to miss the first week because of a previous commitment. Nevertheless, we opened on schedule on August 12th, for what was originally scheduled to be a four-week engagement, but that, as a result of our reviews, was extended far into October. After the first week, when I felt the show was in relatively good shape, I began again to think about the future. We were fortunate that Walter Kerr came up from New York and wrote a very moving review, admitting that he came prepared to dismiss *Shenandoah* as clichéd and sentimental, and suddenly found himself in tears halfway into the first act when John sang "The Pickers Are Comin'," about the young suitors courting his only daughter. He wrote a long and beautiful piece which appeared in the *New York Times* even though he was, unfortunately, no longer their daily theatre critic.

Kerr's review got a good deal of attention and attracted New York theatregoers, many of whom came to Goodspeed prepared to offer advice on how to fix the show. I thought we were doing quite well, and I had already made it clear to John Cullum that the only way he would be replaced for Broadway was by my being replaced as both producer and director. It was encouraging that local people offered some small investments in the Broadway production. On the other hand, when John Cullum's agent came to see the show, he assured his client not to worry about his future because he was immediately returning to New York to try to get other work for him. His opinion: "*Shenandoah* will never go beyond Goodspeed." His purpose: to instill John with confidence!

After three weeks, our run was extended for three more, during which time I commuted between my office in New York and my hotel near Goodspeed. One Saturday evening, when my wife and I arrived home from a dinner engagement, there was a message on the machine from a Mr. Louis Sher, asking if I was available for brunch on Sunday. I had no idea who Mr. Sher was, but when I returned his call, he told me that he had seen *Shenandoah* Saturday afternoon and would like to talk to me. After some thought about whether to take the meeting, I decided I would at least be well fed. So the following morning at 11:00 A.M. I arrived at a very expansive apartment on East 57th Street to lunch with Louis Sher, his wife Gloria, and some of their friends.

After introductions, we all sat down at a large table spread with the standard New York Zabar's assortment of lox, bagels, and lots of cheeses, plus champagne and Bloody Marys, creating a very festive atmosphere. I should point out here that while I could happily feast on all of these foods and drinks, the only thing I always avoid is a strong smelling or tasting cheese such as blue or Roquefort. In fact, my wife always screens any dips at cocktail parties because my immediate reaction to them is not pleasant to either see or describe. But I seemed to have no problems with that here. After a very pleasant half hour of food and drink, during which I was flattered, congratulated, and honored, Mr. Sher asked me the cost of a one-unit investment in *Shenandoah*. I replied that it was $10,000, based on a total budget of $500,000, and realized that this might not be a wasted afternoon.

Meanwhile, our hostess Gloria was graciously proceeding around the table to refill plates with more lox on half-bagels and cheese. As I lifted a half-bagel to my mouth and took a large bite, Mr. Sher said he would like to invest $250,000 and become my co-producer. This was just as my taste buds and nose informed me that our hostess had generously smeared my bagel not with cream cheese but with blue cheese. I knew that reacting to Mr. Sher's offer by throwing up on his beautiful table and his guests would not be appropriate. So I swallowed and prayed fervently that the few moments of discomfort would be seen as an indication of how grateful I was for the offer. And indeed I heard admiring comments about my willingness to display emotion, even to the degree of turning very white and then pink again.

All the guests were impressed by Mr. Sher's offer to become my co-producer, to which we drank a toast. Mr. Sher then ushered me into another room, where he wrote a check for $250,000, and we had a brief discussion as to what this would entitle him to, financially and otherwise. He trusted me, he said, to draw up an agreement, which we could sign within a few days. After we shook hands, he tossed his check on the desk in front of me (I noticed that it landed there quietly, without bouncing), and as I deposited it in my pocket, I asked how he could be so quick to make such a substantial investment with somebody he barely knew. He explained that it was not unusual for him to make quick judgments of people, but equally important was his enthusiasm for the show, particularly for its family background and its American values. He also volunteered that I could be of some help to him in his business. I now felt I was on safe ground to inquire what his business was. He said he owned several theatres around the country which showed "soft porn" motion pictures. As a matter of fact, he was the distributor for a film called *The Stewardesses*, which was the first big hit nationwide in that genre. He then admitted candidly that his association with *Shenandoah*, which he was certain would be a smash hit, could help him in states where he was fighting restrictions, or even facing jail time, for showing his films. Mr. Sher proved to be quite prescient, because many months after we opened in New York, there he was, on trial in Tennessee. He offered the success of *Shenandoah* as proof of his non-prurient business interests, and indeed brought me to the Tennessee court to testify on his behalf. He won his case. Mr. Sher remained a close friend and supporter until he died some years later.

I was now in what was, for me, an unusual situation. As soon as Mr. Sher's check cleared I was ready to commit to a New York opening, actually having over half the budget in our bank account. What I lacked was a theatre. A young actor, Konrad Matthaei, who had seen the show at Goodspeed, had recently purchased a major interest in the Alvin Theatre on 52nd Street. He decided not only to make an investment in *Shenandoah* but to offer us his theatre. We closed the deal quickly and set the date for our opening in January 1975. I then also scheduled a rehearsal period in New York and a run in Boston in order to mount the show in a large theatre with new scenery, lighting, costumes, and perhaps even some changes in the material.

As we approached our last week in Goodspeed and the impending New York rehearsals, I was still short about $110,000 when I received a call from the office of Mr. DeWitt Wallace, whom I knew to be the original creator and owner of, and still the power behind, the *Reader's Digest*. When I called him back, he began with a polite but brief compliment about *Shenandoah*, which he and his wife had just seen at Goodspeed. He asked if I still needed money to get the show to Broadway, and if so how much. I said $100,000 dollars. He told me to please give my office address to his secretary and said we should keep in touch. I wasn't quite sure exactly what to make of this short conversation until one hour later, when Lynda told me that a messenger had just arrived with an envelope for me. I opened it to find a check from *Reader's Digest*, signed by DeWitt Wallace, for $100,000.

Mr. Wallace and his wife Lila became avid fans of *Shenan-*

doah, often showing up at Wednesday matinee performances. He instructed his CEO to support us by organizing theatre groups from Pleasantville, New York, their headquarters. I'm certain that employees of the magazine from around the world at one time or another attended our show, their tickets paid for by the *Digest*. The Wallaces stayed in touch with me for the rest of their lives.

We opened in Boston on November 25, 1974, and, of course, the next day the two major Boston papers published their reviews. The first, brought to me at the opening night party by our press agent, Merle Debuskey, was from Elliot Norton of the *Boston Post,* a well-known, highly regarded critic, and therefore very important. His importance only made things worse since his notice was devastatingly negative, as if he were more or less expecting or advising us to close the show as quickly as possible. My staff and I spent a dreadful hour trying to keep the news from spreading to the rest of the party-goers, but then we were brought the equally important review from Kevin Kelly of the *Boston Globe*. His headline and first words were "*Shenandoah*, at the Colonial, is absolutely magnificent." It got better after that: "The script is one of the most searing antiwar statements I've encountered in musical theatre." It was almost as though each of the critics had read the other's review in advance and decided to write as powerful a rebuttal as he could. In any case, the Kelly review made us feel a whole lot better. We were even able to laugh at Norton's comment that John Cullum had a phony southern accent. It so happens that John was born and raised in the Deep South, and was still working hard at hiding it in other productions.

Merle and I proceeded to prepare our "quote ad" from Kelly's and other friendly reviews. But we had an immediate, ticklish decision to make about an appointment we had scheduled. John Cullum, Peter Udell, Gary Geld, and I were all to be interviewed by Elliot Norton on his talk show the following Friday morning. This was an invitation offered to any new play opening in Boston ahead of its New York opening. My first inclination was to cancel the scheduled appearance, but in discussing it, we decided that armed with the other review we might have some fun. When we arrived for the interview, the conversation was polite if not relaxed. On the air, all of us were properly introduced, and the name of the play and the theatre announced. Then Norton, carefully avoiding mention of his negative review, chose to discuss instead the history of the production, including all the vicissitudes and postponements it had been subject to. At the end of that lengthy list, Mr. Norton turned to me, the producer, and said, perhaps as a compliment, "Well, Philip, it's amazing that with all of these problems, you kept on going. I guess you really wanted to do this show in the worst way." I answered, "No, Mr. Norton, I wanted to do it in the best way." We left Boston soon afterwards.

'Shenandoah' absolutely magnificent

"Shenandoah," at the Colonial, is absolutely magnificent. If that sounds like the conventional hype of a deadlining critic, I hope you'll forgive me but, more importantly, remember what I said: absolutely magnificent. Having seen it in its summer tryout at the Goodspeed Opera House, I'm in danger of repeating my initial praise. I don't want to do that because, well, in my ears I sound tongue-tied. So you'll have to accept absolutely magnificent. Accept it and rush to the Colonial, where you'll see what is likely to be the best American musical of the season.

Adapted by James Lee Barrett, Peter Udell and Philip Rose, from Mr. Barrett's 1965 movie, the musical's book is a hardheaded examination of the insanity of war, in this case the Civil War and its devastating effect on a widowed patriarch, Charlie Anderson, his six sons,

KEVIN KELLY

his daughter and daughter-in-law. Charlie Anderson is the rockbed hero of the American spirit, a farmer with 500 acres in the Shenandoah Valley, the kind of man who made this country strong. But he is, in no way, the typical patriot. He is, in fact, a pacificist, an isolationist who would keep himself an his family out of the war. But try as he does to remain apart, to shelter what is his from the howl of madness around him, Charlie Anderson stands on the slipping soil of a national holocaust.

The script is one of the most searing antiwar statements I've encountered in the musical theater. For once, we have a traditional musical, admittedly oldfashioned in its format, that tells us something about the suffering human spirit and tells it with flatout honesty and considerable eloquences, all of which, let me add, is perfectly reflected in the score by Gary Geld and Mr. Udell. Behind the Andersons' story is a lesson about the shaping of our nation, the lesson of a maverick who knows the ultimate futility of shooting strangers, which, as Charlie says, is a definition of war. Strictly speaking our country may not have been built by the Charlie Andersons, but they are clearly our conscience.

I'm aware, right here, that I may be making "Shenandoah" sound heavy and grim. Let me correct or, rather, explain the impression. It is full of harsh truth and hard irony, but that is only one side of the Andersons' full and loving life. We come to know them in their moments of struggle and in their moments of ease. For most of the first act they're a heartwarming and entertaining clan, then, in the second act, their world comes apart. All of this is told with remarkable skill, notably in the superb pace of Mr. Rose's direction; the moss hung, cutout scenery by C. Murawski; the mood-perfect lighting by Thomas Skelton; and the virile choreography by Robert Tucker.

And then there's "Shenandoah's" cast.

John Callum, as Charlie Anderson, gives a performance I can only call absolutely magnificent (there I go again). Mr. Cullum, sandyhaired, workworn, seizes the stage with his first song, a personal protest against war, "I've Heard It All Before," and you know immediately that this is theater on its highest level. Later, in a perhaps more difficult moment, a vocal meditation to his dead wife, Mr. Cullum's sorrow is so overwhelming he touched me, and I'm sure most of the audience, with such anguish that I wept. Throughout the evening his characterization is so honestly projected, so immeasurably felt that there's little wonder about the ovation that finally roars off the walls of the Colonial. It is, to be brief, one of the great performances in the musical theater.

There are wonderful characterizations from everyone, notably Ted Agress, Joel Higgins, Jordan Suffin, David Russell, Robert Rosen and Joseph Shapiro, as the six sons; Penelope Milford, as the daughter; and Donna Theodore, as the daughter-in-law. Chip Ford is marvelous as a black boy, and one of "Shenandoah's" memorable moments is a duet called "Freedom" which he shares with Miss Theodore. Then there's a beautiful number by Mr. Cullum, "The Pickers Are Comin" and an aching ballad ,"The Only Home I Know," and . . . on and on and on. "Shenandoah" is magnificent and does the theater proud.

Philip Rose
being directed by his two young stars.

Philip Rose and
Doris Belack

Philip Rose
and John Cullum

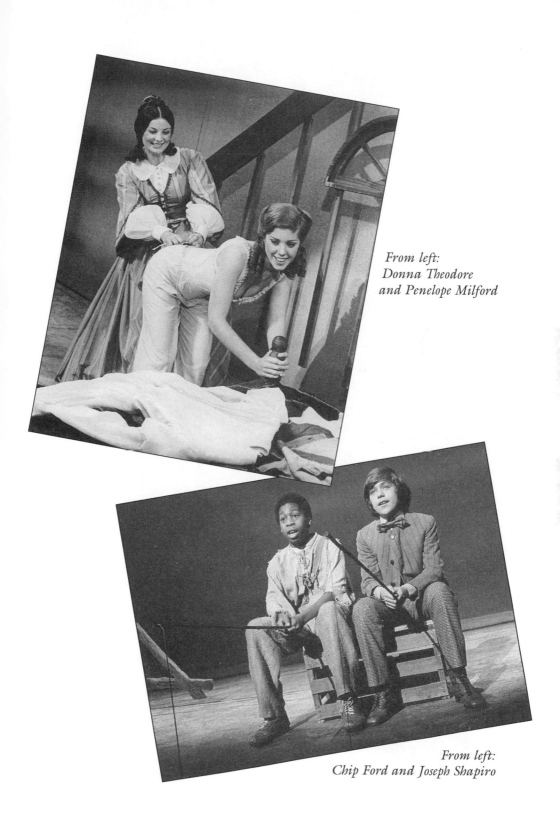

From left:
Donna Theodore
and Penelope Milford

From left:
Chip Ford and Joseph Shapiro

*Donna Theodore
and Chip Ford*

*From Left:
David Russell, Ted Agress,
John Cullum, Joel Higgins,
Jordan Suffin, and Robert Rosen*

We opened at the Alvin Theatre in New York on January 7th, 1975, after just a few previews, because we had a very limited advance sale, actually about $50,000, not even enough to fill the theatre for one week. Our New York reviews were unanimously divided; that is, extremely good or extremely bad. Fortunately, there were enough good ones for some very effective ads. The one most fascinating aspect of almost every positive review related to the music and lyrics: how refreshing it was to once again be moved and entertained in the old-fashioned style of the best of Rodgers and Hammerstein. The one most fascinating aspect of almost every negative review was a reference to the music and lyrics as being as old-fashioned as the worst of Rodgers and Hammerstein. The book divided the critics in much the same way. So we knew we were in for a fight.

After the opening it became apparent that the sophisticated theatre community was not rushing to associate itself with an "old-fashioned" show; and there seemed to be an almost deliberate avoidance of the antiwar aspect of the book. But we began to build our audience through intense word-of-mouth support and the unanimous acclaim that had greeted John Cullum's performance. We had created a star. This was underscored by John's winning the 1975 Tony Award for Best Performance in a Musical. Surprisingly, perhaps, *Shenandoah* won for best musical book.

But it remained a show that had to struggle through many hard times, including the longest musicians' strike in Broadway history, during which, according to the press, *Shenandoah* was "not going to reopen." Of course, it did, and ran for a long time afterwards. We also became one of the most performed musicals on tour throughout the country starring prominent singer-actors such as Howard Keel and John Raitt. The popularity has continued to this very day. One of the more recent landmarks was a brief Broadway revival of *Shenandoah* in August of 1989, at which time John Simon of *New York* magazine chose to review it again, this time more positively than before. His 1989 headline was "Aging Gracefully," and he went on to say, "There is a real story in *Shenandoah*. There are characters that waylay your emotions, and there is a shape to the whole thing." He also wrote, "Philip Rose, co-author of the book and the guiding spirit of such shows as *Raisin in the Sun, Purlie Victorious*, and just plain *Purlie*—is a manifest liberal." I chose to accept the word "manifest" as an approving adjective. A year earlier, in reviewing another show I was connected with, *Checkmates*, Mr. Simon had written, "Philip Rose is an old-time liberal." I wasn't sure if this was a slur or a compliment. In either case I might have preferred a phrase with no possible implicit reference to age. Nevertheless, my press agent prepared a *Checkmates* poster using the line as a prominent quote, and the poster still proudly hangs on the wall of my office.

In his review of the revival, Mr. Simon wrote favorably of "*Shenandoah*, despite its obvious weaknesses." I would like to say of Mr. Simon that, despite his obvious weaknesses, I think he is by far our best theatre critic since Kenneth Tynan or Walter Kerr, and that has been my opinion even through the years when I have often received devastating reviews from him. I thank him for reconsidering his initial reaction to *Shenandoah* (a rare inclination from any critic), and I am particularly grateful for his perceptivity in insisting that I am a liberal. I now assume he meant it to be, and I choose to accept it as, a compliment. And I will go on doing so.

Chapter 26

After the many years spent on *Purlie* and *Shenandoah* performing the triple tasks of producer, director, and writer, the end of the 1970s found me weary of money-raising. So, despite my enormous satisfaction in seeing both shows enter into the canon of classical musicals (still being performed as I write this at the beginning of a new century), I decided never again to become involved in a project which would require me to do that. I should perhaps add that I had reached that decision when my wife informed me of it—that is, she told me that I could spend my days writing and directing shows, but not my nights worrying about financing: not in *our* apartment. Following my new rule, in the early 1980s I directed a small musical called *My Old Friends* at LaMama, an experimental theatre on East 4th Street. The writers, Mel Mandel and Norman Sachs, collaborated on book, music, and lyrics. It was a showcase production, and as such scheduled for only a brief run, but it received enough attention to persuade an old friend of mine, Larry Abrams, to become the producer and to move it to the larger Orpheum Theatre on Second Avenue. While working on this show, I had the good fortune to meet and become friends with two legends.

My Old Friends took place in an old age home and required several actors of advanced years. During the casting period, I got a phone call from a Miss Sullivan. To my "Hello" she replied, in a quiet voice, "You might not know me but I know your work and I would like to audition for your show." I asked, "Are you an actor?" She said, "Not really but I can sing a little bit." I told her about the age requirements and she said, "I think I can fit in." "Well," I said, "Give me your name and phone number and we'll try to set up an audition time for you." "Sullivan" she said, "Maxine Sullivan." I almost dropped the phone but instead I replied, "Just sing a few bars of your song for me, please." She began, "By yon bonny banks and by yon bonny braes," and I broke in: "Enough. You've got the job."

Maxine Sullivan was a great black jazz singer from the 1930s through the '60s who achieved world-wide fame with her swinging recording of the Scottish folk song "Loch Lomond." Retired for many years, during which she did volunteer work, she was drawn to *My Old Friends* because it portrayed older people in a positive way that even included the possibility of romance. Mel and Norman wrote a wonderful song especially for her, based on something she had once said about herself in an interview: "There's Still a Little Starch in the Old Girl Yet." She stopped the show with that number every night. The audience adored this tiny little angel of a woman, as did I, and we remained friends for the too few years until she died.

Some months after *Friends* closed at the Orpheum Theatre, it reopened at the 92nd Street Y. For that production I added another legendary talent to our cast, Imogene Coca. Imogene, the *other* genius of Sid Caesar's television show, was a very shy and self-effacing person. I first met her at the apartment she shared with her husband, the actor King Donovan. Having already read the script, she was a bit frightened by the singing requirements of her role. I eased her fears by assuring her that I needed an actress, not a singer, particularly one who thought she could be funny. She said she would try, and we were off to a good start. I noticed something a bit peculiar, however, about the way she walked around the large living room, which contained a grand piano as well as all the expected furniture. As she went to get me a drink from the kitchen, she seemed to touch the furniture gently. I turned to her husband and, before I could say anything, he volunteered, "Imogene is almost legally blind. It will not affect her performance. All you need to do is protect her entrances and exits. Once she has become familiar with the set she will be fine, and the audience will not have a clue."

He was absolutely right. I soon had her moving around the stage, even dancing, with no fear on her part, and almost none on mine. Except for her insistence that anything that went wrong on stage was her fault, even if she was in her dressing room at the time, she was a joy to direct. When I began staging the Christmas party at the old people's home, I thought it would be nice if Imogene played the piano for a sing-a-long. I knew she could play a little. She went to the piano and did some warmup exercises with her fingers, her hands, her arms, and her body before she even touched the keyboard. It was an enormously funny pantomime, for which many people complimented the director, people no more perceptive in distinguishing the director's contributions from the actor's than are most of the critics who presume to do it professionally. After the play opened, Imogene, Doris, and I became very good friends. (King unfortunately died soon after our opening.) We shared many New Year's Eves at her home where the stroke of midnight was enhanced by Imogene on her patio, facing all of New York and playing "Auld Lang Syne" on her tiny but real trumpet.

Later I directed a musical at the Booth Theatre in Washington, D.C. that was based on James Baldwin's play *The Amen Corner*. It came to New York, where it unfortunately had a short life. However, it gave me the chance to work with Ruth Brown, the great rhythm and blues singer, and to discover a talented young actress named Helena Joyce Wright. Ms. Wright received a great deal of attention at the time and was, I thought, on the verge of an important career. But soon after the show closed, she married and moved to Oakland, California. Many years later I was glad to hear she had not only returned to acting but had become the Producing Artistic Director of the Oakland Ensemble Theatre.

On an ordinary Saturday evening in 1984, while Doris was in California filming a television program, I was home alone and read about a showcase (three weekends only) of a new play called *Split Second*. It was close to curtain time when I decided to dash down to the theatre, and I arrived and took my seat just as the play began. I had no time to wonder whether this would be one of those showcases without an intermission, making it impossible to leave gracefully. Well, all such thoughts disappeared within the play's first minutes, as I watched a black police officer capture a young white man who had broken into a car. The perpetrator began to plead with the cop to let him go, and the cop was amused by his sentimental appeal for compassion. But when his pleas went unanswered, the young man suddenly became an inflamed racist, spewing vulgar personal profanities. After several futile warnings from the officer to stop, and with the insults increasing, the officer lost control, pulled his gun, and shot the young man, killing him instantly. From this point on, the audience was totally engrossed in a very well-written, exciting play, beautifully performed.

During the intermission (there was one, but no one left), I checked my program and discovered that the leading actor, John McDonald, had a background in theatre and television, and the playwright, Dennis McIntyre, had previously written *Modigliani*, which had been produced on Broadway. I decided to go backstage after the performance to meet and congratulate both of them. They then introduced me to Gus Fleming, who was functioning, along with Mr. McDonald, as co-producer of the showcase. During our conversation I learned that McDonald had worked for a number of years as a soap opera star under the name of John Danelle, one of the first black actors to be a regular on an afternoon series. When, after a number of years, he became bored with his role, he commissioned his old friend Dennis to write *Split Second* for him. Gus Fleming, another friend who had been a producer of jazz concerts and similar events, joined John in presenting the showcase. I was also told that, barring some miracle, *Split Second* would be closing after the following weekend.

I expressed my sincere hopes that the miracle they were praying for would indeed occur, and also my regret that since I was no longer a functioning producer, there was nothing I could do for them. Before I left, John McDonald made a point of telling me that if it were not for *A Raisin in the Sun* and Sidney Poitier, he as a black man would never have dreamed of becoming an actor. The implication was clear: having performed that first miracle, I had the responsibility of creating another one.

I left the theatre that night wondering whether I should accept that burden and decided that if I did I should certainly share it with Sidney Poitier. After all, had Sidney been a lousy actor, he would have inspired nobody, and I would never have produced *Raisin*. I then called him in L.A. and happily discovered he was in New York. As miracles go, this turned out to be an important first step. I know that several chapters ago I promised not to write any more about Sidney, but now we're talking about miracles, so what's a promise? I told Sidney I would like him to see this play and get acquainted with the writer. He said he'd try, and we met at the theatre just a few days later. Sidney brought along a friend who also just happened to be in New York. The friend was Berry Gordy, the owner of Motown Records (we're still in the miracle department). Gordy was impressed with the play and arranged for an associate, Suzanne De-Passe (now a respected television and film producer), to see it the following evening. The day after that, she informed me that Mr. Gordy would put up the money to move *Split Second* to another theatre for an open-ended run, with me joining Gus and John as co-producers. Mr. Gordy would also own the film rights, and intended to produce and direct the film.

Split Second reopened some weeks later at Theatre 54, where it ran for several months. It has since been, and continues to be, produced at theatres throughout the country. Unfortunately, Gordy sold Motown before he produced the film, and the rights were later sold to HBO. From time to time there has been talk of other film production plans, but so far none have been realized.

Split Second had reverberations beyond the play, affecting all of us who were involved. Most important, we all became friends, and through our friendships, we have shared times happy and sad. Dennis McIntyre wrote a play, *National Anthem,* that was first showcased in 1988 at the Long Wharf Theatre in New Haven, with Al Pacino starring, followed by a full production with Kevin Spacey, who then optioned it for a play or film. Dennis also worked with Sidney Poitier on developing a film script, and another screenplay of his, *State of Grace,* was filmed and released in early 1990. Dennis was on his way to becoming a very successful writer when this young, gifted man was discovered to have cancer. In spite of all medical efforts, Dennis was lost to us later in 1990, at the age of 47.

Gus Fleming, co-producer of *Split Second,* became Director of Concert Halls at Lincoln Center in 1988. In May of 2000, he too died of cancer, at the age of 56.

John McDonald, now and forever a close friend, has just been appointed Director of Operations for Carnegie Hall. He and I now have a signed contract which guarantees that neither of us will be the next to go.

Chapter 27

In the many years that I was producing and/or directing shows, including some I haven't mentioned, the problems and challenges I faced have, I hope, proved to be interesting. But my next venture became an adventure. In 1988, an old friend, Woody King, had directed a modest production, in Los Angeles, of a play called *Checkmates,* which then moved on to San Francisco. Woody King had been for years a major influence in black theatre around the country, both as a producer and director. He also was, and still is, the force behind the New Federal Theatre in New York. He and the playwright Ron Milner were trying to transplant *Checkmates* to Broadway and called me for help. While I recited my litany that I was no longer functioning as a money-raising producer, I agreed to read the script and perhaps make some suggestions.

The play dealt with two black married couples, one young, the other older, who share a house, the younger as renters and the older as landlords. I was intrigued by the marital problems each couple faced and by the relationship and interaction between the two generations. The play was, I thought, moving and funny, and challenging in *not* being about the "race question." I told Woody I would see what I could do.

I spoke to Jimmy Nederlander, one of Broadway's most prominent theatre owners, whom I respected a great deal for his honesty in never pretending to want to read a play. He was interested only in the package and whether it was likely to fill one of his theatres. Fortunately, however, he felt that while my opinion might be worthless in any other area, it was worth considering if the play was about black people. He agreed to produce *Checkmates*, provided I could land a major star for one of the roles, and that I function as executive producer—in effect, to protect his interests. When I reported all this to Woody and Ron, they were of course delighted by the possibility of moving forward. We proceeded to put a cast together and were pleased to receive immediate commitments from Ruby Dee and Paul Winfield. For Jimmy, this did not supply the star insurance he needed to go ahead. He was satisfied with our choice of my old friend Roy Somlyo to function as general manager.

Denzel Washington's name had come up many times in our casting conversations. While he was not yet the giant box-office star he was soon to become, he was already known from television appearances and his role in the play and film *A Soldier's Story*. I knew he was an extraordinary actor and was hopeful when Somlyo began conversations with Denzel's agent. For many weeks we got no commitment beyond an expression of interest based on availability. Finally, Somlyo told me meaningful negotiations with Denzel had started: I called Nederlander for his approval, and after saying, "Hold the phone," he immediately began his research into Denzel's importance by calling out to his office staff, "Anybody here know Denzel Washington?" I heard several affirmative oohs and aahs from female assistants, and then, his research concluded, he said, "OK, if you get him, we'll go." We got him.

Some days later I received a call from a Michael Harris, a stranger to me, who said he had made a small investment in the original Los Angeles production of the play, and would like to talk with me. He said he was in Los Angeles but could be in New York the following day. I suggested we meet a day later and we made a firm appointment. I then called Woody King, who corroborated that Harris had indeed been a minor backer of that original presentation of *Checkmates*.

The following morning Harris arrived at my office punctually, with an associate, Hayward Collins. Harris was a handsome young black man, in his mid- or late twenties, I guessed, probably over six and a half feet tall and maybe still growing. He was well-dressed, well spoken, and seemed gentle, quite mature, and well educated. As we talked about *Checkmates,* he expressed his pride in having been at least partially responsible for starting the play on its journey to Broadway. He then began to ask about our budget and specifically whether he could repeat his original investment with a comparably small amount. I told him about Nederlander's projected budget of $750,000, and informed him also that one unit in the show would cost $15,000. After posing several more precise, intelligent questions, he asked if he could use a private phone to make a long distance call. I led him to a phone in another room, and within a few minutes he returned and asked me to speak to his Los Angeles attorney, whose name, oddly enough, was also Michael Harris. I picked up the phone in the other room. The attorney, after a brief greeting, said, "My client, Mr. Harris, would like to be co-producer of *Checkmates.* I assume he could have that position for an investment of $375,000." It took a moment before I asked him to repeat what I thought I had heard, which he did. He then volunteered that his client was an impulsive but genuine individual who always stood by and delivered on his quick decisions. I told him I would have to get Nederlander's assent to this partnership, though I was certain he would not put up great resistance, and he would hear from Nederlander's attorney, Dick Ticktin, who was also to be the official attorney for our production.

I returned to my own office to find Mr. Harris with a smile that conveyed how much he was enjoying my surprised reaction to the just-concluded phone conversation. I suggested we go out for lunch, after which I would try to arrange a meeting at Mr. Nederlander's office to introduce these two prospective partners to each other. When we arrived at the restaurant, I excused myself to call Nederlander and tell him I'd be at his office at 2:30 to introduce him to a new friend who might be worth meeting. When he started to protest how busy he was, I rephrased this to "who might be worth $375,000." He graciously became much less occupied, and I returned to our table.

By that time my new friend had already perused the menu and was ready to order, so I made a quick decision and then listened while he ordered two of each item, including the entrées. We had a really good time at lunch, with Michael asking many relevant questions and saying he would like to stay in touch with me to share in and learn about the producing process. I learned that Michael had started out in school intending to be a professional basketball player, but instead had gone into real estate and investments, and now owned one of Los Angeles's most successful car rental services, catering to the Hollywood stars and specializing in custom-made Rolls-Royces, Mercedes, etc. When our food arrived, with the bulk of it placed in front of Michael, I noticed his head drop down and was for a moment concerned that something was wrong—until I realized he was saying grace. Once again, I had a pleasant surprise from this very contemporary young man, who had no reservations about displaying his spirituality in public. That image of him has remained with me for many years.

Harris and Nederlander soon signed their partnership agreement and each deposited $50,000 in the *Checkmates* bank account. They were to match each other's contributions as needed by Roy Somlyo until they reached the guaranteed total of $750,000. Michael Harris and I were now speaking almost daily. I kept him informed of our progress in designing and building scenery, designing costumes, and obtaining a theatre, the 46th Street (now known as the Richard Rodgers), and Michael always knew how Somlyo was expending the money received.

Before we went into rehearsal, Woody King had to fulfill a promise made many months before to bring the Los Angeles production of *Checkmates* to Washington, D.C. for a short engagement. This did not involve most of our New York cast, but since Ruby Dee was in it, it gave us an opportunity to see how wonderful she would be in New York. Michael Harris flew in from Los Angeles for the D.C. opening and he and I had a good time partying afterwards.

As we went into rehearsal I was increasingly concerned about the difficulty I was suddenly having in reaching Harris and by the fact that his matching checks were falling behind. I did manage to talk to his attorney, who assured me that the money would be forthcoming. I then received a call from Michael's associate, Hayward Collins, informing me that Michael's younger brother had drowned and Michael would be in mourning and unavailable for a while. He too assured me that the checks would be arriving, but from a different source. That source turned out to be Michael's car rental company, and checks were once again being received, if a bit late. I made calls to various people trying to locate Michael, but to no avail.

Soon afterwards I was in Los Angeles and decided to visit Michael's car rental company. There I saw its very impressive showroom and beautiful array of limousines, and met the man who now was sending us the checks. I invited him to our New York opening, and even offered to put his name in our playbill as an associate of Michael's, but he declined the honor, saying he was just a friend helping Michael out during his mourning period.

Checkmates opened on the night of August 4th, 1988. We received mixed notices from the mainstream reviewers but tremendous appreciation from the black press and audience. The cast of Denzel Washington, Ruby Dee, Paul Winfield, and Marsha Jackson was brilliant, with Denzel showing a comedic talent that seemed a wonderful surprise. We were playing to enthusiastic black audiences but had not achieved the necessary breakthrough to white theatergoers, which would require further money for television advertising. Though I had not seen or heard from Michael Harris since that night months before in Washington D.C., he had fulfilled his financial obligation. I was certain that if he could see his show he would be proud to make additional money available, but I seemed to have lost all possibility of contact with him while the weeks of struggle went by.

One night while I was at a poker game with a group of friends, I got a phone call from a man who introduced himself as a reporter for the CBS television station in Los Angeles. He was calling to invite me to appear on their network news program at CBS's expense the following evening. "For what?" I asked, and he continued, "Don't you know? Your co-producer, Michael Harris, who has long been in jail in San Francisco for attempted murder, has now been indicted as one of this country's most important drug dealers. We're planning to show a national map pointing out the various states where his activities have been prominent. We thought you'd like to be interviewed about your relationship and feelings about him."

I left the poker game not caring whether I was winning or losing and dashed home to start making phone calls. Waiting for me were invitations from the FBI and IRS also requesting interviews but with no RSVP indicated, informing me that I would be visited very shortly in my office. They were also politely offering to examine the books of the *Checkmates* company and would be going to Roy Somlyo's office to accomplish that.

The following day CBS and the other television networks had the entire story, which also appeared in the print press. It revealed that Michael Harris had indeed been behind bars for months, having been convicted of attempted murder. Apparently he had suspected one of his "employees" of stealing from him, and to discipline the man, Michael had met him in a garage, shot him, and left him for dead. Unfortunately for Michael, the man recovered and went on to become a key trial witness against him.

The FBI and Internal Revenue Service did examine all our books to make certain we were not partners with Michael in any of his other ventures; we were soon exonerated. But they were amused at my naiveté in not having been at all suspicious. The rental car company in Los Angeles locked its doors and was gone the day after the CBS story aired. The uproar aroused by all this inevitably invaded our show, and *Checkmates* was forced to close shortly afterwards.

I never heard from Michael Harris again, but I keep remembering the image of that "gentle" man at lunch saying grace before he would touch his food.

Chapter 28

Sometime after January of 1990, I finally decided to desert Broadway theatre—or perhaps I realized that it had deserted me. In any event, I then found myself advising and counseling young talents, both actors and writers, in furthering their careers. Before long I was acting as a personal manager, and at the request of several of these artists we formalized our relationships.

By the middle of the decade, I had been involved with two playwrights. Gary Richards had written *The Root,* a play that I saw in its first presentation at the George Street Playhouse in New Jersey. The play was produced under the auspices of a Broadway producer, Daryl Roth. I was there at the suggestion of Michael Tolan, a fine actor who had directed an earlier reading of it and was impressed with the writer. At the Playhouse I saw a very professional production—well directed by Matthew Penn—of an interesting play about a crooked cop, his almost equally crooked victim, and their respective cohorts, all caught up in the greed of our society. After the performance I met the playwright, and he requested a meeting which led to my representing him. The play received rave reviews, and I assumed that the production would be brought to Broadway immediately by its producer. Unfortunately, this did not happen, though Gary's play has since been performed in several regional theatres. It's also been published by Samuel French and has been adapted into a screenplay which I hope will someday be filmed.

I had heard about an African-American woman, Anne Thompson-Scretching, who had written and produced *You Shouldn't Have Told* as a non-Equity showcase. The play was a well-written drama about child abuse within a black family. After seeing it I was able to persuade Art McFarland of ABC's news staff to see it and he then covered it as a television story, including scenes from the play plus a positive review; McFarland's story was shown repeatedly. Following that, a close friend of Ms. Scretching's, Neville Pinnock, who had designed the scenery, financed a move to Theatre Row on 42nd Street, where it received generally good notices and enjoyed a run for months with very emotional responses from the audiences. Unfortunately, it was never picked up by any Broadway producer. It has been published by Samuel French.

On September 29th, 1996, an article appeared in the *New York Times* about a statue of a trio of ladies: Elizabeth Cady Stanton, Lucretia Mott, and Susan B. Anthony—the founders of the suffragist movement of this country in the 1850s. The article told the intriguing story of three of the most important people in American history, who in the year 1921 finally received proper recognition by that sculpture in the Rotunda of the Congress of the United States. When the statue was placed there, it became the first representation of women among the hundreds of images of famous men. However, it remained there for all of one day; then, by the vote of an all-male Congress, it was removed to the basement, so that these "unattractive" ladies would not lower the esthetic standards embodied by all the "handsome" men. While I was amused by the story and impressed by the degree of stupidity that could be displayed by an all-male Congress, I didn't at first see this as an ongoing cause—certainly not one that would involve me.

A few days later, I was invited to the reading of a new play written and to be performed by Elizabeth Perry. Elizabeth was an old friend as well as a lovely actress with an extensive stage and television background. Having decided she had reached that "uncertain" age when there is no longer much work for a female actor, she had resolved to create some for herself.

I attended the reading, which was done in a studio on a bare stage, with Elizabeth holding script in hand. As she started, I was surprised to discover that the play, called *Sun Flower,* was about Elizabeth Cady Stanton, to whom I had recently been introduced by the statue story. By the end, I was stunned by both the play and the incredible performance of Elizabeth, who portrayed some twenty well-known figures in American history.

I and many other friends had been invited to this reading because Elizabeth naturally wanted to hear what we all thought of her work. As usual in such a setting, opinions were varied. My own reaction was to encourage her to work further on the piece and to recognize its importance both as history and as a vehicle for herself in the future. I of course offered to help if I could.

As a result, we began to work together very soon afterwards. I undertook the task of being Elizabeth's executive producer/manager, mainly trying to arrange bookings. The first year was very difficult, but with each one-night engagement the word spread, and by 1999, in addition to performing at the Smithsonian, the Senate, and the White House, Elizabeth Perry and Elizabeth Cady Stanton have had impact throughout the country. Incidentally, the statue of the suffragists was returned to its place in the Rotunda on June 26th, 1997 and Elizabeth Perry was a performing guest of honor. So far, there has been no offer of sponsorship for *Sun Flower* from the Broadway community.

I quite often read articles bemoaning the dearth of serious writers for the Broadway theatre, writers who presumably don't exist or who wouldn't attract audiences. What is mostly nonexistent is the individual producer who will welcome and present such writers on Broadway. This is Broadway's loss and off-Broadway's gain. Plays such as *Driving Miss Daisy* or *Dinner with Friends* go Off-Broadway just to find a producer and of course the audience follows the good play. In another era, every Broadway producer would have been fighting to present those plays. In our current climate we have occasional reminders of the past in someone like Robert Whitehead, who recently brought *Master Class* to Broadway with no grandiose special effects, very little scenery, no guarantee of a hit—just a good play that he believed in.

Sun Flower has provided me with an extraordinary education about the 100-year struggle, still ongoing, for women's rights. In the course of my involvement, I have had the pleasure of meeting and working with some remarkable women, among them Linda Muir, who was responsible for bringing *Sun Flower* to Atlanta, not once but twice, under the sponsorship of the Bell South Company; and Joan Wages and Karen Staser, who devote much of their time and efforts to the construction of the National Museum of Women's History in Washington, D.C. I trust I will not offend anyone when I add that I consider all these women immensely attractive.

I guess my devotion to the cause of women's rights is but another proof of my being (to quote John Simon again) "a manifest liberal." I am happy once again to acknowledge that, and to hope that as I grow older, new people and causes will come into my life.

As I come to the end of my story I would like to return briefly to the beginning—by sharing the letter Lorraine delivered to me and the wire I sent to her on the afternoon of March 11th, 1959, the opening day of *A Raisin in the Sun*.

NA 349 GGN DL. PD.

1959 Mar. 11 506

Mr & Mrs Philip Rose

This Ain't No theatre type wire Just to you. What the Hell to Say they can't write anything tonight to take this particular love affair away from me. Champagne won't salute it right nor flowers either. Just; this co ours show Kids. And you did it. But I knew that you would be as you are when I I first fell in love with you both long; long ago.. All my love

Lorraine

289   MAR 11   505P

59 PD   FR

CIR5   2255

MISS LORRAINE HANSBERRY

A RAISIN IN THE SUN ETHEL
BARRYMORE THEATRE WEST 47TH ST   NYC

WHATEVER HAPPENS TONIGHT WE HAVE BEEN, WE HAVE

BECOME, WE WILL BE INEXTRICABLY A PART OF EACH

OTHERS LIVES. I DONT THINK WE COME OUT OF THIS

EXPERIENCE BEING QUITE THE SAME PEOPLE THAT WE

WERE GOING INTO IT. I KNOW THAT I CAN BE GRATEFUL

FOR THE OPPORTUNITY TO BE AFFECTED BY PERHAPS THE

MOST PROFOUND EXPERIENCE THAT LIFE HAS SO FAR OFFERED
TO ME. THANK YOU

PHIL ROSE SDR

PHIL

BOOKED
SKELETON IN KLD

DATE_____
CLERK_____

GLORY RECORDS

WU 550 (1-52)

And one last thought: If this book is distributed and read beyond the realm of this universe, and if Lorraine Hansberry happens upon it, I hope she will approve and be happy with what I've written.

Index